Book of Common Prayer and space for notes on right-hand page

3ook of Common Prayer

August 2021

	Calendar and Holy Communion	Morning Prayer	Evening Prayer	NOTES
	THE TENTH SUNDAY AFTER TRINITY			
G	Jer. 7. 9-15 Ps. 17. 1-8 1 Cor. 12. 1-11 Luke 19. 41-47a	Ps. 89. 1-18 Song of Sol. 8. 5-7 *or* 1 Macc. 14. 4-15 2 Pet. 3. 8-13	Ps. 91 (*or* 91. 1-12) Job 39.1 - 40.4 *or* Ecclus. 43. 13-end Heb. 12. 1-17	
G		Prov. 1. 1-19 Mark 2.23 - 3.6	1 Sam. ch. 24 Acts 3. 11-end	
	Laurence, Deacon at Rome, Martyr, 258			
Gr	Com. Martyr	Prov. 1. 20-end Mark 3. 7-19a	1 Sam. ch. 26 Acts 4. 1-12	

mn 6

gical ur (*see mn 1*).

Column 7

- The name of the Principal Holy Day, Sunday, Festival or Lesser Festival;
- any general note that applies to the whole Prayer Book provision for the day and an indication of points at which users may wish to draw on *Common Worship* material on the opposite page where the BCP has no provision;
- the Lectionary for the Eucharist on any day for which provision is made.

Column 8

This provides the readings for Morning Prayer, together with psalm provision where it varies from the BCP monthly cycle.

Column 9

This provides the readings for Evening Prayer, together with psalm provision where it varies from the BCP monthly cycle.

A letter to indicate liturgical colour in this column indicates a change of colour for Evening Prayer. The symbol in bold lower case, **ct**, indicates that the Collect at Evening Prayer should be that of the following day.

Column 10

Space for notes.

ABBREVIATIONS OF BOOKS OF THE BIBLE

Old Testament

Gen. (Genesis)
Exod. (Exodus)
Lev. (Leviticus)
Num. (Numbers)
Deut. (Deuteronomy)
Josh. (Joshua)
Judg. (Judges)
Ruth
Sam. (Samuel)
Kings
Chron. (Chronicles)
Ezra
Neh. (Nehemiah)
Esth. (Esther)
Job
Ps. (Psalms)
Prov. (Proverbs)
Eccles. (Ecclesiastes)
Song of Sol. (Song of Solomon)
Isa. (Isaiah)
Jer. (Jeremiah)
Lam. (Lamentations)
Ezek. (Ezekiel)
Dan. (Daniel)
Hos. (Hosea)
Joel
Amos
Obad. (Obadiah)
Jonah
Mic. (Micah)
Nahum
Hab. (Habakkuk)
Zeph. (Zephaniah)
Hag. (Haggai)
Zech. (Zechariah)
Mal. (Malachi)

Apocrypha

Esd. (Esdras)
Tobit
Judith
Wisd. (Wisdom of Solomon)
Ecclus. (Ecclesiasticus)
Baruch (Baruch)
Song of the Three (Song of the Three Children)
Susanna (The History of Susanna)
Prayer of Manasseh
Macc. (Maccabees)

New Testament

Matt. (Matthew)
Mark
Luke
John
Acts (Acts of the Apostles)
Rom. (Romans)
Cor. (Corinthians)
Gal. (Galatians)
Eph. (Ephesians)
Phil. (Philippians)
Col. (Colossians)
Thess. (Thessalonians)
Tim. (Timothy)
Titus
Philem. (Philemon)
Heb. (Hebrews)
James
Pet. (Peter)
John (letters of John)
Jude
Rev. (Revelation)

MAKING CHOICES IN *COMMON WORSHIP*

Common Worship makes provision for a variety of pastoral and liturgical circumstances. It needs to, for it has to serve some church communities where Morning Prayer, Holy Communion and Evening Prayer are all celebrated every day, and yet be useful also in a church with only one service a week, and that service varying in form and time from week to week.

At the beginning of the year, some decisions in principle need to be taken.

In relation to the Calendar, whether to keep The Epiphany on Wednesday 6 January or on Sunday 3 January, whether to keep The Presentation of Christ (Candlemas) on Tuesday 2 February or on Sunday 31 January, and whether to keep the Feast of All Saints on Monday 1 November or on Sunday 31 October.

In relation to the Lectionary, the initial choices every year to decide in relation to Sundays are:

- which of the services on a Principal Feast, Principal Holy Day, Sunday or Festival constitutes the 'Principal Service'; then use the Principal Service Lectionary (column 3) consistently for that service through the year;
- during the Sundays after Trinity, whether to use Track I of the Principal Service Lectionary (column 2), where the first reading stays over several weeks with one Old Testament book read semi-continuously, or Track 2 (column 3), where the first reading is chosen for its relationship to the Gospel reading of the day;
- which, if any, service on a Principal Feast, Principal Holy Day, Sunday or Festival constitutes the 'Second Service'; then use the Second Service Lectionary (column 5) consistently for that service through the year;
- which, if any, service on a Principal Feast, Principal Holy Day, Sunday or Festival constitutes the 'Third Service'; then use the Third Service Lectionary (column 4) consistently for that service through the year.

And in relation to weekdays:

- whether to use the Daily Eucharistic Lectionary (column 3) consistently for weekday celebrations of Holy Communion (with the exception of Principal Feasts, Principal Holy Days and Festivals) or to make some use of the Lesser Festival provision;
- whether to follow the first psalm provision in column 4 (morning) and column 5 (evening), where psalms during the seasons have a seasonal flavour but in ordinary time follow a sequential pattern; or to follow the alternative provision in the same columns, where psalms follow the sequential pattern throughout the year, except for the period between 19 December and The Epiphany and from the Monday of Holy Week to the Saturday of Easter Week; or to follow the psalm cycle in the Book of Common Prayer, where they are nearly always used 'in course';
- whether to use the Additional Weekday Lectionary (which begins on page 120) for weekday services (other than Holy Communion). It provides a one-year cycle of two readings for each day (except for Sundays, Principal Feasts, Principal Holy Days, Festivals and during Holy Week). Since each of the readings is designed to 'stand alone' (that is, it is complete in itself and will make sense to the worshipper who has not attended on the previous day and who will not be present on the next day), it is intended particularly for use in those churches and cathedrals that attract occasional rather than regular congregations.

The flexibility of *Common Worship* is intended to enable the church and the minister to find the most helpful provision for them. But once a decision is made it is advisable to stay with that decision through the year or at the very least through a complete season.

All Bible references (except to the psalms) are to the New Revised Standard Version, Anglicized edition (1995). Those who use other Bible translations should check the verse numbers against the NRSV. References to the psalms are to the *Common Worship* Psalter.

BOOK OF COMMON PRAYER

separate Lectionary for the Book of Common Prayer s no longer issued. Provision is made on the right-hand ages of this Lectionary for BCP worship on all Sundays n the year, for the major festivals and for Morning and vening Prayer. The Epistles and Gospels for Holy ommunion are those of 1662, with the additions and ariations of 1928, now authorized under the *Common Vorship* overall provision. The Old Testament readings nd psalms for these services, formerly appended to he Series One Holy Communion service, may be used ut are not mandatory with the 1662 order.

eadings for Morning and Evening Prayer, which are he same as those for *Common Worship*, are set out in he BCP section for Sundays and weekdays. The special salm provision of the BCP is given; however, where he *Common Worship* psalm provision is used, verse umbering may occasionally differ slightly from that in he BCP Psalter, and appropriate adjustment will have o be made (a table of variations in verse numbering an be found at www.churchofengland.org/prayer-nd-worship/worship-texts-and-resources/common-vorship/daily-prayer/psalter/psalter-verse). Otherwise he Psalter is read in course daily through each month.

he Calendar observes BCP dates when these differ rom those of *Common Worship*; for example, St Thomas on 21 December. Additional commemorations in the *Common Worship* Calendar are not included, but those who wish to observe them may use the *Collects and Post Communions in Traditional Language: Lesser Festivals, Common of the Saints, Special Occasions* (Church House Publishing).

The Lectionaries of 1871 and 1922, to be found in many copies of the BCP, are still authorized and may be used, but – with the exception of the psalms and readings for Holy Communion mentioned above – the Additional Alternative Lectionary (1961) is no longer authorized for public worship.

Although those who use the BCP, for private or public worship or both, are free to follow any of the authorized lectionaries, there is much to be said for common usage across the Church of England, so that the same passages are being read by all. It is of course appropriate that BCP readings should be taken from the Authorized or King James Version for harmony of style, with the daily recitation of the BCP Psalter.

The integrity of the BCP as the traditional source of worship in the Church of England is not in any way affected by the use of a common lectionary for the daily offices.

CERTAIN DAYS AND OCCASIONS COMMONLY OBSERVED

lough Sunday may be observed on 10 January 2021.

he Week of Prayer for Christian Unity may be bserved from 18 to 25 January 2021.

ducation Sunday may be observed on 12 September 021.

ogation Sunday may be observed on 9 May 2021.

he Feast of Dedication is observed on the nniversary of the dedication or consecration of church, or, when the actual date is unknown, on October 2021. In *Common Worship*, 24 October 2021 s an alternative date.

mber Days. *Common Worship* encourages the bishop o set the Ember Days in each diocese in the week efore the ordinations, whereas in BCP the dates are xed.

Days of Discipline and Self-Denial in *Common Worship* are the weekdays of Lent and all Fridays in the year, except all Principal Feasts and festivals outside Lent and Fridays between Easter Day and Pentecost. The eves of Principal Feasts are also appropriately kept as days of discipline and self-denial in preparation for the feast.

Days of Fasting and Abstinence according to the BCP are the forty days of Lent, the Ember Days at the four seasons, the three Rogation Days, and all Fridays in the year except Christmas Day. The BCP also orders the observance of the Evens or Vigils before The Nativity of our Lord, The Purification of the Blessed Virgin Mary, The Annunciation of the Blessed Virgin Mary, Easter Day, Ascension Day, Pentecost, and before the following saints' days: Matthias, John the Baptist, Peter, James, Bartholomew, Matthew, Simon and Jude, Andrew, Thomas, and All Saints. (If any of these days falls on Monday, the Vigil is to be kept on the previous Saturday.)

KEY TO LITURGICAL COLOURS

Common Worship suggests appropriate liturgical colours. They are not mandatory, and traditional or local use may be followed.

For a detailed discussion of when colours may be used, see *Common Worship: Services and Prayers for the Church of England* (Church House Publishing), *New Handbook of Pastoral Liturgy* (SPCK) or *A Companion to Common Worship: Volume I* (SPCK).

When a lower-case letter accompanies an upper-case letter, the lower-case letter indicates the liturgical colour appropriate to the Lesser Festival of that day while the upper-case letter indicates the continuing seasonal colour.

W White
𝔚 Gold or white
R Red
P Purple (may vary from 'Roman purple' to violet with blue as an alternative; a Lent array of sackcloth may be used in Lent, and rose pink on The Third Sunday of Advent and Fourth Sunday of Lent)
G Green

PRINCIPAL FEASTS, HOLY DAYS AND FESTIVALS

Principal Feasts and other Principal Holy Days (Ash Wednesday, Maundy Thursday, Good Friday) are printed in **LARGE BOLD CAPITALS** in the Lectionary.

There are no longer proper readings relating to the Holy Spirit on the six days after Pentecost. Instead they have been located on the nine days before Pentecost.

When Patronal and Dedication Festivals are kept as Principal Feasts, they may be transferred to the nearest Sunday, unless that day is already either a Principal Feast or The First Sunday of Advent, The Baptism of Christ, The First Sunday of Lent or Palm Sunday.

Festivals are printed in the Lectionary in **SMALL BOLD CAPITALS.**

For each day there is a full liturgical provision fo the Holy Communion and for Morning and Evening Prayer. Most holy days that are in the category 'Festival' are provided with an optional First Evening Prayer. Its use is entirely at the discretion of the minister. Where it is used, the liturgical colour fo the next day should be used at that First Evening Prayer, and this has been indicated in the provision on the following pages.

LESSER FESTIVALS AND COMMEMORATIONS

Lesser Festivals (printed in **medium-bold roman** typeface) are observed at the level appropriate to a particular church. The readings and psalms for The Common of the Saints are listed on page 10. In addition, there are special readings appropriate to the Festival listed in the first column. The daily psalms and readings at Morning and Evening Prayer are not usually superseded by those for Lesser Festivals, but the readings and psalms for Holy Communion may on occasion be used at Morning or Evening Prayer.

Commemorations are printed in the Lectionary in *italic* typeface. They do not have collect, psalm or readings, but may be observed by mention in prayers of intercession and thanksgiving. For local reasons, or where there is an established tradition in the wide Church, they may be kept as Lesser Festivals using the appropriate material from The Common of the Saints. Equally, it may be desirable to observe some Lesse Festivals as Commemorations.

If a Lesser Festival or a Commemoration falls on a Principal Feast, Principal Holy Day, Sunday or Festival it is not normally observed that year, although i may be celebrated, where there is sufficient reason on the nearest available day. Lesser Festivals and Commemorations which, for this reason, would no be celebrated in 2020–21 are listed on pages 9–10, so that, if desired, they may be mentioned in prayers o intercession and thanksgiving.

LESSER FESTIVALS AND COMMEMORATIONS NOT OBSERVED IN 2020–21

The Lesser Festivals and Commemorations (shown in italics) listed below fall on a Sunday or during Holy Week or Easter Week this year, and are thus not observed in this Lectionary.

COMMON WORSHIP

2020

December

6 Nicholas, Bishop of Myra, c. 326
13 Lucy, Martyr at Syracuse, 304
Samuel Johnson, Moralist, 1784

2021

January

10 *William Laud, Archbishop of Canterbury, 1645*
17 Antony of Egypt, Hermit, Abbot, 356
Charles Gore, Bishop, Founder of the Community of the Resurrection, 1932
24 Francis de Sales, Bishop of Geneva, Teacher, 1622
31 *John Bosco, Priest, Founder of the Salesian Teaching Order, 1888*

February

14 Cyril and Methodius, Missionaries to the Slavs, 869 and 885
Valentine, Martyr at Rome, c. 269
17 Janani Luwum, Archbishop of Uganda, Martyr, 1977

March

7 Perpetua, Felicity and their Companions, Martyrs at Carthage, 203
21 Thomas Cranmer, Archbishop of Canterbury, Reformation Martyr, 1556
31 *John Donne, Priest, Poet, 1631*

April

1 *Frederick Denison Maurice, Priest, Teacher, 1872*
9 *Dietrich Bonhoeffer, Lutheran Pastor, Martyr, 1945*
10 William Law, Priest, Spiritual Writer, 1761
William of Ockham, Friar, Philosopher, Teacher, 1347
11 *George Augustus Selwyn, first Bishop of New Zealand, 1878*

May

2 Athanasius, Bishop of Alexandria, Teacher, 373
16 *Caroline Chisholm, Social Reformer, 1877*
30 Josephine Butler, Social Reformer, 1906
Joan of Arc, Visionary, 1431; Apolo Kivebulaya, Priest, Evangelist in Central Africa, 1933

June

6 *Ini Kopuria, Founder of the Melanesian Brotherhood, 1945*
27 *Cyril, Bishop of Alexandria, Teacher, 444*

July

11 Benedict of Nursia, Abbot of Monte Cassino, Father of Western Monasticism, c. 550
18 *Elizabeth Ferard, first Deaconess of the Church of England, Founder of the Community of St Andrew, 1883*

August

8 Dominic, Priest, Founder of the Order of Preachers, 1221
29 The Beheading of John the Baptist

September

19 *Theodore of Tarsus, Archbishop of Canterbury, 690*
26 *Wilson Carlile, Founder of the Church Army, 1942*

October

3 *George Bell, Bishop of Chichester, Ecumenist, Peacemaker, 1958*
10 Paulinus, Bishop of York, Missionary, 644
Thomas Traherne, Poet, Spiritual Writer, 1674
17 Ignatius, Bishop of Antioch, Martyr, c. 107
31 *Martin Luther, Reformer, 1546*

November

7 Willibrord of York, Bishop, Apostle of Frisia, 739
14 *Samuel Seabury, first Anglican Bishop in North America, 1796*

BOOK OF COMMON PRAYER

2020

December
6 Nicholas, Bishop of Myra, *c.* 326
13 Lucy, Martyr at Syracuse, 304

2021

February
14 Valentine, Martyr at Rome, *c.* 269

March
21 Benedict, Abbot of Monte Cassino, *c.* 550

June
20 Translation of Edward, King of the West Saxons, 979

August
29 The Beheading of John the Baptist

September
26 Cyprian, Bishop of Carthage, Martyr, 258

October
17 Etheldreda, Abbess of Ely, 679

THE COMMON OF THE SAINTS

The Blessed Virgin Mary
Genesis 3. 8–15, 20; Isaiah 7. 10–14; Micah 5. 1–4
Psalms 45. 10–17; 113; 131
Acts 1. 12–14; Romans 8. 18–30; Galatians 4. 4–7
Luke 1. 26–38; l. 39–47; John 19. 25–27

Martyrs
2 Chronicles 24. 17–21; Isaiah 43. 1–7; Jeremiah 11. 18–20; Wisdom 4. 10–15
Psalms 3; 11; 31. 1–5; 44. 18–24; 126
Romans 8. 35–end; 2 Corinthians 4. 7–15; 2 Timothy 2. 3–7 [8–13]; Hebrews 11. 32–end; 1 Peter 4. 12–end; Revelation 12. 10–12a
Matthew 10. 16–22; 10. 28–39; 16. 24–26; John 12. 24–26; 15. 18–21

Teachers of the Faith and Spiritual Writers
I Kings 3. [6–10] 11–14; Proverbs 4. 1–9; Wisdom 7. 7–10, 15–16; Ecclesiasticus 39. 1–10
Psalms 19. 7–10; 34. 11–17; 37. 31–35; 119. 89–96; 119. 97–104
I Corinthians 1. 18–25; 2. 1–10; 2. 9–end; Ephesians 3. 8–12; 2 Timothy 4. 1–8; Titus 2. 1–8
Matthew 5. 13–19; 13. 52–end; 23. 8–12; Mark 4. 1–9; John 16. 12–15

Bishops and Other Pastors
I Samuel 16. I, 6–13; Isaiah 6. 1–8; Jeremiah 1. 4–10; Ezekiel 3. 16–21; Malachi 2. 5–7
Psalms 1; 15; 16. 5–end; 96; 110
Acts 20. 28–35; I Corinthians 4. 1–5; 2 Corinthians 4. 1–10 (*or* 1–2, 5–7); 5. 14–20; 1 Peter 5. 1–4
Matthew 11. 25–end; 24. 42–46; John 10. 11–16; 15. 9–17; 21. 15–17

Members of Religious Communities
I Kings 19. 9–18; Proverbs 10. 27–end; Song of Solomon 8. 6–7; Isaiah 61.10 - 62.5; Hosea 2. 14–15, 19–20
Psalms 34. 1–8; 112. 1–9; 119. 57–64; 123; 131
Acts 4. 32–35; 2 Corinthians 10.17 - 11.2; Philippians 3. 7–14; 1 John 2. 15–17; Revelation 19. 1, 5–9
Matthew 11. 25–end; 19. 3–12; 19. 23–end; Luke 9. 57–end; 12. 32–37

Missionaries
Isaiah 52. 7–10; 61. 1–3a; Ezekiel 34. 11–16; Jonah 3. 1–5
Psalms 67; 87; 97; 100; 117
Acts 2. 14, 22–36; 13. 46–49; 16. 6–10; 26. 19–23; Romans 15. 17–21; 2 Corinthians 5.11 - 6.2
Matthew 9. 35–end; 28. 16–end; Mark 16. 15–20; Luke 5. 1–11; 10. 1–9

Any Saint
Genesis 12. 1–4; Proverbs 8. 1–11; Micah 6. 6–8; Ecclesiasticus 2. 7–13 [14–end]
Psalms 32; 33. 1–5; 119. 1–8; 139. 1–4 [5–12]; 145. 8–14
Ephesians 3. 14–19; 6. 11–18; Hebrews 13. 7–8, 15–16; James 2. 14–17; 1 John 4. 7–16; Revelation 21. [1–4] 5–7
Matthew 19. 16–21; 25. 1–13; 25. 14–30; John 15. 1–8; 17. 20–end

SPECIAL OCCASIONS

The Guidance of the Holy Spirit
Proverbs 24. 3–7; Isaiah 30. 15–21; Wisdom 9. 13–17
Psalms 25. 1–9; 104. 26–33; 143. 8–10
Acts 15. 23–29; Romans 8. 22–27;
1 Corinthians 12. 4–13
Luke 14. 27–33; John 14. 23–26; 16. 13–15

The Commemoration of the Faithful Departed
Lamentations 3. 17–26, 31–33 *or* Wisdom 3. 1–9
Psalm 23 *or* 27. 1–6, 16–end
Romans 5. 5–11 *or* I Peter 1. 3–9
John 5. 19–25 *or* 6. 37–40

Rogation Days
Deuteronomy 8. 1–10; 1 Kings 8. 35–40; Job 28. 1–11
Psalms 104. 21–30; 107. 1–9; 121
Philippians 4. 4–7; 2 Thessalonians 3. 6–13;
1 John 5. 12–15
Matthew 6. 1–15; Mark 11. 22–24; Luke 11. 5–13

Harvest Thanksgiving

Year A
Deuteronomy 8. 7–18 *or* 28. 1–14
Psalm 65
2 Corinthians 9. 6–end
Luke 12. 16–30 *or* 17. 11–19

Year B
Joel 2. 21–27
Psalm 126
1 Timothy 2. 1–7 *or* 6. 6–10
Matthew 6. 25–33

Year C
Deuteronomy 26. 1–11
Psalm 100
Philippians 4. 4–9 *or* Revelation 14. 14–18
John 6. 25–35

Mission and Evangelism
Isaiah 49. 1–6; 52. 7–10; Micah 4. 1–5
Psalms 2; 46; 67
Acts 17. 12–end; 2 Corinthians 5.14 - 6.2;
Ephesians 2. 13–end
Matthew 5. 13–16; 28. 16–end; John 17. 20–end

The Unity of the Church
Jeremiah 33. 6–9a; Ezekiel 36. 23–28;
Zephaniah 3. 16–end
Psalms 100; 122; 133
Ephesians 4. 1–6; Colossians 3. 9–17;
1 John 4. 9–15
Matthew 18. 19–22; John 11. 45–52; 17. 11b–23

The Peace of the World
Isaiah 9. 1–6; 57. 15–19; Micah 4. 1–5
Psalms 40. 14–17; 72. 1–7; 85. 8–13
Philippians 4. 6–9; 1 Timothy 2. 1–6;
James 3. 13–18
Matthew 5. 43–end; John 14. 23–29; 15. 9–17

Social Justice and Responsibility
Isaiah 32. 15–end; Amos 5. 21–24; 8. 4–7;
Acts 5. 1–11
Psalms 31. 21–24; 85. 1–7; 146. 5–10
Colossians 3. 12–15; James 2. 1–4
Matthew 5. 1–12; 25. 31–end;
Luke 16. 19–end

Ministry (including Ember Days)
Numbers 11. 16–17, 24–29; 27. 15–end;
1 Samuel 16. 1–13a; Isaiah 6. 1–8; 61. 1–3;
Jeremiah 1. 4–10
Psalms 40. 8–13; 84. 8–12; 89. 19–25;
101. 1–5, 7; 122
Acts 20. 28–35; 1 Corinthians 3. 3–11;
Ephesians 4. 4–16; Philippians 3. 7–14
Luke 4. 16–21; 12. 35–43; 22. 24–27;
John 4. 31–38; 15. 5–17

In Time of Trouble
Genesis 9. 8–17; Job 1. 13–end; Isaiah 38. 6–11
Psalms 86. 1–7; 107. 4–15; 142. 1–7
Romans 3. 21–26; 8. 18–25;
2 Corinthians 8. 1–5, 9
Mark 4. 35–end; Luke 12. 1–7; John 16. 31–end

For the Sovereign
Joshua 1. 1–9; Proverbs 8. 1–16
Psalms 20; 101; 121
Romans 13. 1–10; Revelation 21.22 - 22.4
Matthew 22. 16–22; Luke 22. 24–30

		Sunday Principal Service Weekday Eucharist	Third Service Morning Prayer	Second Service Evening Prayer
29 Sunday	**THE FIRST SUNDAY OF ADVENT** *Common Worship* Year B begins			
P		Isa. 64. 1–9 Ps. 80. 1–8, 18–20 (*or* 80. 1–8) 1 Cor. 1. 3–9 Mark 13. 24–end	Ps. 44 Isa. 2. 1–5 Luke 12. 35–48	Ps. 25 (*or* 25. 1–9) Isa. 1. 1–20 Matt. 21. 1–13 *or First EP of Andrew the Apostle* Ps. 48 Isa. 49. 1–9a 1 Cor. 4. 9–16 **R ct**
30 Monday	**ANDREW THE APOSTLE**			
R		Isa. 52. 7–10 Ps. 19. 1–6 Rom. 10. 12–18 Matt. 4. 18–22	*MP*: Ps. 47; 147. 1–12 Ezek. 47. 1–12 *or* Ecclus. 14. 20–end John 12. 20–32	*EP*: Ps. 87; 96 Zech. 8. 20–end John 1. 35–42

December 2020

1 Tuesday	*Charles de Foucauld, Hermit in the Sahara, 1916* Daily Eucharistic Lectionary Year 1 begins			
P		Isa. 11. 1–10 Ps. 72. 1–4, 18–19 Luke 10. 21–24	Ps. ***80***; 82 *alt.* Ps. ***5***; 6; (8) Isa. 43. 1–13 Rev. ch. 20	Ps. ***74***; 75 *alt.* ***9***; 10† Isa. 26. 1–13 Matt. 12. 22–37
2 Wednesday				
P		Isa. 25. 6–10a Ps. 23 Matt. 15. 29–37	Ps. 5; ***7*** *alt.* Ps. 119. 1–32 Isa. 43. 14–end Rev. 21. 1–8	Ps. 76; ***77*** *alt.* Ps. ***11***; 12; 13 Isa. 28. 1–13 Matt. 12. 38–end
3 Thursday	*Francis Xavier, Missionary, Apostle of the Indies, 1552*			
P		Isa. 26. 1–6 Ps. 118. 18–27a Matt. 7. 21, 24–27	Ps. ***42***; 43 *alt.* Ps. 14; ***15***; 16 Isa. 44. 1–8 Rev. 21. 9–21	Ps. ***40***; 46 *alt.* Ps. 18† Isa. 28. 14–end Matt. 13. 1–23
4 Friday	*John of Damascus, Monk, Teacher, c. 749; Nicholas Ferrar, Deacon, Founder of the Little Gidding Community, 1637*			
P		Isa. 29. 17–end Ps. 27. 1–4, 16–17 Matt. 9. 27–31	Ps. ***25***; 26 *alt.* Ps. 17; ***19*** Isa. 44. 9–23 Rev. 21.22 – 22.5	Ps. 16; ***17*** *alt.* Ps. 22 Isa. 29. 1–14 Matt. 13. 24–43
5 Saturday				
P		Isa. 30. 19–21, 23–26 Ps. 146. 4–9 Matt. 9.35 – 10.1, 6–8	Ps. ***9***; (10) *alt.* Ps. 20; 21; ***23*** Isa. 44.24 – 45.13 Rev. 22. 6–end	Ps. ***27***; 28 *alt.* Ps. ***24***; 25 Isa. 29. 15–end Matt. 13. 44–end **ct**
6 Sunday	**THE SECOND SUNDAY OF ADVENT**			
P		Isa. 40. 1–11 Ps. 85. 1–2, 8–end (*or* 85. 8–end) 2 Pet. 3. 8–15a Mark 1. 1–8	Ps. 80 Baruch 5. 1–9 *or* Zeph. 3. 14–end Luke 1. 5–20	Ps. 40 (*or* 40. 12–end) 1 Kings 22. 1–28 Rom. 15. 4–13 *Gospel*: Matt. 11. 2–11

	Calendar and Holy Communion	Morning Prayer	Evening Prayer
	THE FIRST SUNDAY IN ADVENT Advent 1 Collect until Christmas Eve		
P	Mic. 4. 1–4, 6–7 Ps. 25. 1–9 Rom. 13. 8–14 Matt. 21. 1–13	Ps. 44 Isa. 2. 1–5 Luke 12. 35–48	Ps. 9 Isa. 1. 1–20 Mark 13. 24–end *or First EP of Andrew the Apostle* Ps. 48 Isa. 49. 1–9a 1 Cor. 4. 9–16 **R ct**
	ANDREW THE APOSTLE		
R	Zech. 8. 20–end Ps. 92. 1–5 Rom. 10. 9–end Matt. 4. 18–22	(Ps. 47; 147. 1–12) Ezek. 47. 1–12 *or* Ecclus. 14. 20–end John 12. 20–32	(Ps. 87; 96) Isa. 52. 7–10 John 1. 35–42
P		Isa. 43. 1–13 Rev. ch. 20	Isa. 26. 1–13 Matt. 12. 22–37
P		Isa. 43. 14–end Rev. 21. 1–8	Isa. 28. 1–13 Matt. 12. 38–end
P		Isa. 44. 1–8 Rev. 21. 9–21	Isa. 28. 14–end Matt. 13. 1–23
P		Isa. 44. 9–23 Rev. 21.22 – 22.5	Isa. 29. 1–14 Matt. 13. 24–43
P		Isa. 44.24 – 45.13 Rev. 22. 6–end	Isa. 29. 15–end Matt. 13. 44–end **ct**
	THE SECOND SUNDAY IN ADVENT		
P	2 Kings 22. 8–10; 23. 1–3 Ps. 50. 1–6 Rom. 15. 4–13 Luke 21. 25–33	Ps. 80 Baruch 5. 1–9 *or* Zeph. 3. 14–end Luke 1. 5–20	Ps. 40 (*or* 40. 12–end) 1 Kings 22. 1–28 2 Pet. 3. 8–15a

NOTES

		Sunday Principal Service Weekday Eucharist	Third Service Morning Prayer	Second Service Evening Prayer
7 Monday	**Ambrose, Bishop of Milan, Teacher, 397**			
Pw	Com. Teacher *or* *also* Isa. 41. 9b-13 Luke 22. 24-30	Isa. ch. 35 Ps. 85. 7-end Luke 5. 17-26	Ps. 44 *alt.* Ps. 27; ***30*** Isa. 45. 14-end 1 Thess. ch. 1	Ps. ***144***; 146 *alt.* Ps. 26; ***28***; 29 Isa. 30. 1-18 Matt. 14. 1-12
8 Tuesday	**The Conception of the Blessed Virgin Mary**			
Pw	Com. BVM *or*	Isa. 40. 1-11 Ps. 96. 1, 10-end Matt. 18. 12-14	Ps. ***56***; 57 *alt.* Ps. 32; ***36*** Isa. ch. 46 1 Thess. 2. 1-12	Ps. ***11***; 12; 13 *alt.* Ps. 33 Isa. 30. 19-end Matt. 14. 13-end
9 Wednesday	Ember Day*			
P		Isa. 40. 25-end Ps. 103. 8-13 Matt. 11. 28-end	Ps. ***62***; 63 *alt.* Ps. 34 Isa. ch. 47 1 Thess. 2. 13-end	Ps. ***10***; 14 *alt.* Ps. 119. 33-56 Isa. ch. 31 Matt. 15. 1-20
10 Thursday				
P		Isa. 41. 13-20 Ps. 145. 1, 8-13 Matt. 11. 11-15	Ps. 53; ***54***; 60 *alt.* Ps. 37† Isa. 48. 1-11 1 Thess. ch. 3	Ps. 73 *alt.* Ps. 39; ***40*** Isa. ch. 32 Matt. 15. 21-28
11 Friday	Ember Day*			
P		Isa. 48. 17-19 Ps. 1 Matt. 11. 16-19	Ps. 85; ***86*** *alt.* Ps. 31 Isa. 48. 12-end 1 Thess. 4. 1-12	Ps. 82; ***90*** *alt.* Ps. 35 Isa. 33. 1-22 Matt. 15. 29-end
12 Saturday	Ember Day*			
P		Ecclus. 48. 1-4, 9-11 *or* 2 Kings 2. 9-12 Ps. 80. 1-4, 18-19 Matt. 17. 10-13	Ps. 145 *alt.* Ps. 41; ***42***; 43 Isa. 49. 1-13 1 Thess. 4. 13-end	Ps. 93; ***94*** *alt.* Ps. 45; ***46*** Isa. ch. 35 Matt. 16. 1-12 **ct**
13 Sunday	**THE THIRD SUNDAY OF ADVENT**			
P		Isa. 61. 1-4, 8-end Ps. 126 *or Canticle*: Magnificat 1 Thess. 5. 16-24 John 1. 6-8, 19-28	Ps. 50. 1-6; 62 Isa. ch. 12 Luke 1. 57-66	Ps. 68. 1-19 (*or* 68. 1-8) Mal. 3. 1-4; ch. 4 Phil. 4. 4-7 *Gospel*: Matt. 14. 1-12
14 Monday	**John of the Cross, Poet, Teacher, 1591**			
Pw	Com. Teacher *or* *esp.* 1 Cor. 2. 1-10 *also* John 14. 18-23	Num. 24. 2-7, 15-17 Ps. 25. 3-8 Matt. 21. 23-27	Ps. 40 *alt.* Ps. 44 Isa. 49. 14-25 1 Thess. 5. 1-11	Ps. 25; ***26*** *alt.* Ps. ***47***; 49 Isa. 38. 1-8, 21-22 Matt. 16. 13-end
15 Tuesday				
P		Zeph. 3. 1-2, 9-13 Ps. 34. 1-6, 21-22 Matt. 21. 28-32	Ps. ***70***; 74 *alt.* Ps. ***48***; 52 Isa. ch. 50 1 Thess. 5. 12-end	Ps. ***50***; 54 *alt.* Ps. 50 Isa. 38. 9-20 Matt. 17. 1-13

*For Ember Day provision, see p. 11.

	Calendar and Holy Communion	Morning Prayer	Evening Prayer	NOTES
P		Isa. 45. 14–end 1 Thess. ch. 1	Isa. 30. 1–18 Matt. 14. 1–12	
	The Conception of the Blessed Virgin Mary			
Pw		Isa. ch. 46 1 Thess. 2. 1–12	Isa. 30. 19–end Matt. 14. 13–end	
P		Isa. ch. 47 1 Thess. 2. 13–end	Isa. ch. 31 Matt. 15. 1–20	
P		Isa. 48. 1–11 1 Thess. ch. 3	Isa. ch. 32 Matt. 15. 21–28	
P		Isa. 48. 12–end 1 Thess. 4. 1–12	Isa. 33. 1–22 Matt. 15. 29–end	
P		Isa. 49. 1–13 1 Thess. 4. 13–end	Isa. ch. 35 Matt. 16. 1–12 **ct**	
	THE THIRD SUNDAY IN ADVENT			
P	Isa. ch. 35 Ps. 80. 1–7 1 Cor. 4. 1–5 Matt. 11. 2–10	Ps. 62 Isa. ch. 12 Luke 1. 57–66	Ps. 68. 1–19 (*or* 68. 1–8) Mal. 3. 1–4; ch. 4 Matt. 14. 1–12	
P		Isa. 49. 14–25 1 Thess. 5. 1–11	Isa. 38. 1–8, 21–22 Matt. 16. 13–end	
P		Isa. ch. 50 1 Thess. 5. 12–end	Isa. 38. 9–20 Matt. 17. 1–13	

		Sunday Principal Service Weekday Eucharist	Third Service Morning Prayer	Second Service Evening Prayer
16 Wednesday				
P		Isa. 45. 6b–8, 18, 21b–end Ps. 85. 7–end Luke 7. 18b–23	Ps. ***75***; 96 *alt.* Ps. 119. 57–80 Isa. 51. 1–8 2 Thess. ch. 1	Ps. 25; ***82*** *alt.* Ps. ***59***; 60; (67) Isa. ch. 39 Matt. 17. 14–21
17 Thursday	O Sapientia* *Eglantyne Jebb, Social Reformer, Founder of 'Save the Children', 1928*			
P		Gen. 49. 2, 8–10 Ps. 72. 1–5, 18–19 Matt. 1. 1–17	Ps. ***76***; 97 *alt.* Ps. 56; ***57***; (63†) Isa. 51. 9–16 2 Thess. ch. 2	Ps. 44 *alt.* Ps. 61; ***62***; 64 Zeph. 1.1 – 2.3 Matt. 17. 22–end
18 Friday				
P		Jer. 23. 5–8 Ps. 72. 1–2, 12–13, 18–end Matt. 1. 18–24	Ps. 77; ***98*** *alt.* Ps. ***51***; 54 Isa. 51. 17–end 2 Thess. ch. 3	Ps. 49 *alt.* Ps. 38 Zeph. 3. 1–13 Matt. 18. 1–20
19 Saturday				
P		Judg. 13. 2–7, 24–end Ps. 71. 3–8 Luke 1. 5–25	Ps. 144; ***146*** Isa. 52. 1–12 Jude	Ps. 10; ***57*** Zeph. 3. 14–end Matt. 18. 21–end **ct**
20 Sunday	**THE FOURTH SUNDAY OF ADVENT**			
P		2 Sam. 7. 1–11, 16 *Canticle*: Magnificat *or* Ps. 89. 1–4, 19–26 (*or* 1–8) Rom. 16. 25–end Luke 1. 26–38	Ps. 144 Isa. 7. 10–16 Rom. 1. 1–7	Ps. 113 [131] Zech. 2. 10–end Luke 1. 39–55
21 Monday**				
P		Zeph. 3. 14–18 Ps. 33. 1–4, 11–12, 20–end Luke 1. 39–45	Ps. ***121***; 122; 123 Isa. 52.13 – 53.end 2 Pet. 1. 1–15	Ps. 80; ***84*** Mal. 1. 1, 6–end Matt. 19. 1–12
22 Tuesday				
P		1 Sam. 1. 24–end Ps. 113 Luke 1. 46–56	Ps. ***124***; 125; 126; 127 Isa. ch. 54 2 Pet. 1.16 – 2.3	Ps. 24; ***48*** Mal. 2. 1–16 Matt. 19. 13–15
23 Wednesday				
P		Mal. 3. 1–4; 4. 5–end Ps. 25. 3–9 Luke 1. 57–66	Ps. 128; 129; ***130***; 131 Isa. ch. 55 2 Pet. 2. 4–end	Ps. 89. 1–37 Mal. 2.17 – 3.12 Matt. 19. 16–end

*Evening Prayer readings from the Additional Weekday Lectionary (see p. 120) may be used from 17 to 23 December.
**Thomas the Apostle may be celebrated on 21 December instead of 3 July.

	Calendar and Holy Communion	Morning Prayer	Evening Prayer	NOTES
	O Sapientia Ember Day			
P	Ember CEG	Isa. 51. 1-8 2 Thess. ch. 1	Isa. ch. 39 Matt. 17. 14-21	
P		Isa. 51. 9-16 2 Thess. ch. 2	Zeph. 1.1 - 2.3 Matt. 17. 22-end	
	Ember Day			
P	Ember CEG	Isa. 51. 17-end 2 Thess. ch. 3	Zeph. 3. 1-13 Matt. 18. 1-20	
	Ember Day			
P	Ember CEG	Isa. 52. 1-12 Jude	Zeph. 3. 14-end Matt. 18. 21-end **ct**	
	THE FOURTH SUNDAY IN ADVENT			
P	Isa. 40. 1-9 Ps. 145. 17-end Phil. 4. 4-7 John 1. 19-28	Ps. 144 Isa. 7. 10-16 Rom. 1. 1-7	Ps. 113 [131] Zech. 2. 10-end Luke 1. 39-55 *or First EP of Thomas* Ps. 27 Isa. ch. 35 Heb. 10.35 - 11.1 **R ct**	
	THOMAS THE APOSTLE			
R	Job 42. 1-6 Ps. 139. 1-11 Eph. 2. 19-end John 20. 24-end	(Ps. 92; 146) 2 Sam. 15. 17-21 *or* Ecclus. ch. 2 John 11. 1-16	(Ps. 139) Hab. 2. 1-4 1 Pet. 1. 3-12	
P		Isa. ch. 54 2 Pet. 1.16 - 2.3	Mal. 2. 1-16 Matt. 19. 13-15	
P		Isa. ch. 55 2 Pet. 2. 4-end	Mal. 2.17 - 3.12 Matt. 19. 16-end	

		Sunday Principal Service Weekday Eucharist	Third Service Morning Prayer	Second Service Evening Prayer
24 Thursday	**CHRISTMAS EVE**			
P		*Morning Eucharist* 2 Sam. 7. 1–5, 8–11, 16 Ps. 89. 2, 19–27 Acts 13. 16–26 Luke 1. 67–79	Ps. ***45***; 113 Isa. 56. 1–8 2 Pet. ch. 3	Ps. 85 Zech. ch. 2 Rev. 1. 1–8
25 Friday	**CHRISTMAS DAY**			
𝔚	*Any of the following sets of readings may be used on the evening of Christmas Eve and on Christmas Day. Set III should be used at some service during the celebration.*	*I* Isa. 9. 2–7 Ps. 96 Titus 2. 11–14 Luke 2. 1–14 [15–20] *II* Isa. 62. 6–end Ps. 97 Titus 3. 4–7 Luke 2. [1–7] 8–20 *III* Isa. 52. 7–10 Ps. 98 Heb. 1. 1–4 [5–12] John 1. 1–14	*MP*: Ps. ***110***; 117 Isa. 62. 1–5 Matt. 1. 18–end	*EP*: Ps. 8 Isa. 65. 17–25 Phil. 2. 5–11 *or* Luke 2. 1–20 *if it has not been used at the principal service of the day*
26 Saturday	**STEPHEN, DEACON, FIRST MARTYR**			
R	*The reading from Acts must be used as either the first or second reading at the Eucharist.*	2 Chron. 24. 20–22 *or* Acts 7. 51–end Ps. 119. 161–168 Acts 7. 51–end *or* Gal. 2. 16b–20 Matt. 10. 17–22	*MP*: Ps. ***13***; 31. 1–8; 150 Jer. 26. 12–15 Acts ch. 6	*EP*: Ps. 57; ***86*** Gen. 4. 1–10 Matt. 23. 34–end
27 Sunday	**JOHN, APOSTLE AND EVANGELIST** (or transferred to 29 December)			
W		Exod. 33. 7–11a Ps. 117 1 John ch. 1 John 21. 19b–end	*MP*: Ps. ***21***; 147. 13–end Exod. 33. 12–end 1 John 2. 1–11	*EP*: Ps. 97 Isa. 6. 1–8 1 John 5. 1–12
	or, for The First Sunday of Christmas:			
W		Isa. 61.10 - 62.3 Ps. 148 (*or* 148. 7–end) Gal. 4. 4–7 Luke 2. 15–21	Ps. 105. 1–11 Isa. 63. 7–9 Eph. 3. 5–12	Ps. 132 Isa. ch. 35 Col. 1. 9–20 *or* Luke 2. 41–end
28 Monday	**THE HOLY INNOCENTS**			
R		Jer. 31. 15–17 Ps. 124 1 Cor. 1. 26–29 Matt. 2. 13–18	*MP*: Ps. ***36***; 146 Baruch 4. 21–27 *or* Gen. 37. 13–20 Matt. 18. 1–10	*EP*: Ps. 123; ***128*** Isa. 49. 14–25 Mark 10. 13–16

	Calendar and Holy Communion	Morning Prayer	Evening Prayer	NOTES
	CHRISTMAS EVE			
P	Collect (1) Christmas Eve (2) Advent 1 Mic. 5. 2–5a Ps. 24 Titus 3. 3–7 Luke 2. 1–14	Isa. 56. 1–8 2 Pet. ch. 3	Zech. ch. 2 Rev. 1. 1–8	
	CHRISTMAS DAY			
𝔚	Isa. 9. 2–7 Ps. 98 Heb. 1. 1–12 John 1. 1–14	Ps. 110; 117 Isa. 62. 1–5 Matt. 1. 18–end	Ps. 8 Isa. 65. 17–25 Phil. 2. 5–11 *or* Luke 2. 1–20	
	STEPHEN, DEACON, FIRST MARTYR			
R	Collect (1) Stephen (2) Christmas 2 Chron. 24. 20–22 Ps. 119. 161–168 Acts 7. 55–end Matt. 23. 34–end	(Ps. 13; 31. 1–8; 150) Jer. 26. 12–15 Acts ch. 6	(Ps. 57; 86) Gen. 4. 1–10 Matt. 10. 17–22	
	JOHN, APOSTLE AND EVANGELIST (or transferred to 29 December)			
W	Collect (1) John (2) Christmas Exod. 33. 18–end Ps. 92. 11–end 1 John ch. 1 John 21. 19b–end	Ps. 21; 147. 13–end Exod. 33. 7–11a 1 John 2. 1–11	Ps. 97 Isa. 6. 1–8 1 John 5. 1–12	
	or, for The Sunday after Christmas Day:			
W	Isa. 62. 10–12 Ps. 45. 1–7 Gal. 4. 1–7 Matt. 1. 18–end	Ps. 105. 1–11 Isa. 63. 7–9 Eph. 3. 5–12	Ps. 132 Isa. ch. 35 1 John 1. 1–7	
	THE HOLY INNOCENTS			
R	Collect (1) Innocents (2) Christmas Jer. 31. 10–17 Ps. 123 Rev. 14. 1–5 Matt. 2. 13–18	(Ps. 36; 146) Baruch 4. 21–27 *or* Gen. 37. 13–20 Matt. 18. 1–10	(Ps. 124; 128) Isa. 49. 14–25 Mark 10. 13–16	

		Sunday Principal Service Weekday Eucharist	Third Service Morning Prayer	Second Service Evening Prayer
29 Tuesday	**Thomas Becket, Archbishop of Canterbury, Martyr, 1170*** (For John, Apostle and Evangelist, see provision on 27 December)			
Wr	Com. Martyr *or* *esp.* Matt. 10. 28–33 *also* Ecclus. 51. 1–8	1 John 2. 3–11 Ps. 96. 1–4 Luke 2. 22–35	Ps. ***19***; 20 Isa. 57. 15–end John 1. 1–18	Ps. 131; ***132*** Jonah ch. 1 Col. 1. 1–14
30 Wednesday				
W		1 John 2. 12–17 Ps. 96. 7–10 Luke 2. 36–40	Ps. 111; 112; ***113*** Isa. 59. 1–15a John 1. 19–28	Ps. ***65***; 84 Jonah ch. 2 Col. 1. 15–23
31 Thursday	*John Wyclif, 1384*			
W		1 John 2. 18–21 Ps. 96. 1, 11–end John 1. 1–18	Ps. 102 Isa. 59. 15b–end John 1. 29–34	Ps. ***90***; 148 Jonah chs 3 & 4 Col. 1.24 - 2.7 *or First EP of The Naming of Jesus* Ps. 148 Jer. 23. 1–6 Col. 2. 8–15 **ct**

January 2021

1 Friday	**THE NAMING AND CIRCUMCISION OF JESUS**			
W		Num. 6. 22–end Ps. 8 Gal. 4. 4–7 Luke 2. 15–21	*MP*: Ps. ***103***; 150 Gen. 17. 1–13 Rom. 2. 17–end	*EP*: Ps. 115 Deut. 30. [1–10] 11–end Acts 3. 1–16
2 Saturday	**Basil the Great and Gregory of Nazianzus, Bishops, Teachers, 379 and 389** *Seraphim, Monk of Sarov, Spiritual Guide, 1833; Vedanayagam Samuel Azariah, Bishop in South India, Evangelist, 1945*			
W	Com. Teacher *or* *esp.* 2 Tim. 4. 1–8 Matt. 5. 13–19	1 John 2. 22–28 Ps. 98. 1–4 John 1. 19–28	Ps. 18. 1–30 Isa. 60. 1–12 John 1. 35–42	Ps. 45; ***46*** Ruth ch. 1 Col. 2. 8–end
3 Sunday	**THE SECOND SUNDAY OF CHRISTMAS** *or* The Epiphany (*see provision on the 6th*)			
W		Jer. 31. 7–14 Ps. 147. 13–end *or* Ecclus. 24. 1–12 *Canticle*: Wisd. of Sol. 10. 15–end Eph. 1. 3–14 John 1. [I–9] 10–18	Ps. 87 Zech. 8. 1–8 Luke 2. 41–end	Ps. 135 (*or* 135. 1–14) Isa. 46. 3–end Rom. 12. 1–8 *Gospel*: Matt. 2. 13–end
4 Monday				
W		1 John 3. 7–10 Ps. 98. I, 8–end John 1. 35–42	Ps. 89. 1–37 Isa. ch. 61 John 2. 1–12	Ps. 85; ***87*** Ruth ch. 3 Col. 3.12 - 4.1
	or, if The Epiphany is celebrated on 3 January:	1 John 3.22 - 4.6 Ps. 2. 7–end Matt. 4. 12–17, 23–end	Ps. 89. 1–37 *alt.* Ps. Ps. 71 Isa. 60. 13–end John 1. 43–end	Ps. 85; ***87*** *alt.* Ps. ***72***; 75 Ruth ch. 2 Col. 3. 1–11

*Thomas Becket may be celebrated on 7 July instead of 29 December.

	Calendar and Holy Communion	Morning Prayer	Evening Prayer	NOTES
	CEG of Christmas			
W		Isa. 57. 15–end John 1. 1–18	Jonah ch. 1 Col. 1. 1–14	
W		Isa. 59. 1–15a John 1. 19–28	Jonah ch. 2 Col. 1. 15–23	
	Silvester, Bishop of Rome, 335			
W	Com. Bishop	Isa. 59. 15b–end John 1. 29–34	Jonah chs 3 & 4 Col. 1.24 – 2.7 *or First EP of The Circumcision of Christ* (Ps. 148) Jer. 23. 1–6 Col. 2. 8–15 **ct**	
	THE CIRCUMCISION OF CHRIST			
W	Additional collect Gen. 17. 3b–10 Ps. 98 Rom. 4. 8–13 *or* Eph. 2. 11–18 Luke 2. 15–21	(Ps. 103; 150) Gen. 17. 1–13 Rom. 2. 17–end	(Ps. 115) Deut. 30. [1–10] 11–end Acts 3. 1–16	
W		Isa. 60. 1–12 John 1. 35–42	Ruth ch. 1 Col. 2. 8–end	
	THE SECOND SUNDAY AFTER CHRISTMAS			
W	Exod. 24. 12–18 Ps. 93 2 Cor. 8. 9 John 1. 14–18	Ps. 87 Zech. 8. 1–8 Luke 2. 41–end	Ps. 135 (*or* 135. 1–14) Eph. 1. 3–14 Rom. 12. 1–8	
W		Isa. ch. 61 John 2. 1–12	Ruth ch. 3 Col. 3.12 – 4.1	

		Sunday Principal Service Weekday Eucharist	Third Service Morning Prayer	Second Service Evening Prayer
5 Tuesday				
W		1 John 3. 11–21 Ps. 100 John 1. 43–end	Ps. 8; ***48*** Isa. ch. 62 John 2. 13–end	*First EP of The Epiphany* Ps. 96; **97** Isa. 49. 1–13 John 4. 7–26 **𝔚 ct**
	or, if The Epiphany is celebrated on 3 January:	1 John 4. 7–10 Ps. 72. 1–8 Mark 6. 34–44	Ps. 8; **48** *alt.* Ps. 73 Isa. ch. 61 John 2. 1–12	Ps. 96; **97** *alt.* Ps. 74 Ruth ch. 3 Col. 3.12 – 4.1
6 Wednesday	**THE EPIPHANY**			
𝔚		Isa. 60. 1–6 Ps. 72 (*or* 72. 10–15) Eph. 3. 1–12 Matt. 2. 1–12	*MP*: Ps. ***132***; 113 Jer. 31. 7–14 John 1. 29–34	*EP*: Ps. ***98***; 100 Baruch 4.36 – 5.end *or* Isa. 60. 1–9 John 2. 1–11
W	*or, if The Epiphany is celebrated on 3 January*:	1 John 4. 11–18 Ps. 72. 1, 10–13 Mark 6. 45–52	Ps. ***127***; 128; 131 *alt.* Ps. 77 Isa. ch. 62 John 2. 13–end	Ps. **2**; 110 *alt.* Ps. 119. 81–104 Ruth 4. 1–17 Col. 4. 2–end
7 Thursday				
W		1 John 3.22 – 4.6 Ps. 2. 7–end Matt. 4. 12–17, 23–end	Ps. ***99***; 147. 1–12 *alt.* Ps. 78. 1–39† Isa. 63. 7–end 1 John ch. 3	Ps. 118 *alt.* Ps. 78. 40–end† Baruch 1.15 – 2.10 *or* Jer. 23. 1–8 Matt. 20. 1–16
	or, if The Epiphany is celebrated on 3 January:	1 John 4.19 – 5.4 Ps. 72. 1, 17–end Luke 4. 14–22	Ps. ***99***; 147. 1–12 *alt.* Ps. 78. 1–39† Isa. 63. 7–end 1 John ch. 3	Ps. 118 *alt.* Ps. 78. 40–end† Baruch 1.15 – 2.10 *or* Jer. 23. 1–8 Matt. 20. 1–16
8 Friday				
W		1 John 4. 7–10 Ps. 72. 1–8 Mark 6. 34–44	Ps. ***46***; 147. 13–end *alt.* Ps. 55 Isa. ch. 64 1 John 4. 7–end	Ps. 145 *alt.* Ps. 69 Baruch 2. 11–end *or* Jer. 30. 1–17 Matt. 20. 17–28
	or, if The Epiphany is celebrated on 3 January:	1 John 5. 5–13 Ps. 147. 13–end Luke 5. 12–16	Ps. ***46***; 147. 13–end *alt.* Ps. 55 Isa. ch. 64 1 John 4. 7–end	Ps. 145 *alt.* Ps. 69 Baruch 2. 11–end *or* Jer. 30. 1–17 Matt. 20. 17–28

	Calendar and Holy Communion	Morning Prayer	Evening Prayer	NOTES
W		Isa. ch. 62 John 2. 13-end	*First EP of The Epiphany* Ps. 96; **97** Isa. 49. 1-13 John 4. 7-26 **𝔚 ct**	
	THE EPIPHANY			
𝔚	Isa. 60. 1-9 Ps. 100 Eph. 3. 1-12 Matt. 2. 1-12	Ps. 132; 113 Jer. 31. 7-14 John 1. 29-34	Ps. 72; 98 Baruch 4.36 - 5.end *or* Isa. 60. 1-9 John 2. 1-11	
W *or* **G**		Isa. 63. 7-end 1 John ch. 3	Baruch 1.15 - 2.10 *or* Jer. 23. 1-8 Matt. 20. 1-16	
	Lucian, Priest and Martyr, 290			
Wr *or* **Gr**	Com. Martyr	Isa. ch. 64 1 John 4. 7-end	Baruch 2. 11-end *or* Jer. 30. 1-17 Matt. 20. 17-28	

		Sunday Principal Service Weekday Eucharist	Third Service Morning Prayer	Second Service Evening Prayer
9 Saturday				
W		1 John 4. 11–18 Ps. 72. 1, 10–13 Mark 6. 45–52	Ps. 2; ***148*** *alt.* Ps. ***76***; 79 Isa. 65. 1–16 1 John 5. 1–12	*First EP of The Baptism* Ps. 36 Isa. ch. 61 Titus 2. 11–14; 3. 4–7 **W ct**
	or, if The Epiphany is celebrated on 3 January:	1 John 5. 14–end Ps. 149. 1–5 John 3. 22–30	Ps. 2; ***148*** *alt.* Ps. ***76***; 79 Isa. 65. 1–16 1 John 5. 1–12	*First EP of The Baptism* Ps. 36 Isa. ch. 61 Titus 2. 11–14; 3. 4–7 **W ct**
10 Sunday	**THE BAPTISM OF CHRIST (THE FIRST SUNDAY OF EPIPHANY)**			
W		Gen. 1. 1–5 Ps. 29 Acts 19. 1–7 Mark 1. 4–11	Ps. 89. 19–29 1 Sam. 16. 1–3, 13 John 1. 29–34	Ps. 46; [47] Isa. 42. 1–9 Eph. 2. 1–10 *Gospel*: Matt. 2. 13–end
11 Monday	*Mary Slessor, Missionary in West Africa, 1915*			
W **DEL 1**		Heb. 1. 1–6 Ps. 97. 1–2, 6–10 Mark 1. 14–20	Ps. **2**; 110 *alt.* Ps. ***80***; 82 Amos ch. 1 1 Cor. 1. 1–17	Ps. ***34***; 36 *alt.* Ps. ***85***; 86 Gen. 1. 1–19 Matt. 21. 1–17
12 Tuesday	**Aelred of Hexham, Abbot of Rievaulx, 1167** *Benedict Biscop, Abbot of Wearmouth, Scholar, 689*			
W	Com. Religious *or* *also* Ecclus. 15. 1–6	Heb. 2. 5–12 Ps. 8 Mark 1. 21–28	Ps. ***8***; 9 *alt.* Ps. 87; ***89. 1–18*** Amos ch. 2 1 Cor. 1. 18–end	Ps. ***45***; 46 *alt.* Ps. 89. 19–end Gen. 1.20 – 2.3 Matt. 21. 18–32
13 Wednesday	**Hilary, Bishop of Poitiers, Teacher, 367** *Kentigern (Mungo), Missionary Bishop in Strathclyde and Cumbria, 603; George Fox, Founder of the Society of Friends (the Quakers), 1691*			
W	Com. Teacher *or* *also* 1 John 2. 18–25 John 8. 25–32	Heb. 2. 14–end Ps. 105. 1–9 Mark 1. 29–39	Ps. 19; ***20*** *alt.* Ps. 119. 105–128 Amos ch. 3 1 Cor. ch. 2	Ps. ***47***; 48 *alt.* Ps. ***91***; 93 Gen. 2. 4–end Matt. 21. 33–end
14 Thursday				
W		Heb. 3. 7–14 Ps. 95. 1, 8–end Mark 1. 40–end	Ps. ***21***; 24 *alt.* Ps. 90; **92** Amos ch. 4 1 Cor. ch. 3	Ps. ***61***; 65 *alt.* Ps. 94 Gen. ch. 3 Matt. 22. 1–14
15 Friday				
W		Heb. 4. 1–5, 11 Ps. 78. 3–8 Mark 2. 1–12	Ps. ***67***; 72 *alt.* Ps. ***88***; (95) Amos 5. 1–17 1 Cor. ch. 4	Ps. 68 *alt.* Ps. 102 Gen. 4. 1–16, 25–26 Matt. 22. 15–33

	Calendar and Holy Communion	Morning Prayer	Evening Prayer	NOTES
W *or* **G**		Isa. 65. 1–16 1 John 5. 1–12	Baruch 3. 1–8 *or* Jer. 30.18 – 31.9 Matt. 20. 29–end **ct**	
	THE FIRST SUNDAY AFTER EPIPHANY To celebrate The Baptism of Christ, see *Common Worship* provision.			
W *or* **G**	Zech. 8. 1–8 Ps. 72. 1–8 Rom. 12. 1–5 Luke 2. 41–end	Ps. 89. 19–29 1 Sam. 16. 1–3, 13 John 1. 29–34	Ps. 46; 47 Isa. 42. 1–9 Eph. 2. 1–10	
W *or* **G**		Amos ch. 1 1 Cor. 1. 1–17	Gen. 1. 1–19 Matt. 21. 1–17	
W *or* **G**		Amos ch. 2 1 Cor. 1. 18–end	Gen. 1.20 – 2.3 Matt. 21. 18–32	
	Hilary, Bishop of Poitiers, Teacher, 367			
W *or* **Gw**	Com. Doctor	Amos ch. 3 1 Cor. ch. 2	Gen. 2. 4–end Matt. 21. 33–end	
W *or* **G**		Amos ch. 4 1 Cor. ch. 3	Gen. ch. 3 Matt. 22. 1–14	
W *or* **G**		Amos 5. 1–17 1 Cor. ch. 4	Gen. 4. 1–16, 25–26 Matt. 22. 15–33	

		Sunday Principal Service Weekday Eucharist	Third Service Morning Prayer	Second Service Evening Prayer
16 Saturday				
W		Heb. 4. 12–end Ps. 19. 7–end Mark 2. 13–17	Ps. 29; ***33*** *alt.* Ps. 96; ***97***; 100 Amos 5. 18–end 1 Cor. ch. 5	Ps. 84; ***85*** *alt.* Ps. 104 Gen. 6. 1–10 Matt. 22. 34–end **ct**
17 Sunday	**THE SECOND SUNDAY OF EPIPHANY**			
W		1 Sam. 3. 1–10 [11–20] Ps. 139. 1–5, 12–18 (*or* 1–9) Rev. 5. 1–10 John 1. 43–end	Ps. 145. 1–12 Isa. 62. 1–5 1 Cor. 6. 11–end	Ps. 96 Isa. 60. 9–end Heb. 6.17 - 7.10 *Gospel*: Matt. 8. 5–13
18 Monday	*Amy Carmichael, founder of the Dohnavur Fellowship, Spiritual Writer, 1951* The Week of Prayer for Christian Unity until 25th			
W **DEL 2**		Heb. 5. 1–10 Ps. 110. 1–4 Mark 2. 18–22	Ps. 145; ***146*** *alt.* Ps. ***98***; 99; 101 Amos ch. 6 1 Cor. 6. 1–11	Ps. 71 *alt.* Ps. 105† (*or* 103) Gen. 6.11 - 7.10 Matt. 24. 1–14
19 Tuesday	**Wulfstan, Bishop of Worcester, 1095**			
W	Com. Bishop *or* *esp.* Matt. 24. 42–46	Heb. 6. 10–end Ps. 111 Mark 2. 23–end	Ps. ***132***; 147. 1–12 *alt.* Ps. 106† (*or* 103) Amos ch. 7 1 Cor. 6. 12–end	Ps. 89. 1–37 *alt.* Ps. 107† Gen. 7. 11–end Matt. 24. 15–28
20 Wednesday	*Richard Rolle of Hampole, Spiritual Writer, 1349*			
W		Heb. 7. 1–3, 15–17 Ps. 110. 1–4 Mark 3. 1–6	Ps. ***81***; 147. 13–end *alt.* Ps. 110; ***111***; 112 Amos ch. 8 1 Cor. 7. 1–24	Ps. ***97***; 98 *alt.* Ps. 119. 129–152 Gen. 8. 1–14 Matt. 24. 29–end
21 Thursday	**Agnes, Child Martyr at Rome, 304**			
Wr	Com. Martyr *or* *also* Rev. 7. 13–end	Heb. 7.25 - 8.6 Ps. 40. 7–10, 17–end Mark 3. 7–12	Ps. ***76***; 148 *alt.* Ps. 113; ***115*** Amos ch. 9 1 Cor. 7. 25–end	Ps. 99; 100; ***111*** *alt.* Ps. 114; ***116***; 117 Gen. 8.15 - 9.7 Matt. 25. 1–13
22 Friday	*Vincent of Saragossa, Deacon, first Martyr of Spain, 304*			
W		Heb. 8. 6–end Ps. 85. 7–end Mark 3. 13–19	Ps. ***27***; 149 *alt.* Ps. 139 Hos. 1.1 - 2.1 1 Cor. ch. 8	Ps. 73 *alt.* Ps. ***130***; 131; 137 Gen. 9. 8–19 Matt. 25. 14–30
23 Saturday				
W		Heb. 9. 2–3, 11–14 Ps. 47. 1–8 Mark 3. 20–21	Ps. ***122***; 128; 150 *alt.* Ps. 120; ***121***; 122 Hos. 2. 2–17 1 Cor. 9. 1–14	Ps. ***61***; 66 *alt.* Ps. 118 Gen. 11. 1–9 Matt. 25. 31–end **ct**

	Calendar and Holy Communion	Morning Prayer	Evening Prayer	NOTES
W *or* **G**		Amos 5. 18–end 1 Cor. ch. 5	Gen. 6. 1–10 Matt. 22. 34–end **ct**	
	THE SECOND SUNDAY AFTER THE EPIPHANY			
W *or* **G**	2 Kings 4. 1–17 Ps. 107. 13–22 Rom. 12. 6–16a John 2. 1–11	Ps. 145. 1–12 Isa. 62. 1–5 1 Cor. 6. 11–end	Ps. 96 Isa. 60. 9–end Heb. 6.17 - 7.10	
	Prisca, Martyr at Rome, c. 265 For the Week of Prayer for Christian Unity, see *Common Worship* provision.			
Wr *or* **Gr**	Com. Virgin Martyr	Amos ch. 6 1 Cor. 6. 1–11	Gen. 6.11 - 7.10 Matt. 24. 1–14	
W *or* **G**		Amos ch. 7 1 Cor. 6. 12–end	Gen. 7. 11–end Matt. 24. 15–28	
	Fabian, Bishop of Rome, Martyr, 250			
Wr *or* **Gr**	Com. Martyr	Amos ch. 8 1 Cor. 7. 1–24	Gen. 8. 1–14 Matt. 24. 29–end	
	Agnes, Child Martyr at Rome, 304			
Wr *or* **Gr**	Com. Virgin Martyr	Amos ch. 9 1 Cor. 7. 25–end	Gen. 8.15 - 9.7 Matt. 25. 1–13	
	Vincent of Saragossa, Deacon, first Martyr of Spain, 304			
Wr *or* **Gr**	Com. Martyr	Hos. 1.1 - 2.1 1 Cor. ch. 8	Gen. 9. 8–19 Matt. 25. 14–30	
W *or* **G**		Hos. 2. 2–17 1 Cor. 9. 1–14	Gen. 11. 1–9 Matt. 25. 31–end **ct**	

		Sunday Principal Service Weekday Eucharist	Third Service Morning Prayer	Second Service Evening Prayer
24 Sunday	**THE THIRD SUNDAY OF EPIPHANY**			
W		Gen. 14. 17–20 Ps. 128 Rev. 19. 6–10 John 2. 1–11	Ps. 113 Jonah 3. 1–5, 10 John 3. 16–21	Ps. 33 (*or* 33. 1–12) Jer. 3.21 - 4.2 Titus 2. 1–8, 11–14 *Gospel*: Matt. 4. 12–23 *or First EP of The Conversion of Paul* Ps. 149 Isa. 49. 1–13 Acts 22. 3–16 **ct**
25 Monday	**THE CONVERSION OF PAUL**			
W **DEL 3**	*The reading from Acts must be used as either the first or second reading at the Eucharist.*	Jer. 1. 4–10 *or* Acts 9. 1–22 Ps. 67 Acts 9. 1–22 *or* Gal. 1. 11–16a Matt. 19. 27–end	*MP*: Ps. 66; 147. 13–end Ezek. 3. 22–end Phil. 3. 1–14	*EP*: Ps. 119. 41–56 Ecclus. 39. 1–10 *or* Isa. 56. 1–8 Col. 1.24 - 2.7
26 Tuesday	**Timothy and Titus, Companions of Paul**			
W	Isa. 61. 1–3a Ps. 100 2 Tim. 2. 1–8 *or* Titus 1. 1–5 Luke 10. 1–9 *or*	Heb. 10. 1–10 Ps. 40. 1–4, 7–10 Mark 3. 31–end	Ps. 34; ***36*** *alt.* Ps. ***132***; 133 Hos. 4. 1–16 1 Cor. 10. 1–13	Ps. 145 *alt.* Ps. (134); ***135*** Gen. 13. 2–end Matt. 26. 17–35
27 Wednesday				
W		Heb. 10. 11–18 Ps. 110. 1–4 Mark 4. 1–20	Ps. 45; ***46*** *alt.* Ps. 119. 153–end Hos. 5. 1–7 1 Cor. 10.14 - 11.1	Ps. 21; ***29*** *alt.* Ps. 136 Gen. ch. 14 Matt. 26. 36–46
28 Thursday	**Thomas Aquinas, Priest, Philosopher, Teacher, 1274**			
W	Com. Teacher *or* *esp.* Wisd. 7. 7–10, 15–16 1 Cor. 2. 9–end John 16. 12–15	Heb. 10. 19–25 Ps. 24. 1–6 Mark 4. 21–25	Ps. ***47***; 48 *alt.* Ps. ***143***; 146 Hos. 5.8 - 6.6 1 Cor. 11. 2–16	Ps. ***24***; 33 *alt.* Ps. ***138***; 140; 141 Gen. ch. 15 Matt. 26. 47–56
29 Friday				
W		Heb. 10. 32–end Ps. 37. 3–6, 40–end Mark 4. 26–34	Ps. 61; ***65*** *alt.* Ps. 142; ***144*** Hos. 6.7 - 7.2 1 Cor. 11. 17–end	Ps. ***67***; 77 *alt.* Ps. 145 Gen. ch. 16 Matt. 26. 57–end
30 Saturday	**Charles, King and Martyr, 1649**			
Wr	Com. Martyr *or* *also* Ecclus. 2. 12–17 1 Tim. 6. 12–16	Heb. 11. 1–2, 8–19 *Canticle*: Luke 1. 69–73 Mark 4. 35–end	Ps. 68 *alt.* Ps. 147 Hos. ch. 8 1 Cor. 12. 1–11	Ps. ***72***; 76 *alt.* ***148***; 149; 150 Gen. 17. 1–22 Matt. 27. 1–10 **ct**

	Calendar and Holy Communion	Morning Prayer	Evening Prayer
	THE THIRD SUNDAY AFTER THE EPIPHANY		
W *or* **G**	2 Kings 6. 14b-23 Ps. 102. 15-22 Rom. 12. 16b-end Matt. 8. 1-13	Ps. 113 Jonah 3. 1-5, 10 John 3. 16-21	Ps. 33 (*or* 33. 1-12) Jer. 3.21 - 4.2 Titus 2. 1-8, 11-14 *or First EP of The Conversion of Paul* Ps. 149 Isa. 49. 1-13 Acts 22. 3-16 **W ct**
	THE CONVERSION OF PAUL		
W	Josh. 5. 13-end Ps. 67 Acts 9. 1-22 Matt. 19. 27-end	(Ps. 66; 147. 13-end) Ezek. 3. 22-end Phil. 3. 1-14	(Ps. 119. 41-56) Ecclus. 39. 1-10 *or* Isa. 56. 1-8 Col. 1.24 - 2.7
W *or* **G**		Hos. 4. 1-16 1 Cor. 10. 1-13	Gen. 13. 2-end Matt. 26. 17-35
W *or* **G**		Hos. 5. 1-7 1 Cor. 10.14 - 11.1	Gen. ch. 14 Matt. 26. 36-46
W *or* **G**		Hos. 5.8 - 6.6 1 Cor. 11. 2-16	Gen. ch. 15 Matt. 26. 47-56
W *or* **G**		Hos. 6.7 - 7.2 1 Cor. 11. 17-end	Gen. ch. 16 Matt. 26. 57-end
	Charles, King and Martyr, 1649		
Wr *or* **Gr**	Com. Martyr	Hos. ch. 8 1 Cor. 12. 1-11	Gen. 17. 1-22 Matt. 27. 1-10 **ct**

NOTES

		Sunday Principal Service Weekday Eucharist	Third Service Morning Prayer	Second Service Evening Prayer
31 Sunday	**THE FOURTH SUNDAY OF EPIPHANY** *or The Presentation of Christ in the Temple (Candlemas)**			
W		Deut. 18. 15–20 Ps. 111 Rev. 12. 1–5a Mark 1. 21–28	Ps. 71. 1–6, 15–17 Jer. 1. 4–10 Mark 1. 40–end	Ps. 34 (*or* 34. 1–10) 1 Sam. 3. 1–20 1 Cor. 14. 12–20 *Gospel*: Matt. 13. 10–17

February 2021

		Sunday Principal Service Weekday Eucharist	Third Service Morning Prayer	Second Service Evening Prayer
1 Monday	*Brigid, Abbess of Kildare, c. 525*			
W **DEL 4**		Heb. 11. 32–end Ps. 31. 19–end Mark 5. 1–20	Ps. ***57***; 96 *alt.* Ps. ***1***; 2; 3 Hos. ch. 9 1 Cor. 12. 12–end	*First EP of The Presentation* Ps. 118 1 Sam. 1. 19b–end Heb. 4. 11–end **W ct**
	or, if The Presentation is kept on 31 Jan.:			
G		Heb. 11. 32–end Ps. 31. 19–end Mark 5. 1–20	Ps. ***1***; 2; 3 Hos. ch. 9 1 Cor. 12. 12–end	Ps. ***4***; 7 Gen. 18. 1–15 Matt. 27. 11–26
2 Tuesday	**THE PRESENTATION OF CHRIST IN THE TEMPLE (CANDLEMAS)**			
W		Mal. 3. 1–5 Ps. 24 (*or* 24. 7–end) Heb. 2. 14–end Luke 2. 22–40	*MP*: Ps. ***48***; 146 Exod. 13. 1–16 Rom. 12. 1–5	*EP*: Ps. 122; ***132*** Hag. 2. 1–9 John 2. 18–22
	or, if The Presentation is observed on 31 January:			
G		Heb. 12. 1–4 Ps. 22. 25b–end Mark 5. 21–43	Ps. ***5***; 6; (8) Hos. ch. 10 1 Cor. ch. 13	Ps. ***9***; 10† Gen. 18. 16–end Matt. 27. 27–44
3 Wednesday	**Anskar, Archbishop of Hamburg, Missionary in Denmark and Sweden, 865** Ordinary Time starts today (or on 1 February if The Presentation is observed on 31 January)			
Gw	Com. Missionary *or* *esp.* Isa. 52. 7–10 *also* Rom. 10. 11–15	Heb. 12. 4–7, 11–15 Ps. 103. 1–2, 13–18 Mark 6. 1–6a	Ps. 119. 1–32 Hos. 11. 1–11 1 Cor. 14. 1–19	Ps. ***11***; 12; 13 Gen. 19. 1–3, 12–29 Matt. 27. 45–56
4 Thursday	*Gilbert of Sempringham, Founder of the Gilbertine Order, 1189*			
G		Heb. 12. 18–19, 21–24 Ps. 48. 1–3, 8–10 Mark 6. 7–13	Ps. 14; ***15***; 16 Hos. 11.12 – 12.end 1 Cor. 14. 20–end	Ps. 18† Gen. 21. 1–21 Matt. 27. 57–end
5 Friday				
G		Heb. 13. 1–8 Ps. 27. 1–6, 9–12 Mark 6. 14–29	Ps. 17; ***19*** Hos. 13. 1–14 1 Cor. 16. 1–9	Ps. 22 Gen. 22. 1–19 Matt. 28. 1–15
6 Saturday	*The Martyrs of Japan, 1597* (The Accession of Queen Elizabeth II may be observed on 6 February, and Collect, Readings and Post-Communion for the sovereign used.)			
G		Heb. 13. 15–17, 20–21 Ps. 23 Mark 6. 30–34	Ps. 20; 21; ***23*** Hos. ch. 14 1 Cor. 16. 10–end	Ps. ***24***; 25 Gen. ch. 23 Matt. 28. 16–end **ct**

*See provision for First EP on 1 February and throughout the day for The Presentation on 2 February.

	Calendar and Holy Communion	Morning Prayer	Evening Prayer
	SEPTUAGESIMA		
W *or* **G**	Gen. 1. 1-5 Ps. 9. 10-20 1 Cor. 9. 24-end Matt. 20. 1-16	Ps. 71. 1-6, 15-17 Jer. 1. 4-10 Mark 1. 40-end	Ps. 34 (*or* 34. 1-10) 1 Sam. 3. 1-20 1 Cor. 14. 12-20
W *or* **G**		Hos. ch. 9 1 Cor. 12. 12-end	*First EP of The Presentation* Ps. 118 1 Sam. 1. 19b-end Heb. 4. 11-end **𝔚 ct**
	THE PRESENTATION OF CHRIST IN THE TEMPLE		
𝔚	Mal. 3. 1-5 Ps. 48. 1-7 Gal. 4. 1-7 Luke 2. 22-40	Ps. 48; 146 Exod. 13. 1-16 Rom. 12. 1-5	Ps. 122; 132 Hag. 2. 1-9 John 2. 18-22
	Blasius, Bishop of Sebastopol, Martyr, c. 316		
Gr	Com. Martyr	Hos. 11. 1-11 1 Cor. 14. 1-19	Gen. 19. 1-3, 12-29 Matt. 27. 45-56
G		Hos. 11.12 - 12.end 1 Cor. 14. 20-end	Gen. 21. 1-21 Matt. 27. 57-end
	Agatha, Martyr in Sicily, 251		
Gr	Com. Virgin Martyr	Hos. 13. 1-14 1 Cor. 16. 1-9	Gen. 22. 1-19 Matt. 28. 1-15
	The Accession of Queen Elizabeth II, 1952		
G	*For Accession Service*: Ps. 20; 101; 121; Josh. 1. 1-9; Prov. 8. 1-16; Rom. 13. 1-10; Rev. 21.22 - 22.4		
	For The Accession: 1 Pet. 2. 11-17 Matt. 22. 16-22	Hos. ch. 14 1 Cor. 16. 10-end	Gen. ch. 23 Matt. 28. 16-end **ct**

NOTES

		Sunday Principal Service Weekday Eucharist	Third Service Morning Prayer	Second Service Evening Prayer
7 Sunday	**THE SECOND SUNDAY BEFORE LENT**			
G		Prov. 8. 1, 22–31 Ps. 104. 26–end Col. 1. 15–20 John 1. 1–14	Ps. 29; 67 Deut. 8. 1–10 Matt. 6. 25–end	Ps. 65 Gen. 2. 4b–end Luke 8. 22–35
8 Monday				
G **DEL 5**		Gen. 1. 1–19 Ps. 104. 1–2, 6–13, 26 Mark 6. 53–end	Ps. 27; ***30*** Eccles. 7. 1–14 John 19. 1–16	Ps. 26; ***28***; 29 Gen. 29.31 – 30.24 2 Tim. 4. 1–8
9 Tuesday				
G		Gen. 1.20 – 2.4a Ps. 8 Mark 7. 1–13	Ps. 32; ***36*** Eccles. 7. 15–end John 19. 17–30	Ps. 33 Gen. 31. 1–24 2 Tim. 4. 9–end
10 Wednesday	*Scholastica, sister of Benedict, Abbess of Plombariola, c. 543*			
G		Gen. 2. 4b–9, 15–17 Ps. 104. 11–12, 29–32 Mark 7. 14–23	Ps. 34 Eccles. ch. 8 John 19. 31–end	Ps. 119. 33–56 Gen. 31.25 – 32.2 Titus ch. 1
11 Thursday				
G		Gen. 2. 18–end Ps. 128 Mark 7. 24–30	Ps. 37† Eccles. ch. 9 John 20. 1–10	Ps. 39; ***40*** Gen. 32. 3–30 Titus ch. 2
12 Friday				
G		Gen. 3. 1–8 Ps. 32. 1–8 Mark 7. 31–end	Ps. 31 Eccles. 11. 1–8 John 20. 11–18	Ps. 35 Gen. 33. 1–17 Titus ch. 3
13 Saturday				
G		Gen. 3. 9–end Ps. 90. 1–12 Mark 8. 1–10	Ps. 41; ***42***; 43 Eccles. 11.9 – 12.end John 20. 19–end	Ps. 45; ***46*** Gen. ch. 35 Philemon **ct**
14 Sunday	**THE SUNDAY NEXT BEFORE LENT**			
G		2 Kings 2. 1–12 Ps. 50. 1–6 2 Cor. 4. 3–6 Mark 9. 2–9	Ps. 27; 150 Exod. 24. 12–end 2 Cor. 3. 12–end	Ps. 2; [99] 1 Kings 19. 1–16 2 Pet. 1. 16–end *Gospel*: Mark 9. [2–8] 9–13
15 Monday	*Sigfrid, Bishop, Apostle of Sweden, 1045; Thomas Bray, Priest, Founder of the SPCK and SPG, 1730*			
G **DEL 6**		Gen. 4. 1–15, 25 Ps. 50. 1, 8, 16–end Mark 8. 11–13	Ps. 44 Jer. ch. 1 John 3. 1–21	Ps. ***47***; 49 Gen. 37. 1–11 Gal. ch. 1
16 Tuesday				
G		Gen. 6. 5–8; 7. 1–5, 10 Ps. 29 Mark 8. 14–21	Ps. ***48***; 52 Jer. 2. 1–13 John 3. 22–end	Ps. 50 Gen. 37. 12–end Gal. 2. 1–10

	Calendar and Holy Communion	Morning Prayer	Evening Prayer	NOTES
	SEXAGESIMA			
G	Gen. 3. 9–19 Ps. 83. 1–2, 13–end 2 Cor. 11. 19–31 Luke 8. 4–15	Ps. 29; 67 Deut. 8. 1–10 Matt. 6. 25–end	Ps. 65 Gen. 2. 4b–end Luke 8. 22–35	
G		Eccles. 7. 1–14 John 19. 1–16	Gen. 29.31 - 30.24 2 Tim. 4. 1–8	
G		Eccles. 7. 15–end John 19. 17–30	Gen. 31. 1–24 2 Tim. 4. 9–end	
G		Eccles. ch. 8 John 19. 31–end	Gen. 31.25 - 32.2 Titus ch. 1	
G		Eccles. ch. 9 John 20. 1–10	Gen. 32. 3–30 Titus ch. 2	
G		Eccles. 11. 1–8 John 20. 11–18	Gen. 33. 1–17 Titus ch. 3	
G		Eccles. 11.9 - 12.end John 20. 19–end	Gen. ch. 35 Philemon **ct**	
	QUINQUAGESIMA			
G	Gen. 9. 8–17 Ps. 77. 11–end 1 Cor. ch. 13 Luke 18. 31–43	Ps. 27; 150 Exod. 24. 12–end 2 Cor. 3. 12–end	Ps. 2; [99] 1 Kings 19. 1–16 2 Pet. 1. 16–end	
G		Jer. ch. 1 John 3. 1–21	Gen. 37. 1–11 Gal. ch. 1	
G		Jer. 2. 1–13 John 3. 22–end	Gen. 37. 12–end Gal. 2. 1–10	

		Sunday Principal Service Weekday Eucharist	Third Service Morning Prayer	Second Service Evening Prayer
17 Wednesday	**ASH WEDNESDAY**			
P		Joel 2. 1–2, 12–17 *or* Isa. 58. 1–12 Ps. 51. 1–18 2 Cor. 5.20b - 6.10 Matt. 6. 1–6, 16–21 *or* John 8. 1–11	*MP*: Ps. 38 Dan. 9. 3–6, 17–19 1 Tim. 6. 6–19	*EP*: Ps. ***51*** *or* Ps. 102 (*or* 102. 1–18) Isa. 1. 10–18 Luke 15. 11–end
18 Thursday				
P		Deut. 30. 15–end Ps. 1 Luke 9. 22–25	Ps. 77 *alt.* Ps. 56; ***57***; (63†) Jer. 2. 14–32 John 4. 1–26	Ps. 74 *alt.* Ps. 61; ***62***; 64 Gen. ch. 39 Gal. 2. 11–end
19 Friday				
P		Isa. 58. 1–9a Ps. 51. 1–5, 17–18 Matt. 9. 14–15	Ps. ***3***; 7 *alt.* Ps. ***51***; 54 Jer. 3. 6–22 John 4. 27–42	Ps. 31 *alt.* Ps. 38 Gen. ch. 40 Gal. 3. 1–14
20 Saturday				
P		Isa. 58. 9b–end Ps. 86. 1–7 Luke 5. 27–32	Ps. 71 *alt.* Ps. 68 Jer. 4. 1–18 John 4. 43–end	Ps. 73 *alt.* Ps. 65; ***66*** Gen. 41. 1–24 Gal. 3. 15–22 **ct**
21 Sunday	**THE FIRST SUNDAY OF LENT**			
P		Gen. 9. 8–17 Ps. 25. 1–9 1 Pet. 3. 18–end Mark 1. 9–15	Ps. 77 Exod. 34. 1–10 Rom. 10. 8b–13	Ps. 119. 17–32 Gen. 2. 15–17; 3. 1–7 Rom. 5. 12–19 *or* Luke 13. 31–end
22 Monday				
P		Lev. 19. 1–2, 11–18 Ps. 19. 7–end Matt. 25. 31–end	Ps. 10; ***11*** *alt.* Ps. 71 Jer. 4. 19–end John 5. 1–18	Ps. 12; ***13***; 14 *alt.* Ps. ***72***; 75 Gen. 41. 25–45 Gal. 3.23 - 4.7
23 Tuesday	**Polycarp, Bishop of Smyrna, Martyr, c. 155**			
Pr	Com. Martyr *or* *also* Rev. 2. 8–11	Isa. 55. 10–11 Ps. 34. 4–6, 21–22 Matt. 6. 7–15	Ps. 44 *alt.* Ps. 73 Jer. 5. 1–19 John 5. 19–29	Ps. 46; ***49*** *alt.* Ps. 74 Gen. 41.46 - 42.5 Gal. 4. 8–20

	Calendar and Holy Communion	Morning Prayer	Evening Prayer	NOTES
	ASH WEDNESDAY			
P	Ash Wednesday Collect until 3 April Commination Joel 2. 12-17 Ps. 57 James 4. 1-10 Matt. 6. 16-21	Ps. 38 Dan. 9. 3-6, 17-19 1 Tim. 6. 6-19	Ps. ***51*** *or* Ps. 102 (*or* 102. 1-18) Isa. 1. 10-18 Luke 15. 11-end	
P	Exod. 24. 12-end Matt. 8. 5-13	Jer. 2. 14-32 John 4. 1-26	Gen. ch. 39 Gal. 2. 11-end	
P	1 Kings 19. 3b-8 Matt. 5.43 - 6.6	Jer. 3. 6-22 John 4. 27-42	Gen. ch. 40 Gal. 3. 1-14	
P	Isa. 38. 1-6a Mark 6. 45-end	Jer. 4. 1-18 John 4. 43-end	Gen. 41. 1-24 Gal. 3. 15-22 **ct**	
	THE FIRST SUNDAY IN LENT			
P	Collect (1) Lent 1 (2) Ash Wednesday Ember until 27 Feb. Gen. 3. 1-6 Ps. 91. 1-12 2 Cor. 6. 1-10 Matt. 4. 1-11	Ps. 77 Exod. 34. 1-10 Rom. 10. 8b-13	Ps. 119. 17-32 Gen. 2. 15-17; 3. 1-7 Rom. 5. 12-19 *or* Luke 13. 31-end	
P	Ezek. 34. 11-16a Matt. 25. 31-end	Jer. 4. 19-end John 5. 1-18	Gen. 41. 25-45 Gal. 3.23 - 4.7	
P	Isa. 55. 6-11 Matt. 21. 10-16	Jer. 5. 1-19 John 5. 19-29	Gen. 41.46 - 42.5 Gal. 4. 8-20 *or First EP of Matthias* (Ps. 147) Isa. 22. 15-22 Phil. 3.13b - 4.1 **R ct**	

		Sunday Principal Service Weekday Eucharist	Third Service Morning Prayer	Second Service Evening Prayer
24 Wednesday*	Ember Day**			
P		Jonah ch. 3 Ps. 51. 1-5, 17-18 Luke 11. 29-32	Ps. ***6***; 17 *alt.* Ps. 77 Jer. 5. 20-end John 5. 30-end	Ps. 9; ***28*** *alt.* Ps. 119. 81-104 Gen. 42. 6-17 Gal. 4.21 - 5.1
25 Thursday				
P		Esther 14. 1-5, 12-14 *or* Isa. 55. 6-9 Ps. 138 Matt. 7. 7-12	Ps. ***42***; 43 *alt.* Ps. 78. 1-39† Jer. 6. 9-21 John 6. 1-15	Ps. 137; 138; ***142*** *alt.* Ps. 78. 40-end† Gen. 42. 18-28 Gal. 5. 2-15
26 Friday	Ember Day**			
P		Ezek. 18. 21-28 Ps. 130 Matt. 5. 20-26	Ps. 22 *alt.* Ps. 55 Jer. 6. 22-end John 6. 16-27	Ps. 54; ***55*** *alt.* Ps. 69 Gen. 42. 29-end Gal. 5. 16-end
27 Saturday	**George Herbert, Priest, Poet, 1633** Ember Day**			
Pw	Com. Pastor *or* *esp.* Mal. 2. 5-7 Matt. 11. 25-end *also* Rev. 19. 5-9	Deut. 26. 16-end Ps. 119. 1-8 Matt. 5. 43-end	Ps. 59; ***63*** *alt.* Ps. ***76***; 79 Jer. 7. 1-20 John 6. 27-40	Ps. ***4***; 16 *alt.* Ps. 81; ***84*** Gen. 43. 1-15 Gal. ch. 6 **ct**
28 Sunday	**THE SECOND SUNDAY OF LENT**			
P		Gen. 17. 1-7, 15-16 Ps. 22. 23-end Rom. 4. 13-end Mark 8. 31-end	Ps. 105. 1-6, 37-end Isa. 51. 1-11 Gal. 3. 1-9, 23-end	Ps. 135 (*or* 135. 1-14) Gen. 12. 1-9 Heb. 11. 1-3, 8-16 *Gospel*: John 8. 51-end

March 2021

1 Monday	**David, Bishop of Menevia, Patron of Wales, c. 601**			
Pw	Com. Bishop *or* *also* 2 Sam. 23. 1-4 Ps. 89. 19-22, 24	Dan. 9. 4-10 Ps. 79. 8-9, 12, 14 Luke 6. 36-38	Ps. 26; ***32*** *alt.* Ps. ***80***; 82 Jer. 7. 21-end John 6. 41-51	Ps. 70; ***74*** *alt.* Ps. ***85***; 86 Gen. 43. 16-end Heb. ch. 1
2 Tuesday	**Chad, Bishop of Lichfield, Missionary, 672*** **			
Pw	Com. Missionary *or* *also* 1 Tim. 6. 11b-16	Isa. 1. 10, 16-20 Ps. 50. 8, 16-end Matt. 23. 1-12	Ps. 50 *alt.* Ps. 87; ***89. 1-18*** Jer. 8. 1-15 John 6. 52-59	Ps. ***52***; 53; 54 *alt.* Ps. 89. 19-end Gen. 44. 1-17 Heb. 2. 1-9
3 Wednesday				
P		Jer. 18. 18-20 Ps. 31. 4-5, 14-18 Matt. 20. 17-28	Ps. 35 *alt.* Ps. 119. 105-128 Jer. 8.18 - 9.11 John 6. 60-end	Ps. ***3***; 51 *alt.* Ps. ***91***; 93 Gen. 44. 18-end Heb. 2. 10-end

*Matthias may be celebrated on 24 February instead of 14 May.
**For Ember Day provision, see p. 11.
***Chad may be celebrated with Cedd on 26 October instead of 2 March.

	Calendar and Holy Communion	Morning Prayer	Evening Prayer	NOTES
	MATTHIAS THE APOSTLE			
R	Ember Day 1 Sam. 2. 27–35 Ps. 16. 1–7 Acts 1. 15–end Matt. 11. 25–end	(Ps. 15) Jonah 1. 1–9 Acts 2. 37–end	(Ps. 80) 1 Sam. 16. 1–13a Matt. 7. 15–27	
P	Isa. 58. 9b–end John 8. 31–45	Jer. 6. 9–21 John 6. 1–15	Gen. 42. 18–28 Gal. 5. 2–15	
	Ember Day			
P	Ember CEG *or* Ezek. 18. 20–25 John 5. 2–15	Jer. 6. 22–end John 6. 16–27	Gen. 42. 29–end Gal. 5. 16–end	
P	Ember Day Ember CEG *or* Ezek. 18. 26–end Matt. 17. 1–9 *or* Luke 4. 16–21 *or* John 10. 1–16	Jer. 7. 1–20 John 6. 27–40	Gen. 43. 1–15 Gal. ch. 6 **ct**	
	THE SECOND SUNDAY IN LENT			
P	Jer. 17. 5–10 Ps. 25. 13–end 1 Thess. 4. 1–8 Matt. 15. 21–28	Ps. 105. 1–6, 37–end Isa. 51. 1–11 Gal. 3. 1–9, 23–end	Ps. 135 (*or* 135. 1–14) Gen. 12. 1–9 Heb. 11. 1–3, 8–16	
	David, Bishop of Menevia, Patron of Wales, c. 601			
Pw	Com. Bishop *or* Heb. 2. 1–10 John 8. 21–30	Jer. 7. 21–end John 6. 41–51	Gen. 43. 16–end Heb. ch. 1	
	Chad, Bishop of Lichfield, Missionary, 672			
Pw	Com. Bishop *or* Heb. 2. 11–end Matt. 23. 1–12	Jer. 8. 1–15 John 6. 52–59	Gen. 44. 1–17 Heb. 2. 1–9	
P	Heb. 3. 1–6 Matt. 20. 17–28	Jer. 8.18 – 9.11 John 6. 60–end	Gen. 44. 18–end Heb. 2. 10–end	

		Sunday Principal Service Weekday Eucharist	Third Service Morning Prayer	Second Service Evening Prayer
4 Thursday				
P		Jer. 17. 5–10 Ps. 1 Luke 16. 19–end	Ps. 34 *alt.* Ps. 90; ***92*** Jer. 9. 12–24 John 7. 1–13	Ps. 71 *alt.* Ps. 94 Gen. 45. 1–15 Heb. 3. 1–6
5 Friday				
P		Gen. 37. 3–4, 12–13, 17–28 Ps. 105. 16–22 Matt. 21. 33–43, 45–46	Ps. 40; ***41*** *alt.* Ps. ***88***; (95) Jer. 10. 1–16 John 7. 14–24	Ps. ***6***; 38 *alt.* Ps. 102 Gen. 45. 16–end Heb. 3. 7–end
6 Saturday				
P		Mic. 7. 4–15, 18–20 Ps. 103. 1–4, 9–12 Luke 15. 1–3, 11–end	Ps. 3; ***25*** *alt.* Ps. 96; ***97***; 100 Jer. 10. 17–24 John 7. 25–36	Ps. ***23***; 27 *alt.* Ps. 104 Gen. 46. 1–7, 28–end Heb. 4. 1–13 **ct**
7 Sunday	**THE THIRD SUNDAY OF LENT**			
P		Exod. 20. 1–17 Ps. 19 (*or* 19. 7–end) 1 Cor. 1. 18–25 John 2. 13–22	Ps. 18. 1–25 Jer. ch. 38 Phil. 1. 1–26	Ps. 11; 12 Exod. 5.1 - 6.1 Phil. 3. 4b–14 *or* Matt. 10. 16–22
8 Monday*	**Edward King, Bishop of Lincoln, 1910** *Felix, Bishop, Apostle to the East Angles, 647; Geoffrey Studdert Kennedy, Priest, Poet, 1929*			
Pw	Com. Bishop *or* *also* Heb. 13. 1–8	2 Kings 5. 1–15 Ps. 42. 1–2; 34. 1–4 Luke 4. 24–30	Ps. ***5***; 7 *alt.* Ps. ***98***; 99; 101 Jer. 11. 1–17 John 7. 37–52	Ps. 11; ***17*** *alt.* Ps. ***105***† (*or* 103) Gen. 47. 1–27 Heb. 4.14 - 5.10
9 Tuesday				
P		Song of the Three 2, 11–20 *or* Dan. 2. 20–23 Ps. 25. 3–10 Matt. 18. 21–end	Ps. 6; ***9*** *alt.* Ps. ***106***† (*or* 103) Jer. 11.18 - 12.6 John 7.53 - 8.11	Ps. 61; 62; ***64*** *alt.* Ps. 107† Gen. 47.28 - 48.end Heb. 5.11 - 6.12
10 Wednesday				
P		Deut. 4. 1, 5–9 Ps. 147. 13–end Matt. 5. 17–19	Ps. 38 *alt.* Ps. 110; ***111***; 112 Jer. 13. 1–11 John 8. 12–30	Ps. 36; ***39*** *alt.* Ps. 119. 129–152 Gen. 49. 1–32 Heb. 6. 13–end
11 Thursday				
P		Jer. 7. 23–28 Ps. 95. 1–2, 6–end Luke 11. 14–23	Ps. ***56***; 57 *alt.* Ps. 113; ***115*** Jer. ch. 14 John 8. 31–47	Ps. ***59***; 60 *alt.* Ps. 114; ***116***; 117 Gen. 49.33 - 50.end Heb. 7. 1–10
12 Friday				
P		Hos. ch. 14 Ps. 81. 6–10, 13, 16 Mark 12. 28–34	Ps. 22 *alt.* Ps. 139 Jer. 15. 10–end John 8. 48–end	Ps. 69 *alt.* Ps. ***130***; 131; 137 Exod. 1. 1–14 Heb. 7. 11–end

*The following readings may replace those provided for Holy Communion on any day during the Third Week of Lent, especially in Years B and C when the Gospel of the Samaritan woman is not read on The Third Sunday of Lent: Exod. 17. 1–7; Ps. 95. 1–2, 6–end; John 4. 5–42.

	Calendar and Holy Communion	Morning Prayer	Evening Prayer	NOTES
P	Heb. 3. 7-end John 5. 30-end	Jer. 9. 12-24 John 7. 1-13	Gen. 45. 1-15 Heb. 3. 1-6	
P	Heb. ch. 4 Matt. 21. 33-end	Jer. 10. 1-16 John 7. 14-24	Gen. 45. 16-end Heb. 3. 7-end	
P	Heb. ch. 5 Luke 15. 11-end	Jer. 10. 17-24 John 7. 25-36	Gen. 46. 1-7, 28-end Heb. 4. 1-13 **ct**	
	THE THIRD SUNDAY IN LENT			
P	Num. 22. 21-31 Ps. 9. 13-end Eph. 5. 1-14 Luke 11. 14-28	Ps. 18. 1-25 Jer. ch. 38 Phil. 1. 1-26	Ps. 11; 12 Exod. 5.1 - 6.1 Phil. 3. 4b-14 *or* Matt. 10. 16-22	
P	Heb. 6. 1-10 Luke 4. 23-30	Jer. 11. 1-17 John 7. 37-52	Gen. 47. 1-27 Heb. 4.14 - 5.10	
P	Heb. 6. 11-end Matt. 18. 15-22	Jer. 11.18 - 12.6 John 7.53 - 8.11	Gen. 47.28 - 48.end Heb. 5.11 - 6.12	
P	Heb. 7. 1-10 Matt. 15. 1-20	Jer. 13. 1-11 John 8. 12-30	Gen. 49. 1-32 Heb. 6. 13-end	
P	Heb. 7. 11-25 John 6. 26-35	Jer. ch. 14 John 8. 31-47	Gen. 49.33 - 50.end Heb. 7. 1-10	
	Gregory the Great, Bishop of Rome, 604			
Pw	Com. Doctor *or* Heb. 7. 26-end John 4. 5-26	Jer. 15. 10-end John 8. 48-end	Exod. 1. 1-14 Heb. 7. 11-end	

		Sunday Principal Service Weekday Eucharist	Third Service Morning Prayer	Second Service Evening Prayer
13 Saturday				
P		Hos. 5.15 - 6.6 Ps. 51. 1-2, 17-end Luke 18. 9-14	Ps. 31 *alt.* Ps. 120; ***121***; 122 Jer. 16.10 - 17.4 John 9. 1-17	Ps. ***116***; 130 *alt.* Ps. 118 Exod. 1.22 - 2.10 Heb. ch. 8 **ct**
14 Sunday	**THE FOURTH SUNDAY OF LENT** (Mothering Sunday)			
P		Num. 21. 4-9 Ps. 107. 1-3, 17-22 (*or* 107. 1-9) Eph. 2. 1-10 John 3. 14-21	Ps. 27 1 Sam. 16. 1-13 John 9. 1-25	Ps. 13; 14 Exod. 6. 2-13 Rom. 5. 1-11 *Gospel*: John 12. 1-8 *If the Principal Service readings for The Fourth Sunday of Lent are displaced by Mothering Sunday provisions, they may be used at the Second Service.*
	or, for Mothering Sunday:	Exod. 2. 1-10 *or* 1 Sam. 1. 20-end Ps. 34. 11-20 *or* Ps. 127. 1-4 2 Cor. 1. 3-7 *or* Col. 3. 12-17 Luke 2. 33-35 *or* John 19. 25b-27		
15 Monday*				
P		Isa. 65. 17-21 Ps. 30. 1-5, 8, 11-end John 4. 43-end	Ps. 70; ***77*** *alt.* Ps. 123; 124; 125; ***126*** Jer. 17. 5-18 John 9. 18-end	Ps. ***25***; 28 *alt.* Ps. ***127***; 128; 129 Exod. 2. 11-22 Heb. 9. 1-14
16 Tuesday				
P		Ezek. 47. 1-9, 12 Ps. 46. 1-8 John 5. 1-3, 5-16	Ps. 54; ***79*** *alt.* Ps. ***132***; 133 Jer. 18. 1-12 John 10. 1-10	Ps. ***80***; 82 *alt.* Ps. (134); ***135*** Exod. 2.23 - 3.20 Heb. 9. 15-end
17 Wednesday	**Patrick, Bishop, Missionary, Patron of Ireland, c. 460**			
Pw	Com. Missionary *or* *also* Ps. 91. 1-4, 13-end Luke 10. 1-12, 17-20	Isa. 49. 8-15 Ps. 145. 8-18 John 5. 17-30	Ps. 63; ***90*** *alt.* Ps. 119. 153-end Jer. 18. 13-end John 10. 11-21	Ps. 52; ***91*** *alt.* Ps. 136 Exod. 4. 1-23 Heb. 10. 1-18

*The following readings may replace those provided for Holy Communion on any day (except Joseph of Nazareth) during the Fourth Week of Lent, especially in Years B and C when the Gospel of the man born blind is not read on The Fourth Sunday of Lent: Mic. 7. 7-9; Ps. 27. 1, 9-10, 16-17; John ch. 9.

	Calendar and Holy Communion	Morning Prayer	Evening Prayer	NOTES
P	Heb. 8. 1–6 John 8. 1–11	Jer. 16.10 – 17.4 John 9. 1–17	Exod. 1.22 – 2.10 Heb. ch. 8 **ct**	
	THE FOURTH SUNDAY IN LENT To celebrate Mothering Sunday, see *Common Worship* provision.			
P	Exod. 16. 2–7a Ps. 122 Gal. 4. 21–end *or* Heb. 12. 22–24 John 6. 1–14	Ps. 27 1 Sam. 16. 1–13 John 9. 1–25	Ps. 13; 14 Exod. 6. 2–13 Rom. 5. 1–11	
P	Heb. 11. 1–6 John 2. 13–end	Jer. 17. 5–18 John 9. 18–end	Exod. 2. 11–22 Heb. 9. 1–14	
P	Heb. 11. 13–16a John 7. 14–24	Jer. 18. 1–12 John 10. 1–10	Exod. 2.23 – 3.20 Heb. 9. 15–end	
P	Heb. 12. 1–11 John 9. 1–17	Jer. 18. 13–end John 10. 11–21	Exod. 4. 1–23 Heb. 10. 1–18	

		Sunday Principal Service Weekday Eucharist	Third Service Morning Prayer	Second Service Evening Prayer
18 Thursday	*Cyril, Bishop of Jerusalem, Teacher, 386*			
P		Exod. 32. 7–14 Ps. 106. 19–23 John 5. 31–end	Ps. 53; ***86*** *alt.* Ps. ***143***; 146 Jer. 19. 1–13 John 10. 22–end	Ps. 94 *alt.* Ps. ***138***; 140; 141 Exod. 4.27 – 6.1 Heb. 10. 19–25 *or First EP of Joseph* Ps. 132 Hos. 11. 1–9 Luke 2. 41–end **W ct**
19 Friday	**JOSEPH OF NAZARETH**			
W		2 Sam. 7. 4–16 Ps. 89. 27–36 Rom. 4. 13–18 Matt. 1. 18–end	*MP*: Ps. 25; 147. 1–12 Isa. 11. 1–10 Matt. 13. 54–end	*EP*: Ps. 1; 112 Gen. 50. 22–end Matt. 2. 13–end
20 Saturday	**Cuthbert, Bishop of Lindisfarne, Missionary, 687***			
Pw	Com. Missionary *or* *esp.* Ezek. 34. 11–16 *also* Matt. 18. 12–14	Jer. 11. 18–20 Ps. 7. 1–2, 8–10 John 7. 40–52	Ps. 32 *alt.* Ps. 147 Jer. 20. 7–end John 11. 17–27	Ps. ***140***; 141; 142 *alt.* Ps. ***148***; 149; 150 Exod. 7. 8–end Heb. 11. 1–16 **ct**
21 Sunday	**THE FIFTH SUNDAY OF LENT (Passiontide begins)**			
P		Jer. 31. 31–34 Ps. 51. 1–13 *or* Ps. 119. 9–16 Heb. 5. 5–10 John 12. 20–33	Ps. 107. 1–22 Exod. 24. 3–8 Heb. 12. 18–end	Ps. 34 (*or* 34. 1–10) Exod. 7. 8–24 Rom. 5. 12–end *Gospel*: Luke 22. 1–13
22 Monday**				
P		Susanna 1–9, 15–17, 19–30, 33–62 (*or* 41b–62) *or* Josh. 2. 1–14 Ps. 23 John 8. 1–11	Ps. ***73***; 121 *alt.* Ps. ***1***; 2; 3 Jer. 21. 1–10 John 11. 28–44	Ps. ***26***; 27 *alt.* Ps. ***4***; 7 Exod. 8. 1–19 Heb. 11. 17–31
23 Tuesday				
P		Num. 21. 4–9 Ps. 102. 1–3, 16–23 John 8. 21–30	Ps. ***35***; 123 *alt.* Ps. ***5***; 6; (8) Jer. 22. 1–5, 13–19 John 11. 45–end	Ps. ***61***; 64 *alt.* Ps. ***9***; 10† Exod. 8. 20–end Heb. 11.32 – 12.2
24 Wednesday	*Walter Hilton of Thurgarton, Augustinian Canon, Mystic, 1396; Paul Couturier, Priest, Ecumenist, 1953; Oscar Romero, Archbishop of San Salvador, Martyr, 1980*			
P		Dan. 3. 14–20, 24–25, 28 *Canticle*: Bless the Lord John 8. 31–42	Ps. ***55***; 124 *alt.* Ps. 119. 1–32 Jer. 22.20 – 23.8 John 12. 1–11	*First EP of The Annunciation* Ps. 85 Wisd. 9. 1–12 *or* Gen. 3. 8–15 Gal. 4. 1–5 **𝔚 ct**

*Cuthbert may be celebrated on 4 September instead of 20 March.
**The following readings may replace those provided for Holy Communion on any day during the Fifth Week of Lent (except The Annunciation), especially in Years B and C when the Gospel of Lazarus is not read on The Fifth Sunday of Lent: 2 Kings 4. 18–21, 32–37; Ps. 17. 1–8, 16; John 11. 1–45.

	Calendar and Holy Communion	Morning Prayer	Evening Prayer	NOTES
	Edward, King of the W. Saxons, 978			
Pr	Com. Martyr *or* Heb. 12. 12-17 John 5. 17-27	Jer. 19. 1-13 John 10. 22-end	Exod. 4.27 - 6.1 Heb. 10. 19-25	
	To celebrate Joseph, see *Common Worship* provision.			
P	Heb. 12. 22-end John 11. 33-46	Jer. 19.14 - 20.6 John 11. 1-16	Exod. 6. 2-13 Heb. 10. 26-end	
P	Heb. 13. 7-21 John 8. 12-20	Jer. 20. 7-end John 11. 17-27	Exod. 7. 8-end Heb. 11. 1-16 **ct**	
	THE FIFTH SUNDAY IN LENT			
P	Exod. 24. 4-8 Ps. 143 Heb. 9. 11-15 John 8. 46-end	Ps. 107. 1-22 Jer. 31. 31-34 Heb. 5. 5-10	Ps. 34 (*or* 34. 1-10) Exod. 7. 8-24 Rom. 5. 12-end	
P	Col. 1. 13-23a John 7. 1-13	Jer. 21. 1-10 John 11. 28-44	Exod. 8. 1-19 Heb. 11. 17-31	
P	Col. 2. 8-12 John 7. 32-39	Jer. 22. 1-5, 13-19 John 11. 45-end	Exod. 8. 20-end Heb. 11.32 - 12.2	
P	Col. 2. 13-19 John 7. 40-end	Jer. 22.20 - 23.8 John 12. 1-11	*First EP of The Annunciation* Ps. 85 Wisd. 9. 1-12 *or* Gen. 3. 8-15 Gal. 4. 1-5 **W ct**	

		Sunday Principal Service Weekday Eucharist	Third Service Morning Prayer	Second Service Evening Prayer
25 Thursday	**THE ANNUNCIATION OF OUR LORD TO THE BLESSED VIRGIN MARY**			
W		Isa. 7. 10–14 Ps. 40. 5–11 Heb. 10. 4–10 Luke 1. 26–38	*MP*: Ps. 111; 113 1 Sam. 2. 1–10 Rom. 5. 12–end	*EP*: Ps. 131; 146 Isa. 52. 1–12 Heb. 2. 5–end
26 Friday	*Harriet Mansell, Founder of the Community of St John the Baptist, Clewer, 1883*			
P		Jer. 20. 10–13 Ps. 18. 1–6 John 10. 31–end	Ps. ***22***; 126 *alt.* Ps. 17; ***19*** Jer. ch. 24 John 12. 20–36a	Ps. 31 *alt.* Ps. 22 Exod. ch. 10 Heb. 13. 1–16
27 Saturday				
P		Ezek. 37. 21–end *Canticle*: Jer. 31. 10–13 *or* Ps. 121 John 11. 45–end	Ps. ***23***; 127 *alt.* Ps. 20; 21; ***23*** Jer. 25. 1–14 John 12. 36b–end	Ps. 128; 129; ***130*** *alt.* Ps. ***24***; 25 Exod. ch. 11 Heb. 13. 17–end **ct**
28 Sunday	**PALM SUNDAY**			
R	*Liturgy of the Palms* Mark 11. 1–11 *or* John 12. 12–16 Ps. 118. 1–2, 19–end (*or* 118. 19–end)	*Liturgy of the Passion* Isa. 50. 4–9a Ps. 31. 9–16 (*or* 31. 9–18) Phil. 2. 5–11 Mark 14.1 - 15.end *or* Mark 15. 1–39 [40–end]	Ps. 61; 62 Zech. 9. 9–12 1 Cor. 2. 1–12	Ps. 69. 1–20 Isa. 5. 1–7 Mark 12. 1–12
29 Monday	**MONDAY OF HOLY WEEK**			
R		Isa. 42. 1–9 Ps. 36. 5–11 Heb. 9. 11–15 John 12. 1–11	*MP*: Ps. 41 Lam. 1. 1–12a Luke 22. 1–23	*EP*: Ps. 25 Lam. 2. 8–19 Col. 1. 18–23
30 Tuesday	**TUESDAY OF HOLY WEEK**			
R		Isa. 49. 1–7 Ps. 71. 1–14 (*or* 71. 1–8) 1 Cor. 1. 18–31 John 12. 20–36	*MP*: Ps. 27 Lam. 3. 1–18 Luke 22. [24–38] 39–53	*EP*: Ps. 55. 13–24 Lam. 3. 40–51 Gal. 6. 11–end
31 Wednesday	**WEDNESDAY OF HOLY WEEK**			
R		Isa. 50. 4–9a Ps. 70 Heb. 12. 1–3 John 13. 21–32	*MP*: Ps. 102 (*or* 102. 1–18) Wisd. 1.16 - 2.1, 12–22 *or* Jer. 11. 18–20 Luke 22. 54–end	*EP*: Ps. 88 Isa. 63. 1–9 Rev. 14.18 - 15.4

April 2021

1 Thursday	**MAUNDY THURSDAY**			
W (HC) R		Exod. 12. 1–4 [5–10], 11–14 Ps. 116. 1, 10–end (*or* 116. 9–end) 1 Cor. 11. 23–26 John 13. 1–17, 31b–35	*MP*: Ps. 42; 43 Lev. 16. 2–24 Luke 23. 1–25	*EP*: Ps. 39 Exod. ch. 11 Eph. 2. 11–18

	Calendar and Holy Communion	Morning Prayer	Evening Prayer
	THE ANNUNCIATION OF THE BLESSED VIRGIN MARY		
𝔚	Isa. 7. 10–14 [15] Ps. 113 Rom. 5. 12–19 Luke 1. 26–38	Ps. 111 1 Sam. 2. 1–10 Heb. 10. 4–10	Ps. 131; 146 Isa. 52. 1–12 Heb. 2. 5–end
P	Col. 3. 12–17 John 11. 47–54	Jer. ch. 24 John 12. 20–36a	Exod. ch. 10 Heb. 13. 1–16
P	Col. 4. 2–6 John 6. 53–end	Jer. 25. 1–14 John 12. 36b–end	Exod. ch. 11 Heb. 13. 17–end **ct**
	THE SUNDAY NEXT BEFORE EASTER (PALM SUNDAY)		
R	Zech. 9. 9–12 Ps. 73. 22–end Phil. 2. 5–11 Passion acc. to Matthew Matt. 27. 1–54 *or* Matt. 26.1 - 27.61 *or* Matt. 21. 1–13	Ps. 61; 62 Isa. 42. 1–9 1 Cor. 2. 1–12	Ps. 69. 1–20 Isa. 5. 1–7 Mark 12. 1–12
	MONDAY IN HOLY WEEK		
R	Isa. 63. 1–19 Ps. 55. 1–8 Gal. 6. 1–11 Mark ch. 14	Ps. 41 Lam. 1. 1–12a John 12. 1–11	Ps. 25 Lam. 2. 8–19 Col. 1. 18–23
	TUESDAY IN HOLY WEEK		
R	Isa. 50. 5–11 Ps. 13 Rom. 5. 6–19 Mark 15. 1–39	Ps. 27 Lam. 3. 1–18 John 12. 20–36	Ps. 55. 13–24 Lam. 3. 40–51 Gal. 6. 11–end
	WEDNESDAY IN HOLY WEEK		
R	Isa. 49. 1–9a Ps. 54 Heb. 9. 16–end Luke ch. 22	Ps. 102 (*or* 102. 1–18) Wisd. 1.16 - 2.1, 12–22 *or* Jer. 11. 18–20 John 13. 21–32	Ps. 88 Isa. 63. 1–9 Rev. 14.18 - 15.4
	MAUNDY THURSDAY		
W **(HC)** **R**	Exod. 12. 1–11 Ps. 43 1 Cor. 11. 17–end Luke 23. 1–49	Ps. 42; 43 Lev. 16. 2–24 John 13. 1–17, 31b–35	Ps. 39 Exod. ch. 11 Eph. 2. 11–18

NOTES

		Sunday Principal Service Weekday Eucharist	Third Service Morning Prayer	Second Service Evening Prayer
2 Friday	**GOOD FRIDAY**			
R		Isa. 52.13 - 53.end Ps. 22 (*or* 22. 1-11 *or* 22. 1-21) Heb. 10. 16-25 *or* Heb. 4. 14-16; 5. 7-9 John 18.1 - 19.end	*MP*: Ps. 69 Gen. 22. 1-18 *A part of* John 18 - 19 *if not read at the Principal Service* *or* Heb. 10. 1-10	*EP*: Ps. 130; 143 Lam. 5. 15-end *A part of* John 18 - 19 *if not read at the Principal Service, especially* John 19. 38-end *or* Col. 1. 18-23
3 Saturday	**EASTER EVE**			
	These readings are for use at services other than the Easter Vigil.	Job 14. 1-14 *or* Lam. 3. 1-9, 19-24 Ps. 31. 1-4, 15-16 (*or* 31. 1-5) 1 Pet. 4. 1-8 Matt. 27. 57-end *or* John 19. 38-end	Ps. 142 Hos. 6. 1-6 John 2. 18-22	Ps. 116 Job 19. 21-27 1 John 5. 5-12
4 Sunday	**EASTER DAY**			
𝔚	*The following readings and psalms (or canticles) are provided for use at the Easter Vigil. A minimum of three Old Testament readings should be chosen. The reading from* Exodus ch. 14 *should always be used.*	Gen. 1.1 - 2.4a & Ps. 136. 1-9, 23-end Gen. 7. 1-5, 11-18; 8. 6-18; 9. 8-13 & Ps. 46 Gen. 22. 1-18 & Ps. 16 Exod. 14. 10-end; 15. 20-21 & *Canticle*: Exod. 15. 1b-13, 17-18 Isa. 55. 1-11 & *Canticle*: Isa. 12. 2-end Baruch 3.9-15, 32 - 4.4 & Ps. 19 *or* Prov. 8. 1-8, 19-21; 9. 4b-6 & Ps. 19 Ezek. 36. 24-28 & Ps. 42; 43 Ezek. 37. 1-14 & Ps. 143 Zeph. 3. 14-end & Ps. 98 Rom. 6. 3-11 & Ps. 114 Mark 16. 1-8		
𝔚	*Easter Day Services The reading from Acts must be used as either the first or second reading at the Principal Service.*	Acts 10. 34-43 *or* Isa. 25. 6-9 Ps. 118. 1-2, 14-24 (*or* 118. 14-24) 1 Cor. 15. 1-11 *or* Acts 10. 34-43 John 20. 1-18 *or* Mark 16. 1-8	*MP*: Ps. 114; 117 Gen. 1. 1-5, 26-end 2 Cor. 5.14 - 6.2	*EP*: Ps. 105 *or* Ps. 66. 1-11 Ezek. 37. 1-14 Luke 24. 13-35
5 Monday	**MONDAY OF EASTER WEEK**			
W		Acts 2. 14, 22-32 Ps. 16. 1-2, 6-end Matt. 28. 8-15	Ps. ***111***; 117; 146 Song of Sol. 1.9 - 2.7 Mark 16. 1-8	Ps. 135 Exod. 12. 1-14 1 Cor. 15. 1-11
6 Tuesday	**TUESDAY OF EASTER WEEK**			
W		Acts 2. 36-41 Ps. 33. 4-5, 18-end John 20. 11-18	Ps. ***112***; 147. 1-12 Song of Sol. 2. 8-end Luke 24. 1-12	Ps. 136 Exod. 12. 14-36 1 Cor. 15. 12-19
7 Wednesday	**WEDNESDAY OF EASTER WEEK**			
W		Acts 3. 1-10 Ps. 105. 1-9 Luke 24. 13-35	Ps. ***113***; 147. 13-end Song of Sol. ch. 3 Matt. 28. 16-end	Ps. 105 Exod. 12. 37-end 1 Cor. 15. 20-28

	Calendar and Holy Communion	Morning Prayer	Evening Prayer	NOTES
	GOOD FRIDAY			
R	Alt. Collect Passion acc. to John Alt. Gospel, if Passion is read Num. 21. 4–9 Ps. 140. 1–9 Heb. 10. 1–25 John 19. 1–37 *or* John 19. 38–end	Ps. 69 Gen. 22. 1–18 John ch. 18	Ps. 130; 143 Lam. 5. 15–end John 19. 38–end	
	EASTER EVE			
	Job 14. 1–14 1 Pet. 3. 17–22 Matt. 27. 57–end	Ps. 142 Hos. 6. 1–6 John 2. 18–22	Ps. 116 Job 19. 21–27 1 John 5. 5–12	
	EASTER DAY			
𝔚	Exod. 12. 21–28 Ps. 111 Col. 3. 1–7 John 20. 1–10	Ps. 114; 117 Gen. 1. 1–5, 26–end 2 Cor. 5.14 - 6.2	Ps. 105 *or* Ps. 66. 1–11 Isa. 25. 6–9 Luke 24. 13–35	
	MONDAY IN EASTER WEEK			
W	Hos. 6. 1–6 Easter Anthems Acts 10. 34–43 Luke 24. 13–35	Song of Sol. 1.9 - 2.7 Mark 16. 1–8	Exod. 12. 1–14 1 Cor. 15. 1–11	
	TUESDAY IN EASTER WEEK			
W	1 Kings 17. 17–end Ps. 16. 9–end Acts 13. 26–41 Luke 24. 36b–48	Song of Sol. 2. 8–end Luke 24. 1–12	Exod. 12. 14–36 1 Cor. 15. 12–19	
W	Isa. 42. 10–16 Ps. 111 Acts 3. 12–18 John 20. 11–18	Song of Sol. ch. 3 Matt. 28. 16–end	Exod. 12. 37–end 1 Cor. 15. 20–28	

		Sunday Principal Service Weekday Eucharist	Third Service Morning Prayer	Second Service Evening Prayer
8 Thursday	**THURSDAY OF EASTER WEEK**			
W		Acts 3. 11-end Ps. 8 Luke 24. 35-48	Ps. ***114***; 148 Song of Sol. 5.2 - 6.3 Luke 7. 11-17	Ps. 106 Exod. 13. 1-16 1 Cor. 15. 29-34
9 Friday	**FRIDAY OF EASTER WEEK**			
W		Acts 4. 1-12 Ps. 118. 1-4, 22-26 John 21. 1-14	Ps. ***115***; 149 Song of Sol. 7.10 - 8.4 Luke 8. 41-end	Ps. 107 Exod. 13.17 - 14.14 1 Cor. 15. 35-50
10 Saturday	**SATURDAY OF EASTER WEEK**			
W		Acts 4. 13-21 Ps. 118. 1-4, 14-21 Mark 16. 9-15	Ps. ***116***; 150 Song of Sol. 8. 5-7 John 11. 17-44	Ps. 145 Exod. 14. 15-end 1 Cor. 15. 51-end **ct**
11 Sunday	**THE SECOND SUNDAY OF EASTER**			
W	*The reading from Acts must be used as either the first or second reading at the Principal Service.*	Acts 4. 32-35 [*or* Exod. 14. 10-end; 15. 20-21] Ps. 133 1 John 1.1 - 2.2 John 20. 19-end	Ps. 22. 20-end Isa. 53. 6-12 Rom. 4. 13-25	Ps. 143. 1-11 Isa. 26. 1-9, 19 Luke 24. 1-12
12 Monday				
W		Acts 4. 23-31 Ps. 2. 1-9 John 3. 1-8	Ps. 2; ***19*** *alt.* Ps. ***1***; 2; 3 Deut. 1. 3-18 John 20. 1-10	Ps. 139 *alt.* Ps. ***4***; 7 Exod. 15. 1-21 Col. 1. 1-14
13 Tuesday				
W		Acts 4. 32-end Ps. 93 John 3. 7-15	Ps. ***8***; 20; 21 *alt.* Ps. ***5***; 6; (8) Deut. 1. 19-40 John 20. 11-18	Ps. 104 *alt.* Ps. 9; ***10***† Exod. 15.22 - 16.10 Col. 1. 15-end
14 Wednesday				
W		Acts 5. 17-26 Ps. 34. 1-8 John 3. 16-21	Ps. 16; ***30*** *alt.* Ps. 119. 1-32 Deut. 3. 18-end John 20. 19-end	Ps. 33 *alt.* Ps. ***11***; 12; 13 Exod. 16. 11-end Col. 2. 1-15
15 Thursday				
W		Acts 5. 27-33 Ps. 34. 1, 15-end John 3. 31-end	Ps. ***28***; 29 *alt.* Ps. 14; ***15***; 16 Deut. 4. 1-14 John 21. 1-14	Ps. 34 *alt.* Ps. 18† Exod. ch. 17 Col. 2.16 - 3.11
16 Friday	*Isabella Gilmore, Deaconess, 1923*			
W		Acts 5. 34-42 Ps. 27. 1-5, 16-17 John 6. 1-15	Ps. 57; ***61*** *alt.* Ps. 17; ***19*** Deut. 4. 15-31 John 21. 15-19	Ps. 118 *alt.* Ps. 22 Exod. 18. 1-12 Col. 3.12 - 4.1

	Calendar and Holy Communion	Morning Prayer	Evening Prayer	NOTES
W	Isa. 43. 16–21 Ps. 113 Acts 8. 26–end John 21. 1–14	Song of Sol. 5.2 – 6.3 Luke 7. 11–17	Exod. 13. 1–16 1 Cor. 15. 29–34	
W	Ezek. 37. 1–14 Ps. 116. 1–9 1 Pet. 3. 18–end Matt. 28. 16–end	Song of Sol. 7.10 – 8.4 Luke 8. 41–end	Exod. 13.17 – 14.14 1 Cor. 15. 35–50	
W	Zech. 8. 1–8 Ps. 118. 14–21 1 Pet. 2. 1–10 John 20. 24–end	Song of Sol. 8. 5–7 John 11. 17–44	Exod. 14. 15–end 1 Cor. 15. 51–end **ct**	
	THE FIRST SUNDAY AFTER EASTER			
W	Ezek. 37. 1–10 Ps. 81. 1–4 1 John 5. 4–12 John 20. 19–23	Ps. 22. 20–end Isa. 53. 6–12 Rom. 4. 13–25	Ps. 143. 1–11 Isa. 26. 1–9, 19 Luke 24. 1–12	
W		Deut. 1. 3–18 John 20. 1–10	Exod. 15. 1–21 Col. 1. 1–14	
W		Deut. 1. 19–40 John 20. 11–18	Exod. 15.22 – 16.10 Col. 1. 15–end	
W		Deut. 3. 18–end John 20. 19–end	Exod. 16. 11–end Col. 2. 1–15	
W		Deut. 4. 1–14 John 21. 1–14	Exod. ch. 17 Col. 2.16 – 3.11	
W		Deut. 4. 15–31 John 21. 15–19	Exod. 18. 1–12 Col. 3.12 – 4.1	

		Sunday Principal Service Weekday Eucharist	Third Service Morning Prayer	Second Service Evening Prayer
17 Saturday				
W		Acts 6. 1–7 Ps. 33. 1–5, 18–19 John 6. 16–21	Ps. 63; ***84*** *alt.* Ps. 20; 21; ***23*** Deut. 4. 32–40 John 21. 20–end	Ps. 66 *alt.* Ps. ***24***; 25 Exod. 18. 13–end Col. 4. 2–end **ct**
18 Sunday	**THE THIRD SUNDAY OF EASTER**			
W	*The reading from Acts must be used as either the first or second reading at the Principal Service.*	Acts 3. 12–19 [or Zeph. 3. 14–end] Ps. 4 1 John 3. 1–7 Luke 24. 36b–48	Ps. 77. 11–20 Isa. 63. 7–15 1 Cor. 10. 1–13	Ps. 142 Deut. 7. 7–13 Rev. 2. 1–11 *Gospel*: Luke 16. 19–end
19 Monday	**Alphege, Archbishop of Canterbury, Martyr, 1012**			
Wr	Com. Martyr *or* *also* Heb. 5. 1–4	Acts 6. 8–15 Ps. 119. 17–24 John 6. 22–29	Ps. ***96***; 97 *alt.* Ps. 27; ***30*** Deut. 5. 1–22 Eph. 1. 1–14	Ps. ***61***; 65 *alt.* Ps. 26; ***28***; 29 Exod. ch. 19 Luke 1. 1–25
20 Tuesday				
W		Acts 7.51 - 8.1a Ps. 31. 1–5, 16 John 6. 30–35	Ps. ***98***; 99; 100 *alt.* Ps. 32; ***36*** Deut. 5. 22–end Eph. 1. 15–end	Ps. 71 *alt.* Ps. 33 Exod. 20. 1–21 Luke 1. 26–38
21 Wednesday	**Anselm, Abbot of Le Bec, Archbishop of Canterbury, Teacher, 1109**			
W	Com. Teacher *or* *also* Wisd. 9. 13–end Rom. 5. 8–11	Acts 8. 1b–8 Ps. 66. 1–6 John 6. 35–40	Ps. 105 *alt.* Ps. 34 Deut. ch. 6 Eph. 2. 1–10	Ps. 67; ***72*** *alt.* Ps. 119. 33–56 Exod. ch. 24 Luke 1. 39–56
22 Thursday				
W		Acts 8. 26–end Ps. 66. 7–8, 14–end John 6. 44–51	Ps. 136 *alt.* Ps. 37† Deut. 7. 1–11 Eph. 2. 11–end	Ps. 73 *alt.* Ps. 39; ***40*** Exod. 25. 1–22 Luke 1. 57–end *or First EP of George* Ps. 111; 116 Jer. 15. 15–end Heb. 11.32 - 12.2 **R ct**
23 Friday	**GEORGE, MARTYR, PATRON OF ENGLAND, c. 304**			
R		1 Macc. 2. 59–64 *or* Rev. 12. 7–12 Ps. 126 2 Tim. 2. 3–13 John 15. 18–21	*MP*: Ps. 5; 146 Josh. 1. 1–9 Eph. 6. 10–20	*EP*: Ps. 3; 11 Isa. 43. 1–7 John 15. 1–8
24 Saturday	*Mellitus, Bishop of London, first Bishop at St Paul's, 624; The Seven Martyrs of the Melanesian Brotherhood, Solomon Islands, 2003*			
W		Acts 9. 31–42 Ps. 116. 10–15 John 6. 60–69	Ps. 108; ***110***; 111 *alt.* Ps. 41; ***42***; 43 Deut. ch. 8 Eph. 3. 14–end	Ps. 23; ***27*** *alt.* Ps. 45; ***46*** Exod. 29. 1–9 Luke 2. 21–40 **ct**

	Calendar and Holy Communion	Morning Prayer	Evening Prayer	NOTES
W		Deut. 4. 32–40 John 21. 20–end	Exod. 18. 13–end Col. 4. 2–end **ct**	
	THE SECOND SUNDAY AFTER EASTER			
W	Ezek. 34. 11–16a Ps. 23 1 Pet. 2. 19–end John 10. 11–16	Ps. 77. 11–20 Isa. 63. 7–15 1 Cor. 10. 1–13	Ps. 142 Deut. 7. 7–13 Rev. 2. 1–11	
	Alphege, Archbishop of Canterbury, Martyr, 1012			
Wr	Com. Martyr	Deut. 5. 1–22 Eph. 1. 1–14	Exod. ch. 19 Luke 1. 1–25	
W		Deut. 5. 22–end Eph. 1. 15–end	Exod. 20. 1–21 Luke 1. 26–38	
W		Deut. ch. 6 Eph. 2. 1–10	Exod. ch. 24 Luke 1. 39–56	
W		Deut. 7. 1–11 Eph. 2. 11–end	Exod. 25. 1–22 Luke 1. 57–end	
	To celebrate George, see *Common Worship* provision. **George, Martyr, Patron of England, c. 304**			
Wr	Com. Martyr	Deut. 7. 12–end Eph. 3. 1–13	Exod. 28. 1–4a, 29–38 Luke 2. 1–20	
W		Deut. ch. 8 Eph. 3. 14–end	Exod. 29. 1–9 Luke 2. 21–40 **ct**	

		Sunday Principal Service Weekday Eucharist	Third Service Morning Prayer	Second Service Evening Prayer
25 Sunday	**THE FOURTH SUNDAY OF EASTER** (Mark transferred to 26th)			
W	*The reading from Acts must be used as either the first or second reading at the Principal Service.*	Acts 4. 5–12 [Gen. 7. 1–5, 11–18; 8. 6–18; 9. 8–13] Ps. 23 1 John 3. 16–end John 10. 11–18	Ps. 119. 89–96 Neh. 7.73b – 8.12 Luke 24. 25–32	Ps. 81. 8–16 Exod. 16. 4–15 Rev. 2. 12–17 *Gospel*: John 6. 30–40 *or First EP of Mark* Ps. 19 Isa. 52. 7–10 Mark 1. 1–15 **R ct**
26 Monday	**MARK THE EVANGELIST** (transferred from 25th)			
R		Prov. 15. 28–end *or* Acts 15. 35–end Ps. 119. 9–16 Eph. 4. 7–16 Mark 13. 5–13	*MP*: Ps. 37. 23–end; 148 Isa. 62. 6–10 *or* Ecclus. 51. 13–end Acts 12.25 – 13.13	*EP*: Ps. 45 Ezek. 1. 4–14 2 Tim. 4. 1–11
27 Tuesday	*Christina Rossetti, Poet, 1894*			
W		Acts 11. 19–26 Ps. 87 John 10. 22–30	Ps. 139 *alt.* Ps. ***48***; 52 Deut. 9.23 – 10.5 Eph. 4. 17–end	Ps. 115; ***116*** *alt.* Ps. 50 Exod. 32. 15–34 Luke 3. 1–14
28 Wednesday	*Peter Chanel, Missionary in the South Pacific, Martyr, 1841*			
W		Acts 12.24 – 13.5 Ps. 67 John 12. 44–end	Ps. 135 *alt.* Ps. 119. 57–80 Deut. 10. 12–end Eph. 5. 1–14	Ps. ***47***; 48 *alt.* Ps. ***59***; 60; (67) Exod. ch. 33 Luke 3. 15–22
29 Thursday	**Catherine of Siena, Teacher, 1380**			
W	Com. Teacher *or* *also* Prov. 8. 1, 6–11 John 17. 12–26	Acts 13. 13–25 Ps. 89. 1–2, 20–26 John 13. 16–20	Ps. 118 *alt.* Ps. 56; ***57***; (63†) Deut. 11. 8–end Eph. 5. 15–end	Ps. 81; ***85*** *alt.* Ps. 61; ***62***; 64 Exod. 34. 1–10, 27–end Luke 4. 1–13
30 Friday	*Pandita Mary Ramabai, Translator of the Scriptures, 1922*			
W		Acts 13. 26–33 Ps. 2 John 14. 1–6	Ps. 33 *alt.* Ps. ***51***; 54 Deut. 12. 1–14 Eph. 6. 1–9	Ps. ***36***; 40 *alt.* Ps. 38 Exod. 35.20 – 36.7 Luke 4. 14–30 *or First EP of Philip and James* Ps. 25 Isa. 40. 27–end John 12. 20–26 **R ct**

May 2021

1 Saturday	**PHILIP AND JAMES, APOSTLES**			
R		Isa. 30. 15–21 Ps. 119. 1–8 Eph. 1. 3–10 John 14. 1–14	*MP*: Ps. 139; 146 Prov. 4. 10–18 James 1. 1–12	*EP*: Ps. 149 Job 23. 1–12 John 1. 43–end

	Calendar and Holy Communion	Morning Prayer	Evening Prayer	NOTES
	THE THIRD SUNDAY AFTER EASTER (Mark transferred to 26th)			
W	Gen. 45. 3–10 Ps. 57 1 Pet. 2. 11–17 John 16. 16–22	Ps. 119. 89–96 Neh. 7.73b – 8.12 Luke 24. 25–32	Ps. 81. 8–16 Exod. 16. 4–15 Rev. 2. 12–17 *or First EP of Mark* (Ps. 19) Isa. 52. 7–10 Mark 1. 1–15 **R ct**	
	MARK THE EVANGELIST			
R	Prov. 15. 28–end Ps. 119. 9–16 Eph. 4. 7–16 John 15. 1–11	(Ps. 37. 23–end; 148) Isa. 62. 6–10 *or* Ecclus. 51. 13–end Acts 12.25 – 13.13	(Ps. 45) Ezek. 1. 4–14 2 Tim. 4. 1–11	
W		Deut. 9.23 – 10.5 Eph. 4. 17–end	Exod. 32. 15–34 Luke 3. 1–14	
W		Deut. 10. 12–end Eph. 5. 1–14	Exod. ch. 33 Luke 3. 15–22	
W		Deut. 11. 8–end Eph. 5. 15–end	Exod. 34. 1–10, 27–end Luke 4. 1–13	
W		Deut. 12. 1–14 Eph. 6. 1–9	Exod. 35.20 – 36.7 Luke 4. 14–30 *or First EP of Philip and James* (Ps. 119. 1–8) Isa. 40. 27–end John 12. 20–26 **R ct**	
	PHILIP AND JAMES, APOSTLES			
R	Prov. 4. 10–18 Ps. 25. 1–9 James 1. [1] 2–12 John 14. 1–14	(Ps. 139; 146) Isa. 30. 1–5 John 12. 20–26	(Ps. 149) Job 23. 1–12 John 1. 43–end	

			Sunday Principal Service Weekday Eucharist	Third Service Morning Prayer	Second Service Evening Prayer
2 Sunday	**THE FIFTH SUNDAY OF EASTER**				
W	*The reading from Acts must be used as either the first or second reading at the Principal Service.*		Acts 8. 26–end [Baruch 3.9–15, 32 – 4.4 *or* Gen. 22. 1–18] Ps. 22. 25–end 1 John 4. 7–end John 15. 1–8	Ps. 44. 16–end 2 Macc. 7. 7–14 *or* Dan. 3. 16–28 Heb. 11.32 – 12.2	Ps. 96 Isa. 60. 1–14 Rev. 3. 1–13 *Gospel*: Mark 16. 9–16
3 Monday					
W			Acts 14. 5–18 Ps. 118. 1–3, 14–15 John 14. 21–26	Ps. 145 *alt*. Ps. 71 Deut. 16. 1–20 1 Pet. 1. 1–12	Ps. 105 *alt*. Ps. ***72***; 75 Num. 9. 15–end; 10. 33–end Luke 4. 38–end
4 Tuesday	**English Saints and Martyrs of the Reformation Era**				
W	Isa. 43. 1–7 *or* Ecclus. 2. 10–17 Ps. 87 2 Cor. 4. 5–12 John 12. 20–26	*or*	Acts 14. 19–end Ps. 145. 10–end John 14. 27–end	Ps. ***19***; 147. 1–12 *alt*. Ps. 73 Deut. 17. 8–end 1 Pet. 1. 13–end	Ps. 96; **97** *alt*. Ps. 74 Num. 11. 1–33 Luke 5. 1–11
5 Wednesday					
W			Acts 15. 1–6 Ps. 122. 1–5 John 15. 1–8	Ps. ***30***; 147. 13–end *alt*. Ps. 77 Deut. 18. 9–end 1 Pet. 2. 1–10	Ps. 98; **99**; 100 *alt*. Ps. 119. 81–104 Num. ch. 12 Luke 5. 12–26
6 Thursday					
W			Acts 15. 7–21 Ps. 96. 1–3, 7–10 John 15. 9–11	Ps. ***57***; 148 *alt*. Ps. 78. 1–39† Deut. ch. 19 1 Pet. 2. 11–end	Ps. 104 *alt*. Ps. 78. 40–end† Num. 13. 1–3, 17–end Luke 5. 27–end
7 Friday					
W			Acts 15. 22–31 Ps. 57. 8–end John 15. 12–17	Ps. ***138***; 149 *alt*. Ps. 55 Deut. 21.22 – 22.8 1 Pet. 3. 1–12	Ps. 66 *alt*. Ps. 69 Num. 14. 1–25 Luke 6. 1–11
8 Saturday	**Julian of Norwich, Spiritual Writer, *c*. 1417**				
W	Com. Religious *also* 1 Cor. 13. 8–end Matt. 5. 13–16	*or*	Acts 16. 1–10 Ps. 100 John 15. 18–21	Ps. ***146***; 150 *alt*. Ps. ***76***; 79 Deut. 24. 5–end 1 Pet. 3. 13–end	Ps. 118 *alt*. Ps. 81; ***84*** Num. 14. 26–end Luke 6. 12–26 **ct**
9 Sunday	**THE SIXTH SUNDAY OF EASTER**				
W	*The reading from Acts must be used as either the first or second reading at the Principal Service.*		Acts 10. 44–end [Isa. 55. 1–11] Ps. 98 1 John 5. 1–6 John 15. 9–17	Ps. 104. 26–32 Ezek. 47. 1–12 John 21. 1–19	Ps. 45 Song of Sol. 4.16 – 5.2; 8. 6–7 Rev. 3. 14–end *Gospel*: Luke 22. 24–30

	Calendar and Holy Communion	Morning Prayer	Evening Prayer	NOTES
	THE FOURTH SUNDAY AFTER EASTER			
W	Job 19. 21–27a Ps. 66. 14–end James 1. 17–21 John 16. 5–15	Ps. 44. 16–end 2 Macc. 7. 7–14 *or* Dan. 3. 16–28 Heb. 11.32 - 12.2	Ps. 96 Isa. 60. 1–14 Rev. 3. 1–13	
	The Invention of the Cross			
Wr		Deut. 16. 1–20 1 Pet. 1. 1–12	Num. 9. 15–end; 10. 33–end Luke 4. 38–end	
W		Deut. 17. 8–end 1 Pet. 1. 13–end	Num. 11. 1–33 Luke 5. 1–11	
W		Deut. 18. 9–end 1 Pet. 2. 1–10	Num. ch. 12 Luke 5. 12–26	
	John the Evangelist, ante Portam Latinam			
W	CEG of 27 December	Deut. ch. 19 1 Pet. 2. 11–end	Num. 13. 1–3, 17–end Luke 5. 27–end	
W		Deut. 21.22 - 22.8 1 Pet. 3. 1–12	Num. 14. 1–25 Luke 6. 1–11	
W		Deut. 24. 5–end 1 Pet. 3. 13–end	Num. 14. 26–end Luke 6. 12–26 **ct**	
	THE FIFTH SUNDAY AFTER EASTER Rogation Sunday			
W	Joel 2. 21–26 Ps. 66. 1–8 James 1. 22–end John 16. 23b–end	Ps. 104. 26–32 Ezek. 47. 1–12 John 21. 1–19	Ps. 45 Song of Sol. 4.16 - 5.2; 8. 6–7 Rev. 3. 14–end	

		Sunday Principal Service Weekday Eucharist	Third Service Morning Prayer	Second Service Evening Prayer
10 Monday	Rogation Day*			
W		Acts 16. 11-15 Ps. 149. 1-5 John 15.26 - 16.4	Ps. ***65***; 67 *alt.* Ps. ***80***; 82 Deut. ch. 26 1 Pet. 4. 1-11	Ps. ***121***; 122; 123 *alt.* Ps. ***85***; 86 Num. 16. 1-35 Luke 6. 27-38
11 Tuesday	Rogation Day*			
W		Acts 16. 22-34 Ps. 138 John 16. 5-11	Ps. 124; 125; ***126***; 127 *alt.* Ps. 87; ***89. 1-18*** Deut. 28. 1-14 1 Pet. 4. 12-end	Ps. ***128***; 129; 130; 131 *alt.* Ps. 89. 19-end Num. 16. 36-end Luke 6. 39-end
12 Wednesday	*Gregory Dix, Priest, Monk, Scholar, 1952* Rogation Day*			
W		Acts 17.15, 22 - 18.1 Ps. 148. 1-2, 11-end John 16. 12-15	Ps. ***132***; 133 *alt.* Ps. 119. 105-128 Deut. 28. 58-end 1 Pet. ch. 5	*First EP of Ascension Day* Ps. 15; 24 2 Sam. 23. 1-5 Col. 2.20 - 3.4 **𝔚 ct**
13 Thursday	**ASCENSION DAY**			
𝔚	*The reading from Acts must be used as either the first or second reading at the Eucharist.*	Acts 1. 1-11 *or* Dan. 7. 9-14 Ps. 47 *or* Ps. 93 Eph. 1. 15-end *or* Acts 1. 1-11 Luke 24. 44-end	*MP*: Ps. 110; 150 Isa. 52. 7-end Heb. 7. [11-25] 26-end	*EP*: Ps. 8 Song of the Three 29-37 *or* 2 Kings 2. 1-15 Rev. ch. 5 *Gospel*: Matt. 28. 16-end
14 Friday	**MATTHIAS THE APOSTLE****			
R	*The reading from Acts must be used as either the first or second reading at the Eucharist.*	Isa. 22. 15-end *or* Acts 1. 15-end Ps. 15 Acts 1. 15-end *or* 1 Cor. 4. 1-7 John 15. 9-17	*MP*: Ps. 16; 147. 1-12 1 Sam. 2. 27-35 Acts 2. 37-end	*EP*: Ps. 80 1 Sam. 16. 1-13a Matt. 7. 15-27
	or, if Matthias is celebrated on 24 February:			
W		Acts 18. 9-18 Ps. 47. 1-6 John 16. 20-23	Ps. 20; ***81*** *alt.* Ps. ***88***; (95) Deut. 29. 2-15 1 John 1.1 - 2.6 [Exod. 35.30 - 36.1 Gal. 5. 13-end]***	Ps. 145 *alt.* Ps. 102 Num. 20. 1-13 Luke 7. 11-17
15 Saturday				
W		Acts 18. 22-end Ps. 47. 1-2, 7-end John 16. 23-28	Ps. 21; ***47*** *alt.* Ps. 96; ***97***; 100 Deut. ch. 30 1 John 2. 7-17 [Num. 11. 16-17, 24-29 1 Cor. ch. 2]***	Ps. 84; ***85*** *alt.* Ps. 104 Num. 21. 4-9 Luke 7. 18-35 **ct**

*For Rogation Day provision, see p. 11.
**Matthias may be celebrated on 24 February instead of 14 May.
***The alternative readings in square brackets may be used at one of the offices, in preparation for the Day of Pentecost.

	Calendar and Holy Communion	Morning Prayer	Evening Prayer	NOTES
	Rogation Day			
W	Job 28. 1-11 Ps. 107. 1-9 James 5. 7-11 Luke 6. 36-42	Deut. ch. 26 1 Pet. 4. 1-11	Num. 16. 1-35 Luke 6. 27-38	
	Rogation Day			
W	Deut. 8. 1-10 Ps. 121 James 5. 16-end Luke 11. 5-13	Deut. 28. 1-14 1 Pet. 4. 12-end	Num. 16. 36-end Luke 6. 39-end	
	Rogation Day			
W	Deut. 34. 1-7 Ps. 108. 1-6 Eph. 4. 7-13 John 17. 1-11	Deut. 28. 58-end 1 Pet. ch. 5	*First EP of Ascension Day* Ps. 15; 24 2 Sam. 23. 1-5 Col. 2.20 - 3.4 **𝔚 ct**	
	ASCENSION DAY			
𝔚	Dan. 7. 13-14 Ps. 68. 1-6 Acts 1. 1-11 Mark 16. 14-end *or* Luke 24. 44-end	Ps. 110; 150 Isa. 52. 7-end Heb. 7. [11-25] 26-end	Ps. 8 Song of the Three 29-37 *or* 2 Kings 2. 1-15 Rev. ch. 5	
W	Ascension CEG	Deut. 29. 2-15 1 John 1.1 - 2.6	Num. 20. 1-13 Luke 7. 11-17	
W		Deut. ch. 30 1 John 2. 7-17 [Num. 11. 16-17, 24-29 1 Cor. ch. 2]***	Num. 21. 4-9 Luke 7. 18-35 **ct**	

		Sunday Principal Service Weekday Eucharist	Third Service Morning Prayer	Second Service Evening Prayer
16 Sunday	**THE SEVENTH SUNDAY OF EASTER (SUNDAY AFTER ASCENSION DAY)**			
W	*The reading from Acts must be used as either the first or second reading at the Principal Service.*	Acts 1. 15–17, 21–end [Ezek. 36. 24–28] Ps. 1 1 John 5. 9–13 John 17. 6–19	Ps. 76 Isa. 14. 3–15 Rev. 14. 1–13	Ps. 147. 1–12 Isa. ch. 61 Luke 4. 14–21
17 Monday				
W		Acts 19. 1–8 Ps. 68. 1–6 John 16. 29–end	Ps. ***93***; 96; 97 *alt.* Ps. ***98***; 99; 101 Deut. 31. 1–13 1 John 2. 18–end [Num. 27. 15–end 1 Cor. ch. 3]*	Ps. 18 *alt.* Ps. ***105†*** (*or* 103) Num. 22. 1–35 Luke 7. 36–end
18 Tuesday				
W		Acts 20. 17–27 Ps. 68. 9–10, 18–19 John 17. 1–11	Ps. 98; ***99***; 100 *alt.* Ps. ***106†*** (*or* 103) Deut. 31. 14–29 1 John 3. 1–10 [1 Sam. 10. 1–10 1 Cor. 12. 1–13]*	Ps. 68 *alt.* Ps. 107† Num. 22.36 - 23.12 Luke 8. 1–15
19 Wednesday	**Dunstan, Archbishop of Canterbury, Restorer of Monastic Life, 988**			
W	Com. Bishop *or* *esp.* Matt. 24. 42–46 *also* Exod. 31. 1–5	Acts 20. 28–end Ps. 68. 27–28, 32–end John 17. 11–19	Ps. 2; ***29*** *alt.* Ps. 110; ***111***; 112 Deut. 31.30 - 32.14 1 John 3. 11–end [1 Kings 19. 1–18 Matt. 3. 13–end]*	Ps. 36; ***46*** *alt.* Ps. 119. 129–152 Num. 23. 13–end Luke 8. 16–25
20 Thursday	**Alcuin of York, Deacon, Abbot of Tours, 804**			
W	Com. Religious *or* *also* Col. 3. 12–16 John 4. 19–24	Acts 22. 30; 23. 6–11 Ps. 16. 1, 5–end John 17. 20–end	Ps. ***24***; 72 *alt.* Ps. 113; ***115*** Deut. 32. 15–47 1 John 4. 1–6 [Ezek. 11. 14–20 Matt. 9.35 - 10.20]*	Ps. 139 *alt.* Ps. 114; ***116***; 117 Num. ch. 24 Luke 8. 26–39
21 Friday	*Helena, Protector of the Holy Places, 330*			
W		Acts 25. 13–21 Ps. 103. 1–2, 11–12, 19–20 John 21. 15–19	Ps. ***28***; 30 *alt.* Ps. 139 Deut. ch. 33 1 John 4. 7–end [Ezek. 36. 22–28 Matt. 12. 22–32]*	Ps. 147 *alt.* Ps. ***130***; 131; 137 Num. 27. 12–end Luke 8. 40–end
22 Saturday				
W		Acts 28. 16–20, 30–end Ps. 11. 4–end John 21. 20–end	Ps. 42; ***43*** *alt.* Ps. 120; ***121***; 122 Deut. 32. 48–end; ch. 34 1 John ch. 5 [Mic. 3. 1–8 Eph. 6. 10–20]*	*First EP of Pentecost* Ps. 48 Deut. 16. 9–15 John 7. 37–39 **R ct**

*The alternative readings in square brackets may be used at one of the offices, in preparation for the Day of Pentecost.

	Calendar and Holy Communion	Morning Prayer	Evening Prayer	NOTES
	THE SUNDAY AFTER ASCENSION DAY			
W	2 Kings 2. 9–15 Ps. 68. 32–end 1 Pet. 4. 7–11 John 15.26 – 16.4a	Ps. 76 Isa. 14. 3–15 Rev. 14. 1–13	Ps. 147. 1–12 Isa. ch. 61 Luke 4. 14–21	
W		Deut. 31. 1–13 1 John 2. 18–end [Num. 27. 15–end 1 Cor. ch. 3]*	Num. 22. 1–35 Luke 7. 36–end	
W		Deut. 31. 14–29 1 John 3. 1–10 [1 Sam. 10. 1–10 1 Cor. 12. 1–13]*	Num. 22.36 – 23.12 Luke 8. 1–15	
	Dunstan, Archbishop of Canterbury, Restorer of Monastic Life, 988			
W	Com. Bishop	Deut. 31.30 – 32.14 1 John 3. 11–end [1 Kings 19. 1–18 Matt. 3. 13–end]*	Num. 23. 13–end Luke 8. 16–25	
W		Deut. 32. 15–47 1 John 4. 1–6 [Ezek. 11. 14–20 Matt. 9.35 – 10.20]*	Num. ch. 24 Luke 8. 26–39	
W		Deut. ch. 33 1 John 4. 7–end [Ezek. 36. 22–28 Matt. 12. 22–32]*	Num. 27. 12–end Luke 8. 40–end	
W		Deut. 32. 48–end; ch. 34 1 John ch. 5 [Mic. 3. 1–8 Eph. 6. 10–20]*	*First EP of Whit Sunday* Ps. 48 Deut. 16. 9–15 John 7. 37–39 **R ct**	

		Sunday Principal Service Weekday Eucharist	Third Service Morning Prayer	Second Service Evening Prayer
23 Sunday	**DAY OF PENTECOST (Whit Sunday)**			
R	*The reading from Acts must be used as either the first or second reading at the Principal Service.*	Acts 2. 1–21 *or* Ezek. 37. 1–14 Ps. 104. 26–36, 37b (*or* 26–end) Rom. 8. 22–27 *or* Acts 2. 1–21 John 15. 26–27; 16. 4b–15	*MP*: Ps. 145 Isa. 11. 1–9 *or* Wisd. 7. 15–23 [24–27] 1 Cor. 12. 4–13	*EP*: Ps. 139. 1–11, 13–18, 23–24 (*or* 139. 1–11) Ezek. 36. 22–28 Acts 2. 22–38 *Gospel*: John 20. 19–23
24 Monday	**John and Charles Wesley, Evangelists, Hymn Writers, 1791 and 1788** Ordinary Time resumes today			
Gw **DEL 8**	Com. Pastor *or* *also* Eph. 5. 15–20	Ecclus. 17. 24–29 *or* James 3. 13–end Ps. 32. 1–8 *or* Ps. 19. 7–end Mark 10. 17–27	Ps. 123; 124; 125; ***126*** Job ch. 1 Rom. 1. 1–17	Ps. ***127***; 128; 129 Josh. ch. 1 Luke 9. 18–27
25 Tuesday	**The Venerable Bede, Monk at Jarrow, Scholar, Historian, 735** *Aldhelm, Bishop of Sherborne, 709*			
Gw	Com. Religious *or* *also* Ecclus. 39. 1–10	Ecclus. 35. 1–12 *or* James 4. 1–10 Ps. 50. 1–6 *or* Ps. 55. 7–9, 24 Mark 10. 28–31	Ps. ***132***; 133 Job ch. 2 Rom. 1. 18–end	Ps. (134); ***135*** Josh. ch. 2 Luke 9. 28–36
26 Wednesday	**Augustine, first Archbishop of Canterbury, 605** *John Calvin, Reformer, 1564; Philip Neri, Founder of the Oratorians, Spiritual Guide, 1595*			
Gw	Com. Bishop *or* *also* 1 Thess. 2. 2b–8 Matt. 13. 31–33	Ecclus. 36. 1–2, 4–5, 10–17 *or* James 4. 13–end Ps. 79. 8–9, 12, 14 *or* Ps. 49. 1–2, 5–10 Mark 10. 32–45	Ps. 119. 153–end Job ch. 3 Rom. 2. 1–16	Ps. 136 Josh. ch. 3 Luke 9. 37–50
27 Thursday				
G		Ecclus. 42. 15–end *or* James 5. 1–6 Ps. 33. 1–9 *or* Ps. 49. 12–20 Mark 10. 46–end	Ps. ***143***; 146 Job ch. 4 Rom. 2. 17–end	Ps. ***138***; 140; 141 Josh. 4.1 - 5.1 Luke 9. 51–end
28 Friday	*Lanfranc, Prior of Le Bec, Archbishop of Canterbury, Scholar, 1089*			
G		Ecclus. 44. 1, 9–13 *or* James 5. 9–12 Ps. 149. 1–5 *or* Ps. 103. 1–4, 8–13 Mark 11. 11–26	Ps. ***142***; 144 Job ch. 5 Rom. 3. 1–20	Ps. 145 Josh. 5. 2–end Luke 10. 1–16
29 Saturday				
G		Ecclus. 51. 12b–20a *or* James 5. 13–end Ps. 19. 7–end *or* Ps. 141. 1–4 Mark 11. 27–end	Ps. 147 Job ch. 6 Rom. 3. 21–end	*First EP of Trinity Sunday* Ps. 97; 98 Isa, 40. 12–end Mark 1. 1–13 **W ct**

	Calendar and Holy Communion	Morning Prayer	Evening Prayer	NOTES
	WHIT SUNDAY			
R	Deut. 16. 9–12 Ps. 122 Acts 2. 1–11 John 14. 15–31a	Ps. 145 Isa. 11. 1–9 *or* Wisd. 7. 15–23 [24–27] 1 Cor. 12. 4–13	Ps. 139. 1–11, 13–18, 23–24 (*or* 139. 1–11) Ezek. 36. 22–28 Acts 2. 22–38	
	Monday in Whitsun Week			
R	Acts 10. 34–end John 3. 16–21	Ezek. 11. 14–20 Acts 2. 12–36	Exod. 35.30 – 36.1 Acts 2. 37–end	
	Tuesday in Whitsun Week			
R	Acts 8. 14–17 John 10. 1–10	Ezek. 37. 1–14 1 Cor. 12. 1–13	2 Sam. 23. 1–5 1 Cor. 12.27 – 13.end	
	Augustine, first Archbishop of Canterbury, 605 Ember Day			
Rw	Com. Bishop *or* Ember CEG *or* Acts 2. 14–21 John 6. 44–51	Job ch. 3 Rom. 2. 1–16	Josh. ch. 3 Luke 9. 37–50	
	The Venerable Bede, Monk at Jarrow, Scholar, Historian, 735			
R	Com. Religious *or* Acts 2. 22–28 Luke 9. 1–6	Job ch. 4 Rom. 2. 17–end	Josh. 4.1 – 5.1 Luke 9. 51–end	
	Ember Day			
R	Ember CEG *or* Acts 8. 5–8 Luke 5. 17–26	Job ch. 5 Rom. 3. 1–20	Josh. 5. 2–end Luke 10. 1–16	
	Ember Day			
R	Ember CEG *or* Acts 13. 44–end Matt. 20. 29–end	Job ch. 6 Rom. 3. 21–end	*First EP of Trinity Sunday* Ps. 97; 98 Isa. 40. 12–end Mark 1. 1–13 **𝔚 ct**	

			Sunday Principal Service Weekday Eucharist	Third Service Morning Prayer	Second Service Evening Prayer
30 Sunday		**TRINITY SUNDAY**			
	𝔚		Isa. 6. 1–8 Ps. 29 Rom. 8. 12–17 John 3. 1–17	*MP*: Ps. 33. 1–12 Prov. 8. 1–4, 22–31 2 Cor. 13. [5–10] 11–end	*EP*: Ps. 104. 1–10 Ezek. 1. 4–10, 22–28a Rev. ch. 4 *Gospel*: Mark 1. 1–13
31 Monday		**THE VISIT OF THE BLESSED VIRGIN MARY TO ELIZABETH***			
	W **DEL 9**		Zeph. 3. 14–18 Ps. 113 Rom. 12. 9–16 Luke 1. 39–49 [50–56]	*MP*: Ps. 85; 150 1 Sam. 2. 1–10 Mark 3. 31–end	*EP*: Ps. 122; 127; 128 Zech. 2. 10–end John 3. 25–30
		or, if The Visitation is celebrated on 2 July:			
	G		Tobit 1. 1–2; 2. 1–8 *or* 1 Pet. 1. 3–9 Ps. 15 *or* Ps. 111 Mark 12. 1–12	Ps. ***1***: 2; 3 Job ch. 7 Rom. 4. 1–12	Ps. ***4***; 7 Josh. 7. 1–15 Luke 10. 25–37

June 2021

1 Tuesday		**Justin, Martyr at Rome, c. 165**			
	Gr	Com. Martyr *or* *esp.* John 15. 18–21 *also* 1 Macc. 2. 15–22 1 Cor. 1. 18–25	Tobit 2. 9–end *or* 1 Pet. 1. 10–16 Ps. 112 *or* Ps. 98. 1–5 Mark 12. 13–17	Ps. ***5***; 6; (8) Job ch. 8 Rom. 4. 13–end	Ps. ***9***; 10† Josh. 7. 16–end Luke 10. 38–end
2 Wednesday					
	G		Tobit 3. 1–11, 16–end *or* 1 Pet. 1. 18–25 Ps. 25. 1–8 *or* Ps. 147. 13–end Mark 12. 18–27	Ps. 119. 1–32 Job ch. 9 Rom. 5. 1–11	Ps. ***11***; 12; 13 Josh. 8. 1–29 Luke 11. 1–13 *or First EP of Corpus Christi* Ps. 110; 111 Exod. 16. 12–15 John 6. 22–35 **W ct**
3 Thursday		**DAY OF THANKSGIVING FOR HOLY COMMUNION (CORPUS CHRISTI)** *The Martyrs of Uganda, 1885–87 and 1977*			
	W		Gen. 14. 18–20 Ps. 116. 10–end 1 Cor. 11. 23–26 John 6. 51–58	*MP*: Ps. 147 Deut. 8. 2–16 1 Cor. 10. 1–17	*EP*: Ps. 23; 42; 43 Prov. 9. 1–5 Luke 9. 11–17
	G	*or the ferial readings for the day*:	Tobit 6. 10–11; 7. 1–15; 8. 4–8 *or* 1 Pet. 2. 2–5, 9–12 Ps. 128 *or* Ps. 100 Mark 12. 28–34	Ps. 14; ***15***; 16 Job. ch. 10 Rom. 5. 12–end	Ps. 18† Josh. 8. 30–end Luke 11. 14–28
4 Friday		*Petroc, Abbot of Padstow, 6th century*			
	G		Tobit 11. 5–15 *or* 1 Pet. 4. 7–13 Ps. 146 *or* Ps. 96. 10–end Mark 12. 35–37	Ps. 17; ***19*** Job ch. 11 Rom. 6. 1–14	Ps. 22 Josh. 9. 3–26 Luke 11. 29–36

*The Visit of the Blessed Virgin Mary to Elizabeth may be celebrated on 2 July instead of 31 May.

	Calendar and Holy Communion	Morning Prayer	Evening Prayer
	TRINITY SUNDAY		
W	Isa. 6. 1–8 Ps. 8 Rev. 4. 1–11 John 3. 1–15	Ps. 33. 1–12 Prov. 8. 1–4, 22–31 2 Cor. 13. [5–10] 11–end	Ps. 104. 1–10 Ezek. 1. 4–10, 22–28a Mark 1. 1–13
G		Job ch. 7 Rom. 4. 1–12	Josh. 7. 1–15 Luke 10. 25–37
	Nicomede, Priest and Martyr at Rome (date unknown)		
Gr	Com. Martyr	Job ch. 8 Rom. 4. 13–end	Josh. 7. 16–end Luke 10. 38–end
G		Job ch. 9 Rom. 5. 1–11	Josh. 8. 1–29 Luke 11. 1–13
	To celebrate Corpus Christi, see *Common Worship* provision.		
G		Job. ch. 10 Rom. 5. 12–end	Josh. 8. 30–end Luke 11. 14–28
G		Job ch. 11 Rom. 6. 1–14	Josh. 9. 3–26 Luke 11. 29–36

NOTES

		Sunday Principal Service Weekday Eucharist	Third Service Morning Prayer	Second Service Evening Prayer
5 Saturday	**Boniface (Wynfrith) of Crediton, Bishop, Apostle of Germany, Martyr, 754**			
Gr	Com. Martyr *or* *also* Acts 20. 24–28	Tobit 12. 1, 5–15, 20a *or* Jude 17, 20–25 Ps. 103. 1, 8–13 *or* Ps. 63. 1–6 Mark 12. 38–end	Ps. 20; 21; ***23*** Job ch. 12 Rom. 6. 15–end	Ps. ***24***; 25 Josh. 10. 1–15 Luke 11. 37–end **ct**
6 Sunday	**THE FIRST SUNDAY AFTER TRINITY (Proper 5)**			
G	*Track 1* 1 Sam. 8. 4–11 [12–15] 16–20; [11. 14–end] Ps. 138 2 Cor. 4.13 - 5.1 Mark 3. 20–end	*Track 2* Gen. 3. 8–15 Ps. 130 2 Cor. 4.13 - 5.1 Mark 3. 20–end	Ps. 36 Deut. 6. 10–end Acts 22.22 - 23.11	Ps. 37. 1–17 (*or* 37. 1–11) Jer. 6. 16–21 Rom. 9. 1–13 *Gospel*: Luke 7. 11–17
7 Monday				
G **DEL 10**		2 Cor. 1. 1–7 Ps. 34. 1–8 Matt. 5. 1–12	Ps. 27; ***30*** Job ch. 13 Rom. 7. 1–6	Ps. 26; ***28***; 29 Josh. ch. 14 Luke 12. 1–12
8 Tuesday	**Thomas Ken, Bishop of Bath and Wells, Nonjuror, Hymn Writer, 1711**			
Gw	Com. Bishop *or* *esp.* 2 Cor. 4. 1–10 Matt. 24. 42–46	2 Cor. 1. 18–22 Ps. 119. 129–136 Matt. 5. 13–16	Ps. 32; ***36*** Job ch. 14 Rom. 7. 7–end	Ps. 33 Josh. 21.43 - 22.8 Luke 12. 13–21
9 Wednesday	**Columba, Abbot of Iona, Missionary, 597** *Ephrem of Syria, Deacon, Hymn Writer, Teacher, 373*			
Gw	Com. Missionary *or* *also* Titus 2. 11–end	2 Cor. 3. 4–11 Ps. 78. 1–4 Matt. 5. 17–19	Ps. 34 Job ch. 15 Rom. 8. 1–11	Ps. 119. 33–56 Josh. 22. 9–end Luke 12. 22–31
10 Thursday				
G		2 Cor. 3.15 - 4.1, 3–6 Ps. 78. 36–40 Matt. 5. 20–26	Ps. 37† Job 16.1 - 17.2 Rom. 8. 12–17	Ps. 39; ***40*** Josh. ch. 23 Luke 12. 32–40 *or First EP of Barnabas* Ps. 1; 15 Isa. 42. 5–12 Acts 14. 8–end **R ct**
11 Friday	**BARNABAS THE APOSTLE**			
R	*The reading from Acts must be used as either the first or second reading at the Eucharist.*	Job 29. 11–16 *or* Acts 11. 19–end Ps. 112 Acts 11. 19–end *or* Gal. 2. 1–10 John 15. 12–17	*MP*: Ps. 100; 101; 117 Jer. 9. 23–24 Acts 4. 32–end	*EP*: Ps. 147 Eccles. 12. 9–end *or* Tobit 4. 5–11 Acts 9. 26–31
12 Saturday				
G		2 Cor. 5. 14–end Ps. 103. 1–12 Matt. 5. 33–37	Ps. 41; ***42***; 43 Job ch. 18 Rom. 8. 31–end	Ps. 45; ***46*** Josh. 24. 29–end Luke 12. 49–end **ct**

	Calendar and Holy Communion	Morning Prayer	Evening Prayer	NOTES
	Boniface (Wynfrith) of Crediton, Bishop, Apostle of Germany, Martyr, 754			
Gr	Com. Martyr	Job ch. 12 Rom. 6. 15–end	Josh. 10. 1–15 Luke 11. 37–end **ct**	
	THE FIRST SUNDAY AFTER TRINITY			
G	2 Sam. 9. 6–end Ps. 41. 1–4 1 John 4. 7–end Luke 16. 19–31	Ps. 36 Deut. 6. 10–end Acts 22.22 – 23.11	Ps. 37. 1–17 (*or* 37. 1–11) Jer. 6. 16–21 Rom. 9. 1–13	
G		Job ch. 13 Rom. 7. 1–6	Josh. ch. 14 Luke 12. 1–12	
G		Job ch. 14 Rom. 7. 7–end	Josh. 21.43 – 22.8 Luke 12. 13–21	
G		Job ch. 15 Rom. 8. 1–11	Josh. 22. 9–end Luke 12. 22–31	
G		Job 16.1 – 17.2 Rom. 8. 12–17	Josh. ch. 23 Luke 12. 32–40 *or First EP of Barnabas* (Ps. 1; 15) Isa. 42. 5–12 Acts 14. 8–end **R ct**	
	BARNABAS THE APOSTLE			
R	Job 29. 11–16 Ps. 112 Acts 11. 22–end John 15. 12–16	(Ps. 100; 101; 117) Jer. 9. 23–24 Acts 4. 32–end	(Ps. 147) Eccles. 12. 9–end *or* Tobit 4. 5–11 Acts 9. 26–31	
G		Job ch. 18 Rom. 8. 31–end	Josh. 24. 29–end Luke 12. 49–end **ct**	

		Sunday Principal Service Weekday Eucharist	Third Service Morning Prayer	Second Service Evening Prayer
13 Sunday	**THE SECOND SUNDAY AFTER TRINITY (Proper 6)**			
G	*Track 1* 1 Sam. 15.34 - 16.13 Ps. 20 2 Cor. 5. 6-10 [11-13] 14-17 Mark 4. 26-34	*Track 2* Ezek. 17. 22-end Ps. 92. 1-4, 12-end (*or* 1-8) 2 Cor. 5. 6-10 [11-13] 14-17 Mark 4. 26-34	Ps. 42; 43 Deut. 10.12 - 11.1 Acts 23. 12-35	Ps. 39 Jer. 7. 1-16 Rom. 9. 14-26 *Gospel*: Luke 7.36 - 8.3
14 Monday	*Richard Baxter, Puritan Divine, 1691*			
G **DEL 11**		2 Cor. 6. 1-10 Ps. 98 Matt. 5. 38-42	Ps. 44 Job ch. 19 Rom. 9. 1-18	Ps. ***47***; 49 Judg. ch. 2 Luke 13. 1-9
15 Tuesday	*Evelyn Underhill, Spiritual Writer, 1941*			
G		2 Cor. 8. 1-9 Ps. 146 Matt. 5. 43-end	Ps. ***48***; 52 Job ch. 21 Rom. 9. 19-end	Ps. 50 Judg. 4. 1-23 Luke 13. 10-21
16 Wednesday	**Richard, Bishop of Chichester, 1253** *Joseph Butler, Bishop of Durham, Philosopher, 1752*			
Gw	Com. Bishop *or* *also* John 21. 15-19	2 Cor. 9. 6-11 Ps. 112 Matt. 6. 1-6, 16-18	Ps. 119. 57-80 Job ch. 22 Rom. 10. 1-10	Ps. ***59***; 60; (67) Judg. ch. 5 Luke 13. 22-end
17 Thursday	*Samuel and Henrietta Barnett, Social Reformers, 1913 and 1936*			
G		2 Cor. 11. 1-11 Ps. 111 Matt. 6. 7-15	Ps. 56; ***57***; (63†) Job ch. 23 Rom. 10. 11-end	Ps. 61; ***62***; 64 Judg. 6. 1-24 Luke 14. 1-11
18 Friday	*Bernard Mizeki, Apostle of the MaShona, Martyr, 1896*			
G		2 Cor. 11. 18, 21b-30 Ps. 34. 1-6 Matt. 6. 19-23	Ps. ***51***; 54 Job ch. 24 Rom. 11. 1-12	Ps. 38 Judg. 6. 25-end Luke 14. 12-24
19 Saturday	*Sundar Singh of India, Sadhu (holy man), Evangelist, Teacher, 1929*			
G		2 Cor. 12. 1-10 Ps. 89. 20-33 Matt. 6. 24-end	Ps. 68 Job chs 25 & 26 Rom. 11. 13-24	Ps. 65; ***66*** Judg. ch. 7 Luke 14. 25-end **ct**
20 Sunday	**THE THIRD SUNDAY AFTER TRINITY (Proper 7)**			
G	*Track 1* 1 Sam. 17. [1a, 4-11, 19-23] 32-49 *and* Ps. 9. 9-end *or* 1 Sam. 17.57 - 18.5, 10-16 *and* Ps. 133 2 Cor. 6. 1-13 Mark 4. 35-end	*Track 2* Job 38. 1-11 Ps. 107. 1-3, 23-32 (*or* 23-32) 2 Cor. 6. 1-13 Mark 4. 35-end	Ps. 48 Deut. 11. 1-15 Acts 27. 1-12	Ps. 49 Jer. 10. 1-16 Rom. 11. 25-end *Gospel*: Luke 8. 26-39
21 Monday				
G **DEL 12**		Gen. 12. 1-9 Ps. 33. 12-end Matt. 7. 1-5	Ps. 71 Job ch. 27 Rom. 11. 25-end	Ps. ***72***; 75 Judg. 8. 22-end Luke 15. 1-10

	Calendar and Holy Communion	Morning Prayer	Evening Prayer	NOTES
	THE SECOND SUNDAY AFTER TRINITY			
G	Gen. 12. 1-4 Ps. 120 1 John 3. 13-end Luke 14. 16-24	Ps. 42; 43 Deut. 10.12 - 11.1 Acts 23. 12-35	Ps. 39 Jer. 7. 1-16 Rom. 9. 14-26	
G		Job ch. 19 Rom. 9. 1-18	Judg. ch. 2 Luke 13. 1-9	
G		Job ch. 21 Rom. 9. 19-end	Judg. 4. 1-23 Luke 13. 10-21	
G		Job ch. 22 Rom. 10. 1-10	Judg. ch. 5 Luke 13. 22-end	
	Alban, first Martyr of Britain, c. 250			
Gr	Com. Martyr	Job ch. 23 Rom. 10. 11-end	Judg. 6. 1-24 Luke 14. 1-11	
G		Job ch. 24 Rom. 11. 1-12	Judg. 6. 25-end Luke 14. 12-24	
G		Job chs 25 & 26 Rom. 11. 13-24	Judg. ch. 7 Luke 14. 25-end **ct**	
	THE THIRD SUNDAY AFTER TRINITY			
G	2 Chron. 33. 9-13 Ps. 55. 17-23 1 Pet. 5. 5b-11 Luke 15. 1-10	Ps. 48 Deut. 11. 1-15 Acts 27. 1-12	Ps. 49 Jer. 10. 1-16 Rom. 11. 25-end	
G		Job ch. 27 Rom. 11. 25-end	Judg. 8. 22-end Luke 15. 1-10	

		Sunday Principal Service Weekday Eucharist	Third Service Morning Prayer	Second Service Evening Prayer
22 Tuesday	**Alban, first Martyr of Britain, *c.* 250**			
Gr	Com. Martyr *or* *esp.* 2 Tim. 2. 3–13 John 12. 24–26	Gen. 13. 2, 5–end Ps. 15 Matt. 7. 6, 12–14	Ps. 73 Job ch. 28 Rom. 12. 1–8	Ps. 74 Judg. 9. 1–21 Luke 15. 11–end
23 Wednesday	**Etheldreda, Abbess of Ely, *c.* 678** Ember Day*			
Gw *or* **Rw**	Com. Religious *or* *also* Matt. 25. 1–13	Gen. 15. 1–12, 17–18 Ps. 105. 1–9 Matt. 7. 15–20	Ps. 77 Job ch. 29 Rom. 12. 9–end	Ps. 119. 81–104 Judg. 9. 22–end Luke 16. 1–18 *or First EP of The Birth of John the Baptist* Ps. 71 Judges 13. 2–7, 24–end Luke 1. 5–25 **W ct**
24 Thursday	**THE BIRTH OF JOHN THE BAPTIST**			
W		Isa. 40. 1–11 Ps. 85. 7–end Acts 13. 14b–26 *or* Gal. 3. 23–end Luke 1. 57–66, 80	*MP*: Ps. 50; 149 Ecclus. 48. 1–10 *or* Mal. 3. 1–6 Luke 3. 1–17	*EP*: Ps. 80; 82 Mal. ch. 4 Matt. 11. 2–19
25 Friday	Ember Day*			
G *or* **R**		Gen. 17. 1, 9–10, 15–22 Ps. 128 Matt. 8. 1–4	Ps. 55 Job ch. 31 Rom. 13. 8–end	Ps. 69 Judg. 11. 29–end Luke 17. 1–10
26 Saturday	Ember Day*			
G *or* **R**		Gen. 18. 1–15 *Canticle*: Luke 1. 46b–55 Matt. 8. 5–17	Ps. ***76***; 79 Job ch. 32 Rom. 14. 1–12	Ps. 81; ***84*** Judg. 12. 1–7 Luke 17. 11–19 **ct**
27 Sunday	**THE FOURTH SUNDAY AFTER TRINITY (Proper 8)**			
G	*Track 1* 2 Sam. 1. 1, 17–end Ps. 130 2 Cor. 8. 7–end Mark 5. 21–end	*Track 2* Wisd. of Sol. 1. 13–15; 2. 23–24 *Canticle*: Lam. 3. 22–33 *or* Ps. 30 2 Cor. 8. 7–end Mark 5. 21–end	Ps. 56 Deut. 15. 1–11 Acts 27. [13–32] 33–end	Ps. [52]; 53 Jer. 11. 1–14 Rom. 13. 1–10 *Gospel*: Luke 9. 51–end
28 Monday	**Irenaeus, Bishop of Lyons, Teacher, *c.* 200**			
Gw **DEL 13**	Com. Teacher *or* *also* 2 Pet. 1. 16–21	Gen. 18. 16–end Ps. 103. 6–17 Matt. 8. 18–22	Ps. ***80***; 82 Job ch. 33 Rom. 14. 13–end	Ps. ***85***; 86 Judg. 13. 1–24 Luke 17. 20–end *or First EP of Peter and Paul* Ps. 66; 67 Ezek. 3. 4–11 Gal. 1.13 - 2.8 *or, for Peter alone*: Acts 9. 32–end **R ct**

*For Ember Day provision, see p. 11.

	Calendar and Holy Communion	Morning Prayer	Evening Prayer	NOTES
G		Job ch. 28 Rom. 12. 1–8	Judg. 9. 1–21 Luke 15. 11–end	
G		Job ch. 29 Rom. 12. 9–end	Judg. 9. 22–end Luke 16. 1–18 *or First EP of The Nativity of John the Baptist* (Ps. 71) Judges 13. 2–7, 24–end Luke 1. 5–25 **W ct**	
	THE NATIVITY OF JOHN THE BAPTIST			
W	Isa. 40. 1–11 Ps. 80. 1–7 Acts 13. 22–26 Luke 1. 57–80	(Ps. 50; 149) Ecclus. 48. 1–10 *or* Mal. 3. 1–6 Luke 3. 1–17	(Ps. 82) Mal. ch. 4 Matt. 11. 2–19	
G		Job ch. 31 Rom. 13. 8–end	Judg. 11. 29–end Luke 17. 1–10	
G		Job ch. 32 Rom. 14. 1–12	Judg. 12. 1–7 Luke 17. 11–19 **ct**	
	THE FOURTH SUNDAY AFTER TRINITY			
G	Gen. 3. 17–19 Ps. 79. 8–10 Rom. 8. 18–23 Luke 6. 36–42	Ps. 56 Deut. 15. 1–11 Acts 27. [13–32] 33–end	Ps. [52]; 53 Jer. 11. 1–14 Rom. 13. 1–10	
G		Job ch. 33 Rom. 14. 13–end	Judg. 13. 1–24 Luke 17. 20–end *or First EP of Peter* (Ps. 66; 67) Ezek. 3. 4–11 Acts 9. 32–end **R ct**	

		Sunday Principal Service Weekday Eucharist	Third Service Morning Prayer	Second Service Evening Prayer
29 Tuesday	**PETER AND PAUL, APOSTLES**			
R	*The reading from Acts must be used as either the first or second reading at the Eucharist.*	Zech. 4. 1–6a, 10b–end *or* Acts 12. 1–11 Ps. 125 Acts 12. 1–11 *or* 2 Tim. 4. 6–8, 17–18 Matt. 16. 13–19	*MP*: Ps. 71; 113 Isa. 49. 1–6 Acts 11. 1–18	*EP*: Ps. 124; 138 Ezek. 34. 11–16 John 21. 15–22
	or, if Peter is commemorated alone:			
R	*The reading from Acts must be used as either the first or second reading at the Eucharist.*	Ezek. 3. 22–end *or* Acts 12. 1–11 Ps. 125 Acts 12. 1–11 *or* 1 Pet. 2. 19–end Matt. 16. 13–19	*MP*: Ps. 71; 113 Isa. 49. 1–6 Acts 11. 1–18	*EP*: Ps. 124; 138 Ezek. 34. 11–16 John 21. 15–22
30 Wednesday				
G		Gen. 21. 5, 8–20 Ps. 34. 1–12 Matt. 8. 28–end	Ps. 119. 105–128 Job ch. 39 Rom. 15. 14–21	Ps. ***91***; 93 Judg. 15.1 - 16.3 Luke 18. 15–30

July 2021

1 Thursday	*Henry, John and Henry Venn the Younger, Priests, Evangelical Divines, 1797, 1813 and 1873*			
G		Gen. 22. 1–19 Ps. 116. 1–7 Matt. 9. 1–8	Ps. 90; **92** Job ch. 40 Rom. 15. 22–end	Ps. 94 Judg. 16. 4–end Luke 18. 31–end
2 Friday				
G		Gen. 23. 1–4, 19; 24. 1–8, 62–end Ps. 106. 1–5 Matt. 9. 9–13	Ps. ***88***; (95) Job ch. 41 Rom. 16. 1–16	Ps. 102 Judg. ch. 17 Luke 19. 1–10 *or First EP of Thomas* Ps. 27 Isa. ch. 35 Heb. 10.35 - 11.1 **R ct**
3 Saturday	**THOMAS THE APOSTLE****			
R		Hab. 2. 1–4 Ps. 31. 1–6 Eph. 2. 19–end John 20. 24–29	*MP*: Ps. 92; 146 2 Sam. 15. 17–21 *or* Ecclus. ch. 2 John 11. 1–16	*EP*: Ps. 139 Job 42. 1–6 1 Pet. 1. 3–12
	or, if Thomas is not celebrated:			
G		Gen. 27. 1–5a, 15–29 Ps. 135. 1–6 Matt. 9. 14–17	Ps. 96; ***97***; 100 Job ch. 42 Rom. 16. 17–end	Ps. 104 Judg. 18. 1–20, 27–end Luke 19. 11–27 **ct**
4 Sunday	**THE FIFTH SUNDAY AFTER TRINITY (Proper 9)**			
G	*Track 1* 2 Sam. 5. 1–5, 9–10 Ps. 48 2 Cor. 12. 2–10 Mark 6. 1–13	*Track 2* Ezek. 2. 1–5 Ps. 123 2 Cor. 12. 2–10 Mark 6. 1–13	Ps. 57 Deut. 24. 10–end Acts 28. 1–16	Ps. [63]; 64 Jer. 20. 1–11a Rom. 14. 1–17 *Gospel*: Luke 10. 1–11, 16–20

**Common Worship* Morning and Evening Prayer provision for 31 May may be used.
**Thomas the Apostle may be celebrated on 21 December instead of 3 July.

	Calendar and Holy Communion	Morning Prayer	Evening Prayer	NOTES
	PETER THE APOSTLE			
R	Ezek. 3. 4-11 Ps. 125 Acts 12. 1-11 Matt. 16. 13-19	(Ps. 71; 113) Isa. 49. 1-6 Acts 11. 1-18	(Ps. 124; 138) Ezek. 34. 11-16 John 21. 15-22	
G		Job ch. 39 Rom. 15. 14-21	Judg. 15.1 - 16.3 Luke 18. 15-30	
G		Job ch. 40 Rom. 15. 22-end	Judg. 16. 4-end Luke 18. 31-end	
	The Visitation of the Blessed Virgin Mary*			
Gw	1 Sam. 2. 1-3 Ps. 113 Gal. 4. 1-5 Luke 1. 39-45	Job ch. 41 Rom. 16. 1-16	Judg. ch. 17 Luke 19. 1-10	
G		Job ch. 42 Rom. 16. 17-end	Judg. 18. 1-20, 27-end Luke 19. 11-27 ct	
	THE FIFTH SUNDAY AFTER TRINITY			
G	1 Kings 19. 19-21 Ps. 84. 8-end 1 Pet. 3. 8-15a Luke 5. 1-11	Ps. 57 Deut. 24. 10-end Acts 28. 1-16	Ps. [63]; 64 Jer. 20. 1-11a Rom. 14. 1-17	

		Sunday Principal Service Weekday Eucharist	Third Service Morning Prayer	Second Service Evening Prayer
5 Monday				
G **DEL 14**		Gen. 28. 10-end Ps. 91. 1-10 Matt. 9. 18-26	Ps. ***98***; 99; 101 Ezek. 1. 1-14 2 Cor. 1. 1-14	Ps. ***105***† (*or* 103) 1 Sam. 1. 1-20 Luke 19. 28-40
6 Tuesday	*Thomas More, Scholar, and John Fisher, Bishop of Rochester, Reformation Martyrs, 1535*			
G		Gen. 32. 22-end Ps. 17. 1-8 Matt. 9. 32-end	Ps. ***106***† (*or* 103) Ezek. 1.15 - 2.2 2 Cor. 1.15 - 2.4	Ps. 107† 1 Sam. 1.21 - 2.11 Luke 19. 41-end
7 Wednesday*				
G		Gen. 41. 55-end; 42. 5-7, 17-end Ps. 33. 1-4, 18-end Matt. 10. 1-7	Ps. 110; ***111***; 112 Ezek. 2.3 - 3.11 2 Cor. 2. 5-end	Ps. 119. 129-152 1 Sam. 2. 12-26 Luke 20. 1-8
8 Thursday				
G		Gen. 44. 18-21, 23-29; 45. 1-5 Ps. 105. 11-17 Matt. 10. 7-15	Ps. 113; ***115*** Ezek. 3. 12-end 2 Cor. ch. 3	Ps. 114; ***116***; 117 1 Sam. 2. 27-end Luke 20. 9-19
9 Friday				
G		Gen. 46. 1-7, 28-30 Ps. 37. 3-6, 27-28 Matt. 10. 16-23	Ps. 139 Ezek. ch. 8 2 Cor. ch. 4	Ps. ***130***; 131; 137 1 Sam. 3.1 - 4.1a Luke 20. 20-26
10 Saturday				
G		Gen. 49. 29-end; 50. 15-25 Ps. 105. 1-7 Matt. 10. 24-33	Ps. 120; ***121***; 122 Ezek. ch. 9 2 Cor. ch. 5	Ps. 118 1 Sam. 4. 1b-end Luke 20. 27-40 **ct**
11 Sunday	**THE SIXTH SUNDAY AFTER TRINITY (Proper 10)**			
G	*Track 1* 2 Sam. 6. 1-5, 12b-19 Ps. 24 Eph. 1. 3-14 Mark 6. 14-29	*Track 2* Amos 7. 7-15 Ps. 85. 8-end Eph. 1. 3-14 Mark 6. 14-29	Ps. 65 Deut. 28. 1-14 Acts 28. 17-end	Ps. 66 (*or* 66. 1-8) Job 4. 1; 5. 6-end *or* Ecclus. 4. 11-end Rom. 15. 14-29 *Gospel*: Luke 10. 25-37
12 Monday				
G **DEL 15**		Exod. 1. 8-14, 22 Ps. 124 Matt. 10.34 - 11.1	Ps. 123; 124; 125; ***126*** Ezek. 10. 1-19 2 Cor. 6.1 - 7.1	Ps. ***127***; 128; 129 1 Sam. ch. 5 Luke 20.41 - 21.4
13 Tuesday				
G		Exod. 2. 1-15 Ps. 69. 1-2, 31-end Matt. 11. 20-24	Ps. ***132***; 133 Ezek. 11. 14-end 2 Cor. 7. 2-end	Ps. (134); ***135*** 1 Sam. 6. 1-16 Luke 21. 5-19
14 Wednesday	**John Keble, Priest, Tractarian, Poet, 1866**			
Gw	Com. Pastor *or* *also* Lam. 3. 19-26 Matt. 5. 1-8	Exod. 3. 1-6, 9-12 Ps. 103. 1-7 Matt. 11. 25-27	Ps. 119. 153-end Ezek. 12. 1-16 2 Cor. 8. 1-15	Ps. 136 1 Sam. ch. 7 Luke 21. 20-28

*Thomas Becket may be celebrated on 7 July instead of 29 December.

	Calendar and Holy Communion	Morning Prayer	Evening Prayer	NOTES
G		Ezek. 1. 1–14 2 Cor. 1. 1–14	1 Sam. 1. 1–20 Luke 19. 28–40	
G		Ezek. 1.15 - 2.2 2 Cor. 1.15 - 2.4	1 Sam. 1.21 - 2.11 Luke 19. 41–end	
G		Ezek. 2.3 - 3.11 2 Cor. 2. 5–end	1 Sam. 2. 12–26 Luke 20. 1–8	
G		Ezek. 3. 12–end 2 Cor. ch. 3	1 Sam. 2. 27–end Luke 20. 9–19	
G		Ezek. ch. 8 2 Cor. ch. 4	1 Sam. 3.1 - 4.1a Luke 20. 20–26	
G		Ezek. ch. 9 2 Cor. ch. 5	1 Sam. 4. 1b–end Luke 20. 27–40 **ct**	
	THE SIXTH SUNDAY AFTER TRINITY			
G	Gen. 4. 2b–15 Ps. 90. 12–end Rom. 6. 3–11 Matt. 5. 20–26	Ps. 65 Deut. 28. 1–14 Acts 28. 17–end	Ps. 66 (*or* 66. 1–8) Job 4. 1; 5. 6–end *or* Ecclus. 4. 11–end Luke 10. 21–24	
G		Ezek. 10. 1–19 2 Cor. 6.1 - 7.1	1 Sam. ch. 5 Luke 20.41 - 21.4	
G		Ezek. 11. 14–end 2 Cor. 7. 2–end	1 Sam. 6. 1–16 Luke 21. 5–19	
G		Ezek. 12. 1–16 2 Cor. 8. 1–15	1 Sam. ch. 7 Luke 21. 20–28	

		Sunday Principal Service Weekday Eucharist	Third Service Morning Prayer	Second Service Evening Prayer
15 Thursday	**Swithun, Bishop of Winchester, c. 862** *Bonaventure, Friar, Bishop, Teacher, 1274*			
Gw	Com. Bishop *or* *also* James 5. 7-11, 13-18	Exod. 3. 13-20 Ps. 105. 1, 5, 8-9, 24-27 Matt. 11. 28-end	Ps. ***143***; 146 Ezek. 12. 17-end 2 Cor. 8.16 - 9.5	Ps. ***138***; 140; 141 1 Sam. ch. 8 Luke 21. 29-end
16 Friday	*Osmund, Bishop of Salisbury, 1099*			
G		Exod. 11.10 - 12.14 Ps. 116. 10-end Matt. 12. 1-8	Ps. 142; ***144*** Ezek. 13. 1-16 2 Cor. 9. 6-end	Ps. 145 1 Sam. 9. 1-14 Luke 22. 1-13
17 Saturday				
G		Exod. 12. 37-42 Ps. 136. 1-4, 10-15 Matt. 12. 14-21	Ps. 147 Ezek. 14. 1-11 2 Cor. ch. 10	Ps. ***148***; 149; 150 1 Sam. 9.15 - 10.1 Luke 22. 14-23 **ct**
18 Sunday	**THE SEVENTH SUNDAY AFTER TRINITY (Proper 11)**			
G	*Track 1* 2 Sam. 7. 1-14a Ps. 89. 20-37 Eph. 2. 11-end Mark 6. 30-34, 53-end	*Track 2* Jer. 23. 1-6 Ps. 23 Eph. 2. 11-end Mark 6. 30-34, 53-end	Ps. 67; 70 Deut. 30. 1-10 1 Pet. 3. 8-18	Ps. 73 (*or* 73. 21-end) Job 13.13 - 14.6 *or* Ecclus. 18. 1-14 Heb. 2. 5-end *Gospel*: Luke 10. 38-end
19 Monday	**Gregory. Bishop of Nyssa, and his sister Macrina, Deaconess, Teachers, c. 394 and 379**			
Gw **DEL 16**	Com. Teacher *or* *esp.* 1 Cor. 2. 9-13 *also* Wisd. 9. 13-17	Exod. 14. 5-18 Ps. 136. 1-4, 10-15 *or Canticle*: Exod. 15. 1-6 Matt. 12. 38-42	Ps. ***1***; 2; 3 Ezek. 14. 12-end 2 Cor. 11. 1-15	Ps. ***4***; 7 1 Sam. 10. 1-16 Luke 22. 24-30
20 Tuesday	*Margaret of Antioch, Martyr, 4th century; Bartolomé de las Casas, Apostle to the Indies, 1566*			
G		Exod. 14.21 - 15.1 Ps. 105. 37-44 *or Canticle*: Exod. 15. 8-10, 12, 17 Matt. 12. 46-end	Ps. ***5***; 6; (8) Ezek. 18. 1-20 2 Cor. 11. 16-end	Ps. ***9***; 10† 1 Sam. 10. 17-end Luke 22. 31-38
21 Wednesday				
G		Exod. 16. 1-5, 9-15 Ps. 78. 17-31 Matt. 13. 1-9	Ps. 119. 1-32 Ezek. 18. 21-32 2 Cor. ch. 12	Ps. ***11***; 12; 13 1 Sam. ch. 11 Luke 22. 39-46 *or First EP of Mary Magdalene* Ps. 139 Isa. 25. 1-9 2 Cor. 1. 3-7 **W ct**
22 Thursday	**MARY MAGDALENE**			
W		Song of Sol. 3. 1-4 Ps. 42. 1-10 2 Cor. 5. 14-17 John 20. 1-2, 11-18	*MP*: Ps. 30; 32; 150 1 Sam. 16. 14-end Luke 8. 1-3	*EP*: Ps. 63 Zeph. 3. 14-end Mark 15.40 - 16.7

	Calendar and Holy Communion	Morning Prayer	Evening Prayer	NOTES
	Swithun, Bishop of Winchester, c. 862			
Gw	Com. Bishop	Ezek. 12. 17–end 2 Cor. 8.16 - 9.5	1 Sam. ch. 8 Luke 21. 29–end	
G		Ezek. 13. 1–16 2 Cor. 9. 6–end	1 Sam. 9. 1–14 Luke 22. 1–13	
G		Ezek. 14. 1–11 2 Cor. ch. 10	1 Sam. 9.15 - 10.1 Luke 22. 14–23 **ct**	
	THE SEVENTH SUNDAY AFTER TRINITY			
G	1 Kings 17. 8–16 Ps. 34. 11–end Rom. 6. 19–end Mark 8. 1–10a	Ps. 67; 70 Deut. 30. 1–10 1 Pet. 3. 13–22	Ps. 73 (*or* 73. 21–end) Job 13.13 - 14.6 *or* Ecclus. 18. 1–14 Heb. 2. 5–end	
G		Ezek. 14. 12–end 2 Cor. 11. 1–15	1 Sam. 10. 1–16 Luke 22. 24–30	
	Margaret of Antioch, Martyr, 4th century			
Gr	Com. Virgin Martyr	Ezek. 18. 1–20 2 Cor. 11. 16–end	1 Sam. 10. 17–end Luke 22. 31–38	
G		Ezek. 18. 21–32 2 Cor. ch. 12	1 Sam. ch. 11 Luke 22. 39–46 *or First EP of Mary Magdalene* (Ps. 139) Isa. 25. 1–9 2 Cor. 1. 3–7 **W ct**	
	MARY MAGDALENE			
W	Zeph. 3. 14–end Ps. 30. 1–5 2 Cor. 5. 14–17 John 20. 11–18	(Ps. 30; 32; 150) 1 Sam. 16. 14–end Luke 8. 1–3	(Ps. 63) Song of Sol. 3. 1–4 Mark 15.40 - 16.7	

		Sunday Principal Service Weekday Eucharist	Third Service Morning Prayer	Second Service Evening Prayer
23 Friday	*Bridget of Sweden, Abbess of Vadstena, 1373*			
G		Exod. 20. 1–17 Ps. 19. 7–11 Matt. 13. 18–23	Ps. 17; ***19*** Ezek. 20. 21–38 James 1. 1–11	Ps. 22 1 Sam. 13. 5–18 Luke 22. 63–end
24 Saturday				
G		Exod. 24. 3–8 Ps. 50. 1–6, 14–15 Matt. 13. 24–30	Ps. 20; 21; ***23*** Ezek. 24. 15–end James 1. 12–end	Ps. ***24***; 25 1 Sam. 13.19 - 14.15 Luke 23. 1–12 **ct** *or First EP of James* Ps. 144 Deut. 30. 11–end Mark 5. 21–end **R ct**
25 Sunday	**JAMES THE APOSTLE** (or transferred to 26 July)			
R	*The reading from Acts must be used as either the first or second reading at the Principal Service.*	Jer. 45. 1–5 *or* Acts 11.27 - 12.2 Ps. 126 Acts 11.27 - 12.2 *or* 2 Cor. 4. 7–15 Matt. 20. 20–28	*MP*: Ps. 7; 29; 117 2 Kings 1. 9–15 Luke 9. 46–56	*EP*: Ps. 94 Jer. 26. 1–15 Mark 1. 14–20
	or, for The Eighth Sunday after Trinity (Proper 12)			
G	*Track 1* 2 Sam. 11. 1–15 Ps. 14 Eph. 3. 14–end John 6. 1–21	*Track 2* 2 Kings 4. 42–end Ps. 145. 10–19 Eph. 3. 14–end John 6. 1–21	Ps. 75 Song of Sol. ch. 2 *or* 1 Macc. 2. [1–14] 15–22 1 Pet. 4. 7–14	Ps. 74 (*or* 74. 11–16) Job 19. 1–27a *or* Ecclus. 38. 24–end Heb. ch. 8 *Gospel*: Luke 11. 1–13
26 Monday	**Anne and Joachim, Parents of the Blessed Virgin Mary**			
Gw **DEL 17**	Zeph. 3. 14–18a *or* Ps. 127 Rom. 8. 28–30 Matt. 13. 16–17	Exod. 32. 15–24, 30–34 Ps. 106. 19–23 Matt. 13. 31–35	Ps. 27; ***30*** Ezek. 28. 1–19 James 2. 1–13	Ps. 26; ***28***; 29 1 Sam. 14. 24–46 Luke 23. 13–25
27 Tuesday	*Brooke Foss Westcott, Bishop of Durham, Teacher, 1901*			
G		Exod. 33. 7–11; 34. 5–9, 28 Ps. 103. 8–12 Matt. 13. 36–43	Ps. 32; ***36*** Ezek. 33. 1–20 James 2. 14–end	Ps. 33 1 Sam. 15. 1–23 Luke 23. 26–43
28 Wednesday				
G		Exod. 34. 29–end Ps. 99 Matt. 13. 44–46	Ps. 34 Ezek. 33. 21–end James ch. 3	Ps. 119. 33–56 1 Sam. ch. 16 Luke 23. 44–56a
29 Thursday	**Mary, Martha and Lazarus, Companions of Our Lord**			
Gw	Isa. 25. 6–9 *or* Ps. 49. 1–10, 16 Heb. 2. 10–15 John 12. 1–8	Exod. 40. 16–21, 34–end Ps. 84. 1–6 Matt. 13. 47–53	Ps. 37† Ezek. 34. 1–16 James 4. 1–12	Ps. 39; ***40*** 1 Sam. 17. 1–30 Luke 23.56b - 24.12
30 Friday	**William Wilberforce, Social Reformer, Olaudah Equiano and Thomas Clarkson, Anti-Slavery Campaigners, 1833, 1797 and 1846**			
Gw	Com. Saint *or* *also* Job 31. 16–23 Gal. 3. 26–end; 4. 6–7 Luke 4. 16–21	Lev. 23. 1, 4–11, 15–16, 27, 34–37 Ps. 81. 1–8 Matt. 13. 54–end	Ps. 31 Ezek. 34. 17–end James 4.13 - 5.6	Ps. 35 1 Sam. 17. 31–54 Luke 24. 13–35

	Calendar and Holy Communion	Morning Prayer	Evening Prayer	NOTES
G		Ezek. 20. 21–38 James 1. 1–11	1 Sam. 13. 5–18 Luke 22. 63–end	
G		Ezek. 24. 15–end James 1. 12–end	1 Sam. 13.19 - 14.15 Luke 23. 1–12 **ct** *or First EP of James* (Ps. 144) Deut. 30. 11–end Mark 5. 21–end **R ct**	
	JAMES THE APOSTLE (or transferred to 26 July)			
R	2 Kings 1. 9–15 Ps. 15 Acts 11.27 - 12.3a Matt. 20. 20–28	(Ps. 7; 29; 117) Jer. 45. 1–5 Luke 9. 46–56	(Ps. 94) Jer. 26. 1–15 Mark 1. 14–20	
	or, for The Eighth Sunday after Trinity			
G	Jer. 23. 16–24 Ps. 31. 1–6 Rom. 8. 12–17 Matt. 7. 15–21	Ps. 75 Song of Sol. ch. 2 *or* 1 Macc. 2. [1–14] 15–22 1 Pet. 4. 7–14	Ps. 74 (*or* 74. 11–16) Job 19. 1–27a *or* Ecclus. 38. 24–end Heb. ch. 8	
	Anne, Mother of the Blessed Virgin Mary			
Gw	Com. Saint	Ezek. 28. 1–19 James 2. 1–13	1 Sam. 14. 24–46 Luke 23. 13–25	
G		Ezek. 33. 1–20 James 2. 14–end	1 Sam. 15. 1–23 Luke 23. 26–43	
G		Ezek. 33. 21–end James ch. 3	1 Sam. ch. 16 Luke 23. 44–56a	
G		Ezek. 34. 1–16 James 4. 1–12	1 Sam. 17. 1–30 Luke 23.56b - 24.12	
G		Ezek. 34. 17–end James 4.13 - 5.6	1 Sam. 17. 31–54 Luke 24. 13–35	

		Sunday Principal Service Weekday Eucharist	Third Service Morning Prayer	Second Service Evening Prayer
31 Saturday	*Ignatius of Loyola, Founder of the Society of Jesus, 1556*			
G		Lev. 25. 1, 8–17 Ps. 67 Matt. 14. 1–12	Ps. 41; ***42***; 43 Ezek. 36. 16–36 James 5. 7–end	Ps. 45; ***46*** 1 Sam. 17.55 - 18.16 Luke 24. 36–end **ct**

August 2021

1 Sunday	**THE NINTH SUNDAY AFTER TRINITY (Proper 13)**			
G	*Track 1* 2 Sam. 11.26 - 12.13a Ps. 51. 1–13 Eph. 4. 1–16 John 6. 24–35	*Track 2* Exod. 16. 2–4, 9–15 Ps. 78. 23–29 Eph. 4. 1–16 John 6. 24–35	Ps. 86 Song of Sol. 5. 2–end *or* 1 Macc. 3. 1–12 2 Pet. 1. 1–15	Ps. 88 (*or* 88. 1–10) Job ch. 28 *or* Ecclus. 42. 15–end Heb. 11. 17–31 *Gospel*: Luke 12. 13–21
2 Monday				
G **DEL 18**		Num. 11. 4–15 Ps. 81. 11–end Matt. 14. 13–21 (*or* 14. 22–end)	Ps. 44 Ezek. 37. 1–14 Mark 1. 1–13	Ps. ***47***; 49 1 Sam. 19. 1–18 Acts 1. 1–14
3 Tuesday				
G		Num. 12. 1–13 Ps. 51. 1–8 Matt. 14. 22–end *or* Matt. 15. 1–2, 10–14	Ps. ***48***; 52 Ezek. 37. 15–end Mark 1. 14–20	Ps. 50 1 Sam. 20. 1–17 Acts 1. 15–end
4 Wednesday	*John-Baptiste Vianney, Curé d'Ars, Spiritual Guide, 1859*			
G		Num. 13.1–2, 25 - 14.1, 26–35 Ps. 106. 14–24 Matt. 15. 21–28	Ps. 119. 57–80 Ezek. 39. 21–end Mark 1. 21–28	Ps. ***59***; 60; (67) 1 Sam. 20. 18–end Acts 2. 1–21
5 Thursday	**Oswald, King of Northumbria, Martyr, 642**			
Gr	Com. Martyr *or* *esp.* 1 Pet. 4. 12–end	Num. 20. 1–13 Ps. 95. 1, 8–end Matt. 16. 13–23	Ps. 56; ***57***; (63†) Ezek. 43. 1–12 Mark 1. 29–end	Ps. 61; ***62***; 64 1 Sam. 21.1 - 22.5 Acts 2. 22–36 *or First EP of The Transfiguration* Ps. 99; 110 Exod. 24. 12–end John 12. 27–36a **𝔚 ct**
6 Friday	**THE TRANSFIGURATION OF OUR LORD**			
𝔚		Dan. 7. 9–10, 13–14 Ps. 97 2 Pet. 1. 16–19 Luke 9. 28–36	*MP*: Ps. 27; 150 Ecclus. 48. 1–10 *or* 1 Kings 19. 1–16 1 John 3. 1–3	*EP*: Ps. 72 Exod. 34. 29–end 2 Cor. ch. 3
7 Saturday	*John Mason Neale, Priest, Hymn Writer, 1866*			
G		Deut. 6. 4–13 Ps. 18. 1–2, 48–end Matt. 17. 14–20	Ps. 68 Ezek. 47. 1–12 Mark 2. 13–22	Ps. 65; ***66*** 1 Sam. ch. 23 Acts 3. 1–10 **ct**

	Calendar and Holy Communion	Morning Prayer	Evening Prayer	NOTES
G		Ezek. 36. 16-36 James 5. 7-end	1 Sam. 17.55 - 18.16 Luke 24. 36-end **ct**	
	THE NINTH SUNDAY AFTER TRINITY Lammas Day			
G	Num. 10.35 - 11.3 Ps. 95 1 Cor. 10. 1-13 Luke 16. 1-9 *or* Luke 15. 11-end	Ps. 86 Song of Sol. 5. 2-end *or* 1 Macc. 3. 1-12 2 Pet. 1. 1-15	Ps. 88 (*or* 88. 1-10) Job ch. 28 *or* Ecclus. 42. 15-end Heb. 11. 17-31	
G		Ezek. 37. 1-14 Mark 1. 1-13	1 Sam. 19. 1-18 Acts 1. 1-14	
G		Ezek. 37. 15-end Mark 1. 14-20	1 Sam. 20. 1-17 Acts 1. 15-end	
G		Ezek. 39. 21-end Mark 1. 21-28	1 Sam. 20. 18-end Acts 2. 1-21	
G		Ezek. 43. 1-12 Mark 1. 29-end	1 Sam. 21.1 - 22.5 Acts 2. 22-36 *or First EP of The Transfiguration* (Ps. 99; 110) Exod. 24. 12-end John 12. 27-36a **𝔚 ct**	
	THE TRANSFIGURATION OF OUR LORD			
𝔚	Exod. 24. 12-end Ps. 84. 1-7 1 John 3. 1-3 Mark 9. 2-7	(Ps. 27; 150) Ecclus. 48. 1-10 *or* 1 Kings 19. 1-16 2 Pet. 1. 16-19	(Ps. 72) Exod. 34. 29-end 2 Cor. ch. 3	
	The Name of Jesus			
Gw	Jer. 14. 7-9 Ps. 8 Acts 4. 8-12 Matt. 1. 20-23	Ezek. 47. 1-12 Mark 2. 13-22	1 Sam. ch. 23 Acts 3. 1-10 **ct**	

		Sunday Principal Service Weekday Eucharist	Third Service Morning Prayer	Second Service Evening Prayer
8 Sunday	**THE TENTH SUNDAY AFTER TRINITY (Proper 14)**			
G	*Track 1* 2 Sam. 18. 5–9, 15, 31–33 Ps. 130 Eph. 4.25 – 5.2 John 6. 35, 41–51	*Track 2* 1 Kings 19. 4–8 Ps. 34. 1–8 Eph. 4.25 – 5.2 John 6. 35, 41–51	Ps. 90 Song of Sol. 8. 5–7 *or* 1 Macc. 14. 4–15 2 Pet. 3. 8–13	Ps. 91 (*or* 91. 1–12) Job 39.1 – 40.4 *or* Ecclus. 43. 13–end Heb. 12. 1–17 *Gospel*: Luke 12. 32–40
9 Monday	**Mary Sumner, Founder of the Mothers' Union, 1921**			
Gw **DEL 19**	Com. Saint *or* *also* Heb. 13. 1–5	Deut. 10. 12–end Ps. 147. 13–end Matt. 17. 22–end	Ps. 71 Prov. 1. 1–19 Mark 2.23 – 3.6	Ps. **72**; 75 1 Sam. ch. 24 Acts 3. 11–end
10 Tuesday	**Laurence, Deacon at Rome, Martyr, 258**			
Gr	Com. Martyr *or* *also* 2 Cor. 9. 6–10	Deut. 31. 1–8 Ps. 107. 1–3, 42–end *or Canticle*: Deut. 32. 3–4, 7–9 Matt. 18. 1–5, 10, 12–14	Ps. 73 Prov. 1. 20–end Mark 3. 7–19a	Ps. 74 1 Sam. ch. 26 Acts 4. 1–12
11 Wednesday	**Clare of Assisi, Founder of the Minoresses (Poor Clares), 1253** *John Henry Newman, Priest, Tractarian, 1890*			
Gw	Com. Religious *or* *esp.* Song of Sol. 8. 6–7	Deut. ch. 34 Ps. 66. 14–end Matt. 18. 15–20	Ps. 77 Prov. ch. 2 Mark 3. 19b–end	Ps. 119. 81–104 1 Sam. 28. 3–end Acts 4. 13–31
12 Thursday				
G		Josh. 3. 7–11, 13–17 Ps. 114 Matt. 18.21 – 19.1	Ps. 78. 1–39† Prov. 3. 1–26 Mark 4. 1–20	Ps. 78. 40–end† 1 Sam. ch. 31 Acts 4.32 – 5.11
13 Friday	**Jeremy Taylor, Bishop of Down and Connor, Teacher, 1667** *Florence Nightingale, Nurse, Social Reformer, 1910; Octavia Hill, Social Reformer, 1912*			
Gw	Com. Teacher *or* *also* Titus 2. 7–8, 11–14	Josh. 24. 1–13 Ps. 136. 1–3, 16–22 Matt. 19. 3–12	Ps. 55 Prov. 3.27 – 4.19 Mark 4. 21–34	Ps. 69 2 Sam. ch. 1 Acts 5. 12–26
14 Saturday	*Maximilian Kolbe, Friar, Martyr, 1941*			
G		Josh. 24. 14–29 Ps. 16. 1, 5–end Matt. 19. 13–15	Ps. ***76***; 79 Prov. 6. 1–19 Mark 4. 35–end	Ps. 81; ***84*** 2 Sam. 2. 1–11 Acts 5. 27–end **ct** *or First EP of The Blessed Virgin Mary* Ps. 72 Prov. 8. 22–31 John 19. 23–27 **W ct**
15 Sunday	**THE BLESSED VIRGIN MARY*** (or transferred to 16 August)			
W		Isa. 61. 10–end *or* Rev. 11.19 – 12.6, 10 Ps. 45. 10–end Gal. 4. 4–7 Luke 1. 46–55	*MP*: Ps. 98; 138; 147. 1–12 Isa. 7. 10–15 Luke 11. 27–28	*EP*: Ps. 132 Song of Sol. 2. 1–7 Acts 1. 6–14 *(continued overleaf)*

*The Blessed Virgin Mary may be celebrated on 8 September instead of 15 August.

	Calendar and Holy Communion	Morning Prayer	Evening Prayer	NOTES
	THE TENTH SUNDAY AFTER TRINITY			
G	Jer. 7. 9–15 Ps. 17. 1–8 1 Cor. 12. 1–11 Luke 19. 41–47a	Ps. 89. 1–18 Song of Sol. 8. 5–7 *or* 1 Macc. 14. 4–15 2 Pet. 3. 8–13	Ps. 91 (*or* 91. 1–12) Job 39.1 - 40.4 *or* Ecclus. 43. 13–end Heb. 12. 1–17	
G		Prov. 1. 1–19 Mark 2.23 - 3.6	1 Sam. ch. 24 Acts 3. 11–end	
	Laurence, Deacon at Rome, Martyr, 258			
Gr	Com. Martyr	Prov. 1. 20–end Mark 3. 7–19a	1 Sam. ch. 26 Acts 4. 1–12	
G		Prov. ch. 2 Mark 3. 19b–end	1 Sam. 28. 3–end Acts 4. 13–31	
G		Prov. 3. 1–26 Mark 4. 1–20	1 Sam. ch. 31 Acts 4.32 - 5.11	
G		Prov. 3.27 - 4.19 Mark 4. 21–34	2 Sam. ch. 1 Acts 5. 12–26	
G		Prov. 6. 1–19 Mark 4. 35–end	2 Sam. 2. 1–11 Acts 5. 27–end **ct**	
	THE ELEVENTH SUNDAY AFTER TRINITY To celebrate The Blessed Virgin Mary, see *Common Worship* provision.			
G	1 Kings 3. 5–15 Ps. 28 1 Cor. 15. 1–11 Luke 18. 9–14	Ps. 106. 1–10 Jonah ch. 1 *or* Ecclus. 3. 1–15 2 Pet. 3. 14–end	Ps. [92]; 100 Exod. 2.23 - 3.10 Heb. 13. 1–15	

		Sunday Principal Service Weekday Eucharist	Third Service Morning Prayer	Second Service Evening Prayer
15 Sunday	**THE BLESSED VIRGIN MARY** (or transferred to 16 August) (*continued*)			
	or, for The Eleventh Sunday after Trinity (Proper 15)			
G	*Track 1* 1 Kings 2. 10–12; 3. 3–14 Ps. 111 Eph. 5. 15–20 John 6. 51–58	*Track 2* Prov. 9. 1–6 Ps. 34. 9–14 Eph. 5. 15–20 John 6. 51–58	Ps. 106. 1–10 Jonah ch. 1 *or* Ecclus. 3. 1–15 2 Pet. 3. 14–end	Ps. [92]; 100 Exod. 2.23 - 3.10 Heb. 13. 1–15 *Gospel*: Luke 12. 49–56
16 Monday				
G **DEL 20**		Judg. 2. 11–19 Ps. 106. 34–42 Matt. 19. 16–22	Ps. ***80***; 82 Prov. 8. 1–21 Mark 5. 1–20	Ps. ***85***; 86 2 Sam. 3. 12–end Acts ch. 6
17 Tuesday				
G		Judg. 6. 11–24 Ps. 85. 8–end Matt. 19. 23–end	Ps. 87; ***89. 1–18*** Prov. 8. 22–end Mark 5. 21–34	Ps. 89. 19–end 2 Sam. 5. 1–12 Acts 7. 1–16
18 Wednesday				
G		Judg. 9. 6–15 Ps. 21. 1–6 Matt. 20. 1–16	Ps. 119. 105–128 Prov. ch. 9 Mark 5. 35–end	Ps. ***91***; 93 2 Sam. 6. 1–19 Acts 7. 17–43
19 Thursday				
G		Judg. 11. 29–end Ps. 40. 4–11 Matt. 22. 1–14	Ps. 90; ***92*** Prov. 10. 1–12 Mark 6. 1–13	Ps. 94 2 Sam. 7. 1–17 Acts 7. 44–53
20 Friday	**Bernard, Abbot of Clairvaux, Teacher, 1153** *William and Catherine Booth, Founders of the Salvation Army, 1912 and 1890*			
Gw	Com. Religious *or* *esp*. Rev. 19. 5–9	Ruth 1. 1, 3–6, 14–16, 22 Ps. 146 Matt. 22. 34–40	Ps. ***88***; (95) Prov. 11. 1–12 Mark 6. 14–29	Ps. 102 2 Sam. 7. 18–end Acts 7.54 - 8.3
21 Saturday				
G		Ruth 2. 1–3, 1–11; 4. 13–17 Ps. 128 Matt. 23. 1–12	Ps. 96; ***97***; 100 Prov. 12. 10–end Mark 6. 30–44	Ps. 104 2 Sam. ch. 9 Acts 8. 4–25 **ct**
22 Sunday	**THE TWELFTH SUNDAY AFTER TRINITY (Proper 16)**			
G	*Track 1* 1 Kings 8. [1, 6, 10–11] 22–30, 41–43 Ps. 84 Eph. 6. 10–20 John 6. 56–69	*Track 2* Josh. 24. 1–2a, 14–18 Ps. 34. 15–end Eph. 6. 10–20 John 6. 56–69	Ps. 115 Jonah ch. 2 *or* Ecclus. 3. 17–29 Rev. ch. 1	Ps. 116 (*or* 116. 10–end) Exod. 4.27 - 5.1 Heb. 13. 16–21 *Gospel*: Luke 13. 10–17

	Calendar and Holy Communion	Morning Prayer	Evening Prayer	NOTES
G		Prov. 8. 1–21 Mark 5. 1–20	2 Sam. 3. 12–end Acts ch. 6	
G		Prov. 8. 22–end Mark 5. 21–34	2 Sam. 5. 1–12 Acts 7. 1–16	
G		Prov. ch. 9 Mark 5. 35–end	2 Sam. 6. 1–19 Acts 7. 17–43	
G		Prov. 10. 1–12 Mark 6. 1–13	2 Sam. 7. 1–17 Acts 7. 44–53	
G		Prov. 11. 1–12 Mark 6. 14–29	2 Sam. 7. 18–end Acts 7.54 – 8.3	
G		Prov. 12. 10–end Mark 6. 30–44	2 Sam. ch. 9 Acts 8. 4–25 **ct**	
	THE TWELFTH SUNDAY AFTER TRINITY			
G	Exod. 34. 29–end Ps. 34. 1–10 2 Cor. 3. 4–9 Mark 7. 31–37	Ps. 115 Jonah ch. 2 *or* Ecclus. 3. 17–29 Rev. ch. 1	Ps. 116 (*or* 116. 10–end) Exod. 4.27 – 5.1 Heb. 13. 16–21	

		Sunday Principal Service Weekday Eucharist	Third Service Morning Prayer	Second Service Evening Prayer
23 Monday				
G **DEL 21**		1 Thess. 1. 1–5, 8–end Ps. 149. 1–5 Matt. 23. 13–22	Ps. ***98***; 99; 101 Prov. 14.31 – 15.17 Mark 6. 45–end	Ps. ***105***† (*or* 103) 2 Sam. ch. 11 Acts 8. 26–end *or First EP of Bartholomew* Ps. 97 Isa. 61. 1–9 2 Cor. 6. 1–10 **R ct**
24 Tuesday	**BARTHOLOMEW THE APOSTLE**			
R	*The reading from Acts must be used as either the first or second reading at the Eucharist.*	Isa. 43. 8–13 *or* Acts 5. 12–16 Ps. 145. 1–7 Acts 5. 12–16 *or* 1 Cor. 4. 9–15 Luke 22. 24–30	*MP*: Ps. 86; 117 Gen. 28. 10–17 John 1. 43–end	*EP*: Ps. 91; 116 Ecclus. 39. 1–10 *or* Deut. 18. 15–19 Matt. 10. 1–22
25 Wednesday				
G		1 Thess. 2. 9–13 Ps. 126 Matt. 23. 27–32	Ps. 110; ***111***; 112 Prov. 18. 10–end Mark 7. 14–23	Ps. 119. 129–152 2 Sam. 15. 1–12 Acts 9. 19b–31
26 Thursday				
G		1 Thess. 3. 7–end Ps. 90. 13–end Matt. 24. 42–end	Ps. 113; ***115*** Prov. 20. 1–22 Mark 7. 24–30	Ps. 114; ***116***; 117 2 Sam. 15. 13–end Acts 9. 32–end
27 Friday	**Monica, Mother of Augustine of Hippo, 387**			
Gw	Com. Saint *or* *also* Ecclus. 26. 1–3, 13–16	1 Thess. 4. 1–8 Ps. 97 Matt. 25. 1–13	Ps. 139 Prov. 22. 1–16 Mark 7. 31–end	Ps. ***130***; 131; 137 2 Sam. 16. 1–14 Acts 10. 1–16
28 Saturday	**Augustine, Bishop of Hippo, Teacher, 430**			
Gw	Com. Teacher *or* *esp.* Ecclus. 39. 1–10 *also* Rom. 13. 11–13	1 Thess. 4. 9–12 Ps. 98. 1–2, 8–end Matt. 25. 14–30	Ps. 120; ***121***; 122 Prov. 24. 23–end Mark 8. 1–10	Ps. 118 2 Sam. 17. 1–23 Acts 10. 17–33 **ct**
29 Sunday	**THE THIRTEENTH SUNDAY AFTER TRINITY (Proper 17)**			
G	*Track 1* Song of Sol. 2. 8–13 Ps. 45. 1–2, 6–9 (*or* 1–7) James 1. 17–end Mark 7. 1–8, 14–15, 21–23	*Track 2* Deut. 4. 1–2, 6–9 Ps. 15 James 1. 17–end Mark 7. 1–8, 14–15, 21–23	Ps. 119. 17–40 Jonah 3. 1–9 *or* Ecclus. 11. 7–28 (*or* 19–28) Rev. 3. 14–end	Ps. 119. 1–16 (*or* 9–16) Exod. 12. 21–27 Matt. 4.23 – 5.20
30 Monday	**John Bunyan, Spiritual Writer, 1688**			
Gw **DEL 22**	Com. Teacher *or* *also* Heb. 12. 1–2 Luke 21. 21, 34–36	1 Thess. 4. 13–end Ps. 96 Luke 4. 16–30	Ps. 123; 124; 125; ***126*** Prov. 25. 1–14 Mark 8. 11–21	Ps. ***127***; 128; 129 2 Sam. 18. 1–18 Acts 10. 34–end
31 Tuesday	**Aidan, Bishop of Lindisfarne, Missionary, 651**			
Gw	Com. Missionary *or* *also* 1 Cor. 9. 16–19	1 Thess. 5. 1–6, 9–11 Ps. 27. 1–8 Luke 4. 31–37	Ps. ***132***; 133 Prov. 25. 15–end Mark 8. 22–26	Ps. (134); ***135*** 2 Sam. 18.19 – 19.8a Acts 11. 1–18

	Calendar and Holy Communion	Morning Prayer	Evening Prayer	NOTES
G		Prov. 14.31 - 15.17 Mark 6. 45-end	2 Sam. ch. 11 Acts 8. 26-end *or First EP of Bartholomew* (Ps. 97) Isa. 61. 1-9 2 Cor. 6. 1-10 **R ct**	
	BARTHOLOMEW THE APOSTLE			
R	Gen. 28. 10-17 Ps. 15 Acts 5. 12-16 Luke 22. 24-30	(Ps. 86; 117) Isa. 43. 8-13 John 1. 43-end	(Ps. 91; 116) Ecclus. 39. 1-10 *or* Deut. 18. 15-19 Matt. 10. 1-22	
G		Prov. 18. 10-end Mark 7. 14-23	2 Sam. 15. 1-12 Acts 9. 19b-31	
G		Prov. 20. 1-22 Mark 7. 24-30	2 Sam. 15. 13-end Acts 9. 32-end	
G		Prov. 22. 1-16 Mark 7. 31-end	2 Sam. 16. 1-14 Acts 10. 1-16	
	Augustine, Bishop of Hippo, Teacher 430			
Gw	Com. Doctor	Prov. 24. 23-end Mark 8. 1-10	2 Sam. 17. 1-23 Acts 10. 17-33 **ct**	
	THE THIRTEENTH SUNDAY AFTER TRINITY			
G	Lev. 19. 13-18 Ps. 74. 20-end Gal. 3. 16-22 *or* Heb. 13. 1-6 Luke 10. 23b-37	Ps. 119. 17-40 Jonah 3. 1-9 *or* Ecclus. 11. 7-28 (*or* 19-28) Rev. 3. 14-end	Ps. 119. 1-16 (*or* 9-16) Exod. 12. 21-27 Matt. 4.23 - 5.20	
G		Prov. 25. 1-14 Mark 8. 11-21	2 Sam. 18. 1-18 Acts 10. 34-end	
G		Prov. 25. 15-end Mark 8. 22-26	2 Sam. 18.19 - 19.8a Acts 11. 1-18	

		Sunday Principal Service Weekday Eucharist	Third Service Morning Prayer	Second Service Evening Prayer
September 2021				
1 Wednesday	*Giles of Provence, Hermit, c. 710*			
G		Col. 1. 1–8 Ps. 34. 11–18 Luke 4. 38–end	Ps. 119. 153–end Prov. 26. 12–end Mark 8.27 - 9.1	Ps. 136 2 Sam. 19. 8b–23 Acts 11. 19–end
2 Thursday	*The Martyrs of Papua New Guinea, 1901 and 1942*			
G		Col. 1. 9–14 Ps. 98. 1–5 Luke 5. 1–11	Ps. ***143***; 146 Prov. 27. 1–22 Mark 9. 2–13	Ps. ***138***; 140; 141 2 Sam. 19. 24–end Acts 12. 1–17
3 Friday	**Gregory the Great, Bishop of Rome, Teacher, 604**			
Gw	Com. Teacher *or* *also* 1 Thess. 2. 3–8	Col. 1. 15–20 Ps. 89. 19b–28 Luke 5. 33–end	Ps. 142; ***144*** Prov. 30. 1–9, 24–31 Mark 9. 14–29	Ps. 145 2 Sam. 23. 1–7 Acts 12. 18–end
4 Saturday	*Birinus, Bishop of Dorchester (Oxon), Apostle of Wessex, 650**			
G		Col. 1. 21–23 Ps. 117 Luke 6. 1–5	Ps. 147 Prov. 31. 10–end Mark 9. 30–37	Ps. ***148***; 149; 150 2 Sam. ch. 24 Acts 13. 1–12 **ct**
5 Sunday	**THE FOURTEENTH SUNDAY AFTER TRINITY (Proper 18)**			
G	*Track 1* Prov. 22. 1–2, 8–9, 22–23 Ps. 125 James 2. 1–10 [11–13] 14–17 Mark 7. 24–end	*Track 2* Isa. 35. 4–7a Ps. 146 James 2. 1–10 [11–13] 14–17 Mark 7. 24–end	Ps. 119. 57–72 Jonah 3.10 - 4.11 *or* Ecclus. 27.30 - 28.9 Rev. 8. 1–5	Ps. 119. 41–56 (*or* 49–56) Exod. 14. 5–end Matt. 6. 1–18
6 Monday	*Allen Gardiner, Founder of the South American Missionary Society, 1851*			
G **DEL 23**		Col. 1.24 - 2.3 Ps. 62. 1–7 Luke 6. 6–11	Ps. ***1***; 2; 3 Wisd. ch. 1 *or* 1 Chron. 10.1 - 11.9 Mark 9. 38–end	Ps. ***4***; 7 1 Kings 1. 5–31 Acts 13. 13–43
7 Tuesday				
G		Col. 2. 6–15 Ps. 8 Luke 6. 12–19	Ps. ***5***; 6; (8) Wisd. ch. 2 *or* 1 Chron. ch. 13 Mark 10. 1–16	Ps. ***9***; 10† 1 Kings 1.32 - 2.4, 10–12 Acts 13.44 - 14.7
8 Wednesday	**The Birth of the Blessed Virgin Mary****			
Gw	Com. BVM *or*	Col. 3. 1–11 Ps. 15 Luke 6. 20–26	Ps. 119. 1–32 Wisd. 3. 1–9 *or* 1 Chron. 15.1 - 16.3 Mark 10. 17–31	Ps. ***11***; 12; 13 1 Kings ch. 3 Acts 14. 8–end
9 Thursday	*Charles Fuge Lowder, Priest, 1880*			
G		Col. 3. 12–17 Ps. 149. 1–5 Luke 6. 27–38	Ps. 14; ***15***; 16 Wisd. 4. 7–end *or* 1 Chron. ch. 17 Mark 10. 32–34	Ps. 18† 1 Kings 4.29 - 5.12 Acts 15. 1–21

*Cuthbert may be celebrated on 4 September instead of 20 March.
**The Blessed Virgin Mary may be celebrated on 8 September instead of 15 August.

	Calendar and Holy Communion	Morning Prayer	Evening Prayer	NOTES
	Giles of Provence, Hermit, c. 710			
Gw	Com. Abbot	Prov. 26. 12–end Mark 8.27 – 9.1	2 Sam. 19. 8b–23 Acts 11. 19–end	
G		Prov. 27. 1–22 Mark 9. 2–13	2 Sam. 19. 24–end Acts 12. 1–17	
G		Prov. 30. 1–9, 24–31 Mark 9. 14–29	2 Sam. 23. 1–7 Acts 12. 18–end	
G		Prov. 31. 10–end Mark 9. 30–37	2 Sam. ch. 24 Acts 13. 1–12 **ct**	
	THE FOURTEENTH SUNDAY AFTER TRINITY			
G	2 Kings 5. 9–16 Ps. 118. 1–9 Gal. 5. 16–24 Luke 17. 11–19	Ps. 119. 57–72 Jonah 3.10 – 4.11 *or* Ecclus. 27.30 – 28.9 Rev. 8. 1–5	Ps. 119. 41–56 (*or* 49–56) Exod. 14. 5–end Matt. 6. 1–18	
G		Wisd. ch. 1 *or* 1 Chron. 10.1 – 11.9 Mark 9. 38–end	1 Kings 1. 5–31 Acts 13. 13–43	
	Evurtius, Bishop of Orleans, 4th century			
Gw	Com. Bishop	Wisd. ch. 2 *or* 1 Chron. ch. 13 Mark 10. 1–16	1 Kings 1.32 – 2.4, 10–12 Acts 13.44 – 14.7	
	The Nativity of the Blessed Virgin Mary			
Gw	Gen. 3. 9–15 Ps. 45. 11–18 Rom. 5. 12–17 Luke 11. 27–28	Wisd. 3. 1–9 *or* 1 Chron. 15.1 – 16.3 Mark 10. 17–31	1 Kings ch. 3 Acts 14. 8–end	
G		Wisd. 4. 7–end *or* 1 Chron. ch. 17 Mark 10. 32–34	1 Kings 4.29 – 5.12 Acts 15. 1–21	

		Sunday Principal Service Weekday Eucharist	Third Service Morning Prayer	Second Service Evening Prayer
10 Friday				
G		1 Tim. 1. 1–2, 12–14 Ps. 16 Luke 6. 39–42	Ps. 17; ***19*** Wisd. 5. 1–16 *or* 1 Chron. 21.1 - 22.1 Mark 10. 35–45	Ps. 22 1 Kings 6. 1, 11–28 Acts 15. 22–35
11 Saturday				
G		1 Tim. 1. 15–17 Ps. 113 Luke 6. 43–end	Ps. 20; 21; ***23*** Wisd. 5.17 - 6.11 *or* 1 Chron. 22. 2–end Mark 10. 46–end	Ps. ***24***; 25 1 Kings 8. 1–30 Acts 15.36 - 16.5 **ct**
12 Sunday	**THE FIFTEENTH SUNDAY AFTER TRINITY (Proper 19)**			
G	*Track 1* Prov. 1. 20–33 Ps. 19 (*or* 19. 1–6) *or Canticle*: Wisd. 7.26 - 8.1 James 3. 1–12 Mark 8. 27–end	*Track 2* Isa. 50. 4–9a Ps. 116. 1–8 James 3. 1–12 Mark 8. 27–end	Ps. 119. 105–120 Isa. 44.24 - 45.8 Rev. 12. 1–12	Ps. 119. 73–88 (*or* 73–80) Exod. 18. 13–26 Matt. 7. 1–14
13 Monday	**John Chrysostom, Bishop of Constantinople, Teacher, 407**			
Gw **DEL 24**	Com. Teacher *or* *esp.* Matt. 5. 13–19 *also* Jer. 1. 4–10	1 Tim. 2. 1–8 Ps. 28 Luke 7. 1–10	Ps. 27; ***30*** Wisd. 6. 12–23 *or* 1 Chron. 28. 1–10 Mark 11. 1–11	Ps. 26; ***28***; 29 1 Kings 8. 31–62 Acts 16. 6–24 *or First EP of Holy Cross Day* Ps. 66 Isa, 52.13 - 53.end Eph. 2. 11–end **R ct**
14 Tuesday	**HOLY CROSS DAY**			
R		Num. 21. 4–9 Ps. 22. 23–28 Phil. 2. 6–11 John 3. 13–17	*MP*: Ps. 2; 8; 146 Gen. 3. 1–15 John 12. 27–36a	*EP*: Ps. 110; 150 Isa. 63. 1–16 1 Cor. 1. 18–25
15 Wednesday	**Cyprian, Bishop of Carthage, Martyr, 258**			
Gr	Com. Martyr *or* *esp.* 1 Pet. 4. 12–end *also* Matt. 18. 18–22	1 Tim. 3. 14–end Ps. 111. 1–5 Luke 7. 31–35	Ps. 34 Wisd. 7.15 - 8.4 *or* 1 Chron. 29. 1–9 Mark 11. 27–end	Ps. 119. 33–56 1 Kings 10. 1–25 Acts 17. 1–15
16 Thursday	**Ninian, Bishop of Galloway, Apostle of the Picts, *c.* 432** *Edward Bouverie Pusey, Priest, Tractarian, 1882*			
Gw	Com. Missionary *or* *esp.* Acts 13. 46–49 Mark 16. 15–end	1 Tim. 4. 12–end Ps. 111. 6–end Luke 7. 36–end	Ps. 37† Wisd. 8. 5–18 *or* 1 Chron. 29. 10–20 Mark 12. 1–12	Ps. 39; ***40*** 1 Kings 11. 1–13 Acts 17. 16–end
17 Friday	**Hildegard, Abbess of Bingen, Visionary, 1179**			
Gw	Com. Religious *or* *also* 1 Cor. 2. 9–13 Luke 10. 21–24	1 Tim. 6. 2b–12 Ps. 49. 1–9 Luke 8. 1–3	Ps. 31 Wisd. 8.21 - 9.end *or* 1 Chron. 29. 21–end Mark 12. 13–17	Ps. 35 1 Kings 11. 26–end Acts 18. 1–21

	Calendar and Holy Communion	Morning Prayer	Evening Prayer
G		Wisd. 5. 1–16 *or* 1 Chron. 21.1 – 22.1 Mark 10. 35–45	1 Kings 6. 1, 11–28 Acts 15. 22–35
G		Wisd. 5.17 – 6.11 *or* 1 Chron. 22. 2–end Mark 10. 46–end	1 Kings 8. 1–30 Acts 15.36 – 16.5 **ct**
	THE FIFTEENTH SUNDAY AFTER TRINITY		
G	Josh. 24. 14–25 Ps. 92. 1–6 Gal. 6. 11–end Matt. 6. 24–end	Ps. 119. 105–120 Isa. 44.24 – 45.8 Rev. 12. 1–12	Ps. 119. 73–88 (*or* 73–80) Exod. 18. 13–26 Matt. 7. 1–14
G		Wisd. 6. 12–23 *or* 1 Chron. 28. 1–10 Mark 11. 1–11	1 Kings 8. 31–62 Acts 16. 6–24
	HOLY CROSS DAY To celebrate Holy Cross as a festival, see *Common Worship* provision.		
Gr	Num. 21. 4–9 Ps. 67 1 Cor. 1. 17–25 John 12. 27–33	Wisd. 7. 1–14 *or* 1 Chron. 28. 11–end Mark 11. 12–26	1 Kings 8.63 – 9.9 Acts 16. 25–end
	Ember Day		
G	Ember CEG	Wisd. 7.15 – 8.4 *or* 1 Chron. 29. 1–9 Mark 11. 27–end	1 Kings 10. 1–25 Acts 17. 1–15
G		Wisd. 8. 5–18 *or* 1 Chron. 29. 10–20 Mark 12. 1–12	1 Kings 11. 1–13 Acts 17. 16–end
	Lambert, Bishop of Maastricht, Martyr, 709 Ember Day		
Gr	Com. Martyr *or* Ember CEG	Wisd. 8.21 – 9.end *or* 1 Chron. 29. 21–end Mark 12. 13–17	1 Kings 11. 26–end Acts 18. 1–21

NOTES

		Sunday Principal Service Weekday Eucharist	Third Service Morning Prayer	Second Service Evening Prayer
18 Saturday				
G		1 Tim. 6. 13–16 Ps. 100 Luke 8. 4–15	Ps. 41; ***42***; 43 Wisd. 10.15 – 11.10 *or* 2 Chron. 1. 1–13 Mark 12. 18–27	Ps. 45; ***46*** 1 Kings 12. 1–24 Acts 18.22 – 19.7 **ct**
19 Sunday	**THE SIXTEENTH SUNDAY AFTER TRINITY (Proper 20)**			
G	*Track 1* Prov. 31. 10–end Ps. 1 James 3.13 – 4.3, 7–8a Mark 9. 30–37	*Track 2* Wisd. 1.16 – 2.1, 12–22 *or* Jer. 11. 18–20 Ps. 54 James 3.13 – 4.3, 7–8a Mark 9. 30–37	Ps. 119. 153–end Isa. 45. 9–22 Rev. 14. 1–5	Ps. 119. 137–152 (*or* 137–144) Exod. 19. 10–end Matt. 8. 23–end
20 Monday	**John Coleridge Patteson, first Bishop of Melanesia, and his Companions, Martyrs, 1871**			
Gr **DEL 25**	Com. Martyr *or* *esp.* 2 Chron. 24. 17–21 *also* Acts 7. 55–end	Ezra 1. 1–6 Ps. 126 Luke 8. 16–18	Ps. 44 Wisd. 11.21 – 12.2 *or* 2 Chron. 2. 1–16 Mark 12. 28–34	Ps. ***47***; 49 1 Kings 12.25 – 13.10 Acts 19. 8–20 *or First EP of Matthew* Ps. 34 Isa. 33. 13–17 Matt. 6. 19–end **R ct**
21 Tuesday	**MATTHEW, APOSTLE AND EVANGELIST**			
R		Prov. 3. 13–18 Ps. 119. 65–72 2 Cor. 4. 1–6 Matt. 9. 9–13	*MP*: Ps. 49; 117 1 Kings 19. 15–end 2 Tim. 3. 14–end	*EP*: Ps. 119. 33–40, 89–96 Eccles. 5. 4–12 Matt. 19. 16–end
22 Wednesday	Ember Day*			
G *or* **R**		Ezra 9. 5–9 *Canticle*: Song of Tobit *or* Ps. 103. 1–6 Luke 9. 1–6	Ps. 119. 57–80 Wisd. 13. 1–9 *or* 2 Chron. ch. 5 Mark 13. 1–13	Ps. ***59***; 60; (67) 1 Kings ch. 17 Acts 20. 1–16
23 Thursday				
G		Hag. 1. 1–8 Ps. 149. 1–5 Luke 9. 7–9	Ps. 56; ***57***; (63†) Wisd. 16.15 – 17.1 *or* 2 Chron. 6. 1–21 Mark 13. 14–23	Ps. 61; ***62***; 64 1 Kings 18. 1–20 Acts 20. 17–end
24 Friday	Ember Day*			
G *or* **R**		Hag. 1.15b – 2.9 Ps. 43 Luke 9. 18–22	Ps. ***51***; 54 Wisd. 18. 6–19 *or* 2 Chron. 6. 22–end Mark 13. 24–31	Ps. 38 1 Kings 18. 21–end Acts 21. 1–16
25 Saturday	**Lancelot Andrewes, Bishop of Winchester, Spiritual Writer, 1626** Ember Day* *Sergei of Radonezh, Russian Monastic Reformer, Teacher, 1392*			
Gw *or* **Rw**	Com. Bishop *or* *esp.* Isa. 6. 1–8	Zech. 2. 1–5, 10–11 Ps. 125 *or Canticle*: Jer. 31. 10–13 Luke 9. 43b–45	Ps. 68 Wisd. ch. 19 *or* 2 Chron. ch. 7 Mark 13. 32–end	Ps. 65; ***66*** 1 Kings ch. 19 Acts 21. 17–36 **ct**

*For Ember Day provision, see p. 11.

	Calendar and Holy Communion	Morning Prayer	Evening Prayer	NOTES
	Ember Day			
G	Ember CEG	Wisd. 10.15 – 11.10 *or* 2 Chron. 1. 1–13 Mark 12. 18–27	1 Kings 12. 1–24 Acts 18.22 – 19.7 **ct**	
	THE SIXTEENTH SUNDAY AFTER TRINITY			
G	1 Kings 17. 17–end Ps. 102. 12–17 Eph. 3. 13–end Luke 7. 11–17	Ps. 119. 153–end Isa. 45. 9–22 Rev. 14. 1–5	Ps. 119. 137–152 (*or* 137–144) Exod. 19. 10–end Matt. 8. 23–end	
G		Wisd. 11.21 – 12.2 *or* 2 Chron. 2. 1–16 Mark 12. 28–34	1 Kings 12.25 – 13.10 Acts 19. 8–20 *or First EP of Matthew* Ps. 34 Prov. 3. 3–18 Matt. 6. 19–end **R ct**	
	MATTHEW, APOSTLE AND EVANGELIST			
R	Isa. 33. 13–17 Ps. 119. 65–72 2 Cor. 4. 1–6 Matt. 9. 9–13	(Ps. 49; 117) 1 Kings 19. 15–end 2 Tim. 3. 14–end	(Ps. 119. 33–40, 89–96) Eccles. 5. 4–12 Matt. 19. 16–end	
G		Wisd. 13. 1–9 *or* 2 Chron. ch. 5 Mark 13. 1–13	1 Kings ch. 17 Acts 20. 1–16	
G		Wisd. 16.15 – 17.1 *or* 2 Chron. 6. 1–21 Mark 13. 14–23	1 Kings 18. 1–20 Acts 20. 17–end	
G		Wisd. 18. 6–19 *or* 2 Chron. 6. 22–end Mark 13. 24–31	1 Kings 18. 21–end Acts 21. 1–16	
G		Wisd. ch. 19 *or* 2 Chron. ch. 7 Mark 13. 32–end	1 Kings ch. 19 Acts 21. 17–36 **ct**	

		Sunday Principal Service Weekday Eucharist	Third Service Morning Prayer	Second Service Evening Prayer
26 Sunday	**THE SEVENTEENTH SUNDAY AFTER TRINITY (Proper 21)**			
G	*Track 1* Esther 7. 1–6, 9–10; 9. 20–22 Ps. 124 James 5. 13–end Mark 9. 38–end	*Track 2* Num. 11. 4–6, 10–16, 24–29 Ps. 19. 7–end James 5. 13–end Mark 9. 38–end	Ps. 122 Isa. 48. 12–end Luke 11. 37–end	Ps. 120; 121 Exod. ch. 24 Matt. 9. 1–8
27 Monday	**Vincent de Paul, Founder of the Congregation of the Mission (Lazarists), 1660**			
Gw **DEL 26**	Com. Religious *or* *also* 1 Cor. 1. 25–end Matt. 25. 34–40	Zech. 8. 1–8 Ps. 102. 12–22 Luke 9. 46–50	Ps. 71 1 Macc. 1. 1–19 *or* 2 Chron. 9. 1–12 Mark 14. 1–11	Ps. **72**; 75 1 Kings ch. 21 Acts 21.37 - 22.21
28 Tuesday				
G		Zech. 8. 20–end Ps. 87 Luke 9. 51–56	Ps. 73 1 Macc. 1. 20–40 *or* 2 Chron. 10.1 - 11.4 Mark 14. 12–25	Ps. 74 1 Kings 22. 1–28 Acts 22.22 - 23.11 *or First EP of Michael and All Angels* Ps. 91 2 Kings 6. 8–17 Matt. 18. 1–6, 10 **W ct**
29 Wednesday	**MICHAEL AND ALL ANGELS** Ember Day*			
W	*The reading from Revelation must be used as either the first or second reading at the Eucharist.*	Gen. 28. 10–17 *or* Rev. 12. 7–12 Ps. 103. 19–end Rev. 12. 7–12 *or* Heb. 1. 5–end John 1. 47–end	*MP*: Ps. 34; 150 Tobit 12. 6–end *or* Dan. 12. 1–4 Acts 12. 1–11	*EP*: Ps. 138; 148 Dan. 10. 4–end Rev. ch. 5
30 Thursday	*Jerome, Translator of the Scriptures, Teacher, 420*			
G		Neh. 8. 1–12 Ps. 19. 7–11 Luke 10. 1–12	Ps. 78. 1–39† 1 Macc. 2. 1–28 *or* 2 Chron. 13.1 - 14.1 Mark 14. 43–52	Ps. 78. 40–end† 2 Kings 1. 2–17 Acts 24. 1–23

October 2021

1 Friday	Ember Day* *Remigius, Bishop of Rheims, Apostle of the Franks, 533; Anthony Ashley Cooper, Earl of Shaftesbury, Social Reformer, 1885*			
G		Baruch 1. 15–end *or* Deut. 31. 7–13 Ps. 79. 1–9 Luke 10. 13–16	Ps. 55 1 Macc. 2. 29–48 *or* 2 Chron. 14. 2–end Mark 14. 53–65	Ps. 69 2 Kings 2. 1–18 Acts 24.24 - 25.12

	Calendar and Holy Communion	Morning Prayer	Evening Prayer	NOTES
	THE SEVENTEENTH SUNDAY AFTER TRINITY			
G	Prov. 25. 6-14 Ps. 33. 6-12 Eph. 4. 1-6 Luke 14. 1-11	Ps. 132 Isa. 48. 12-end Luke 11. 37-end	Ps. 120; 121 Exod. ch. 24 Matt. 9. 1-8	
G		1 Macc. 1. 1-19 *or* 2 Chron. 9. 1-12 Mark 14. 1-11	1 Kings ch. 21 Acts 21.37 - 22.21	
G		1 Macc. 1. 20-40 *or* 2 Chron. 10.1 - 11.4 Mark 14. 12-25	1 Kings 22. 1-28 Acts 22.22 - 23.11 *or First EP of Michael and All Angels* (Ps. 91) 2 Kings 6. 8-17 John 1. 47-51 **W ct**	
	MICHAEL AND ALL ANGELS			
W	Dan. 10. 10-19a Ps. 103. 17-22 Rev. 12. 7-12 Matt. 18. 1-10	(Ps. 34; 150) Tobit 12. 6-end *or* Dan. 12. 1-4 Acts 12. 1-11	(Ps. 138; 148) Gen. 28. 10-17 Rev. ch. 5	
	Jerome, Translator of the Scriptures, Teacher, 420			
Gw	Com. Doctor	1 Macc. 2. 1-28 *or* 2 Chron. 13.1 - 14.1 Mark 14. 43-52	2 Kings 1. 2-17 Acts 24. 1-23	
	Remigius, Bishop of Rheims, Apostle of the Franks, 533			
Gw	Com. Bishop	1 Macc. 2. 29-48 *or* 2 Chron. 14. 2-end Mark 14. 53-65	2 Kings 2. 1-18 Acts 24.24 - 25.12	

			Sunday Principal Service Weekday Eucharist	Third Service Morning Prayer	Second Service Evening Prayer
2 Saturday		Ember Day*			
	G		Baruch 4. 5-12, 27-29 *or* Josh. 22. 1-6 Ps. 69. 33-37 Luke 10. 17-24	Ps. ***76***; 79 1 Macc. 2. 49-end *or* 2 Chron. 15. 1-15 Mark 14. 66-end	Ps. 81; ***84*** 2 Kings 4. 1-37 Acts 25. 13-end **ct** *or First EP of Dedication Festival* Ps. 24 2 Chron. 7. 11-16 John 4. 19-29 **𝔚 ct**
3 Sunday		**THE EIGHTEENTH SUNDAY AFTER TRINITY (Proper 22)**			
	G	*Track 1* Job 1. 1; 2. 1-10 Ps. 26 Heb. 1. 1-4; 2. 5-12 Mark 10. 2-16	*Track 2* Gen. 2. 18-24 Ps. 8 Heb. 1. 1-4; 2. 5-12 Mark 10. 2-16	Ps. 123; 124 Isa. 49. 13-23 Luke 12. 1-12	Ps. 125; 126 Josh. 3. 7-end Matt. 10. 1-22
		or, if observed as Dedication Festival:			
	𝔚		Gen. 28. 11-18 *or* Rev. 21. 9-14 Ps. 122 1 Pet. 2. 1-10 John 10. 22-29	*MP*: Ps. 48; 150 Hag. 2. 6-9 Heb. 10. 19-25	*EP*: Ps. 132 Jer. 7. 1-11 Luke 19. 1-10
4 Monday		**Francis of Assisi, Friar, Founder of the Friars Minor, 1226**			
	Gw **DEL 27**	Com. Religious *or* *also* Gal. 6. 14-end Luke 12. 22-34	Jonah 1.1 - 2.2, 10 *Canticle*: Jonah 2. 2-4, 7 *or* Ps. 69. 1-6 Luke 10. 25-37	Ps. ***80***; 82 1 Macc. 3. 1-26 *or* 2 Chron. 17. 1-12 Mark 15. 1-15	Ps. ***85***; 86 2 Kings ch. 5 Acts 26. 1-23
5 Tuesday					
	G		Jonah ch. 3 Ps. 130 Luke 10. 38-end	Ps. 87; ***89. 1-18*** 1 Macc. 3. 27-41 *or* 2 Chron. 18. 1-27 Mark 15. 16-32	Ps. 89. 19-end 2 Kings 6. 1-23 Acts 26. 24-end
6 Wednesday		**William Tyndale, Translator of the Scriptures, Reformation Martyr, 1536**			
	Gr	Com. Martyr *or* *also* Prov. 8. 4-11 2 Tim. 3. 12-end	Jonah ch. 4 Ps. 86. 1-9 Luke 11. 1-4	Ps. 119. 105-128 1 Macc. 3. 42-end *or* 2 Chron. 18.28 - 19.end Mark 15. 33-41	Ps. ***91***; 93 2 Kings 9. 1-16 Acts 27. 1-26
7 Thursday					
	G		Mal. 3.13 - 4.2a Ps. 1 Luke 11. 5-13	Ps. 90; ***92*** 1 Macc. 4. 1-25 *or* 2 Chron. 20. 1-23 Mark 15. 42-end	Ps. 94 2 Kings 9. 17-end Acts 27. 27-end
8 Friday					
	G		Joel 1. 13-15; 2. 1-2 Ps. 9. 1-7 Luke 11. 15-26	Ps. ***88***; (95) 1 Macc. 4. 26-35 *or* 2 Chron. 22.10 - 23.end Mark 16. 1-8	Ps. 102 2 Kings 12. 1-19 Acts 28. 1-16

*For Ember Day provision, see p. 11.

	Calendar and Holy Communion	Morning Prayer	Evening Prayer
G		1 Macc. 2. 49–end *or* 2 Chron. 15. 1–15 Mark 14. 66–end	2 Kings 4. 1–37 Acts 25. 13–end **ct** *or First EP of Dedication Festival* Ps. 24 2 Chron. 7. 11–16 John 4. 19–29 **𝔚 ct**
	THE EIGHTEENTH SUNDAY AFTER TRINITY		
G	Deut. 6. 4–9 Ps. 122 1 Cor. 1. 4–8 Matt. 22. 34–end	Ps. 123; 124 Isa. 49. 13–23 Luke 12. 1–12	Ps. 125; 126 Josh. 3. 7–end Matt. 10. 1–22
	or, if observed as Dedication Festival:		
𝔚	2 Chron. 7. 11–16 Ps. 122 1 Cor. 3. 9–17 *or* 1 Pet. 2. 1–5 Matt. 21. 12–16 *or* John 10. 22–29	Ps. 48; 150 Hag. 2. 6–9 Heb. 10. 19–25	Ps. 132 Jer. 7. 1–11 Luke 19. 1–10
G		1 Macc. 3. 1–26 *or* 2 Chron. 17. 1–12 Mark 15. 1–15	2 Kings ch. 5 Acts 26. 1–23
G		1 Macc. 3. 27–41 *or* 2 Chron. 18. 1–27 Mark 15. 16–32	2 Kings 6. 1–23 Acts 26. 24–end
	Faith of Aquitaine, Martyr, *c*. 304		
Gr	Com. Virgin Martyr	1 Macc. 3. 42–end *or* 2 Chron. 18.28 – 19.end Mark 15. 33–41	2 Kings 9. 1–16 Acts 27. 1–26
G		1 Macc. 4. 1–25 *or* 2 Chron. 20. 1–23 Mark 15. 42–end	2 Kings 9. 17–end Acts 27. 27–end
G		1 Macc. 4. 26–35 *or* 2 Chron. 22.10 – 23.end Mark 16. 1–8	2 Kings 12. 1–19 Acts 28. 1–16

NOTES

		Sunday Principal Service Weekday Eucharist	Third Service Morning Prayer	Second Service Evening Prayer
9 Saturday	*Denys, Bishop of Paris, and his Companions, Martyrs, c. 250; Robert Grosseteste, Bishop of Lincoln, Philosopher, Scientist, 1253*			
G		Joel 3. 12–end Ps. 97. 1, 8–end Luke 11. 27–28	Ps. 96; ***97***; 100 1 Macc. 4. 36–end *or* 2 Chron. 24. 1–22 Mark 16. 9–end	Ps. 104 2 Kings 17. 1–23 Acts 28. 17–end **ct**
10 Sunday	**THE NINETEENTH SUNDAY AFTER TRINITY (Proper 23)**			
G	*Track 1* Job 23. 1–9, 16–end Ps. 22. 1–15 Heb. 4. 12–end Mark 10. 17–31	*Track 2* Amos 5. 6–7, 10–15 Ps. 90. 12–end Heb. 4. 12–end Mark 10. 17–31	Ps. 129; 130 Isa. 50. 4–10 Luke 13. 22–30	Ps. 127; [128] Josh. 5.13 - 6.20 Matt. 11. 20–end
11 Monday	*Ethelburga, Abbess of Barking 657; James the Deacon, Companion of Paulinus, 7th century*			
G **DEL 28**		Rom. 1. 1–7 Ps. 98 Luke 11. 29–32	Ps. ***98***; 99; 101 1 Macc. 6. 1–17 *or* 2 Chron. 26. 1–21 John 13. 1–11	Ps. ***105***† (*or* 103) 2 Kings 17. 24–end Phil. 1. 1–11
12 Tuesday	**Wilfrid of Ripon, Bishop, Missionary, 709** *Elizabeth Fry, Prison Reformer, 1845; Edith Cavell, Nurse, 1915*			
Gw	Com. Missionary *or* *esp.* Luke 5. 1–11 *also* 1 Cor. 1. 18–25	Rom. 1. 16–25 Ps. 19. 1–4 Luke 11. 37–41	Ps. ***106***† (*or* 103) 1 Macc. 6. 18–47 *or* 2 Chron. ch. 28 John 13. 12–20	Ps. 107† 2 Kings 18. 1–12 Phil. 1. 12–end
13 Wednesday	**Edward the Confessor, King of England, 1066**			
Gw	Com. Saint *or* *also* 2 Sam. 23. 1–5 1 John 4. 13–16	Rom. 2. 1–11 Ps. 62. 1–8 Luke 11. 42–46	Ps. 110; ***111***; 112 1 Macc. 7. 1–20 *or* 2 Chron. 29. 1–19 John 13. 21–30	Ps. 119. 129–152 2 Kings 18. 13–end Phil. 2. 1–13
14 Thursday				
G		Rom. 3. 21–30 Ps. 130 Luke 11. 47–end	Ps. 113; ***115*** 1 Macc. 7. 21–end *or* 2 Chron. 29. 20–end John 13. 31–end	Ps. 114; ***116***; 117 2 Kings 19. 1–19 Phil. 2. 14–end
15 Friday	**Teresa of Avila, Teacher, 1582**			
Gw	Com. Teacher *or* *also* Rom. 8. 22–27	Rom. 4. 1–8 Ps. 32 Luke 12. 1–7	Ps. 139 1 Macc. 9. 1–22 *or* 2 Chron. ch. 30 John 14. 1–14	Ps. ***130***; 131; 137 2 Kings 19. 20–36 Phil. 3.1 - 4.1
16 Saturday	*Nicholas Ridley, Bishop of London, and Hugh Latimer, Bishop of Worcester, Reformation Martyrs, 1555*			
G		Rom. 4. 13, 16–18 Ps. 105. 6–10, 41–44 Luke 12. 8–12	Ps. 120; ***121***; 122 1 Macc. 13. 41–end; 14. 4–15 *or* 2 Chron. 32. 1–22 John 14. 15–end	Ps. 118 2 Kings ch. 20 Phil. 4. 2–end **ct**

	Calendar and Holy Communion	Morning Prayer	Evening Prayer	NOTES
	Denys, Bishop of Paris, Martyr, c. 250			
Gr	Com. Martyr	1 Macc. 4. 36–end *or* 2 Chron. 24. 1–22 Mark 16. 9–end	2 Kings 17. 1–23 Acts 28. 17–end **ct**	
	THE NINETEENTH SUNDAY AFTER TRINITY			
G	Gen. 18. 23–32 Ps. 141. 1–9 Eph. 4. 17–end Matt. 9. 1–8	Ps. 129; 130 Isa. 50. 4–10 Luke 13. 22–30	Ps. 127; [128] Josh. 5.13 - 6.20 Matt. 11. 20–end	
G		1 Macc. 6. 1–17 *or* 2 Chron. 26. 1–21 John 13. 1–11	2 Kings 17. 24–end Phil. 1. 1–11	
G		1 Macc. 6. 18–47 *or* 2 Chron. ch. 28 John 13. 12–20	2 Kings 18. 1–12 Phil. 1. 12–end	
	Edward the Confessor, King of England, 1066, translated 1163			
Gw	Com. Saint	1 Macc. 7. 1–20 *or* 2 Chron. 29. 1–19 John 13. 21–30	2 Kings 18. 13–end Phil. 2. 1–13	
G		1 Macc. 7. 21–end *or* 2 Chron. 29. 20–end John 13. 31–end	2 Kings 19. 1–19 Phil. 2. 14–end	
G		1 Macc. 9. 1–22 *or* 2 Chron. ch. 30 John 14. 1–14	2 Kings 19. 20–36 Phil. 3.1 - 4.1	
G		1 Macc. 13. 41–end; 14. 4–15 *or* 2 Chron. 32. 1–22 John 14. 15–end	2 Kings ch. 20 Phil. 4. 2–end **ct**	

		Sunday Principal Service Weekday Eucharist	Third Service Morning Prayer	Second Service Evening Prayer
17 Sunday	**THE TWENTIETH SUNDAY AFTER TRINITY (Proper 24)**			
G	*Track 1* Job 38. 1–7 [34–end] Ps. 104. 1–10, 26, 35c (*or* 1–10) Heb. 5. 1–10 Mark 10. 35–45	*Track 2* Isa. 53. 4–end Ps. 91. 9–end Heb. 5. 1–10 Mark 10. 35–45	Ps. 133; 134; 137. 1–6 Isa. 54. 1–14 Luke 13. 31–end	Ps. 141 Josh. 14. 6–14 Matt. 12. 1–21 *or First EP of Luke* Ps. 33 Hos. 6. 1–3 2 Tim. 3. 10–end **R ct**
18 Monday	**LUKE THE EVANGELIST**			
R **DEL 29**		Isa. 35. 3–6 *or* Acts 16. 6–12a Ps. 147. 1–7 2 Tim. 4. 5–17 Luke 10. 1–9	*MP*: Ps. 145; 146 Isa. ch. 55 Luke 1. 1–4	*EP*: Ps. 103 Ecclus. 38. 1–14 *or* Isa. 61. 1–6 Col. 4. 7–end
19 Tuesday	**Henry Martyn, Translator of the Scriptures, Missionary in India and Persia, 1812**			
Gw	Com. Missionary *or* *esp.* Mark 16. 15–end *also* Isa. 55. 6–11	Rom. 5. 12, 15, 17–end Ps. 40. 7–12 Luke 12. 35–38	Ps. ***132***; 133 2 Macc. 6. 12–end *or* 2 Chron. 34. 1–18 John 15. 12–17	Ps. (134); ***135*** 2 Kings 22.1 – 23.3 1 Tim. 1.18 – 2.end
20 Wednesday				
G		Rom. 6. 12–18 Ps. 124 Luke 12. 39–48	Ps. 119. 153–end 2 Macc. 7. 1–19 *or* 2 Chron. 34. 19–end John 15. 18–end	Ps. 136 2 Kings 23. 4–25 1 Tim. ch. 3
21 Thursday				
G		Rom. 6. 19–end Ps. 1 Luke 12. 49–53	Ps. ***143***; 146 2 Macc. 7. 20–41 *or* 2 Chron. 35. 1–19 John 16. 1–15	Ps. ***138***; 140; 141 2 Kings. 23.36 – 24.17 1 Tim. ch. 4
22 Friday				
G		Rom. 7. 18–end Ps. 119. 33–40 Luke 12. 54–end	Ps. 142; ***144*** Tobit ch. 1 *or* 2 Chron. 35.20 – 36.10 John 16. 16–22	Ps. 145 2 Kings 24.18 – 25.12 1 Tim. 5. 1–16
23 Saturday				
G		Rom. 8. 1–11 Ps. 24. 1–6 Luke 13. 1–9	Ps. 147 Tobit ch. 2 *or* 2 Chron. 36. 11–end John 16. 23–end	Ps. ***148***; 149; 150 2 Kings 25. 22–end 1 Tim. 5. 17–end **ct**
24 Sunday	**THE LAST SUNDAY AFTER TRINITY***			
G	*Track 1* Job 42. 1–6, 10–end Ps. 34. 1–8, 19–end (*or* 1–8) Heb. 7. 23–end Mark 10. 46–end	*Track 2* Jer. 31. 7–9 Ps. 126 Heb. 7. 23–end Mark 10. 46–end	Ps. 119. 89–104 Isa. 59. 9–20 Luke 14. 1–14	Ps. 119. 121–136 Eccles. chs 11 and 12 2 Tim. 2. 1–7 *Gospel*: Luke 18. 9–14

(continued overleaf)

*If the Dedication Festival is kept on this Sunday, use the provision given on 2 and 3 October.

	Calendar and Holy Communion	Morning Prayer	Evening Prayer	NOTES
	THE TWENTIETH SUNDAY AFTER TRINITY			
G	Prov. 9. 1-6 Ps. 145. 15-end Eph. 5. 15-21 Matt. 22. 1-14	Ps. 133; 134; 137. 1-6 Isa. 54. 1-14 Luke 13. 31-end	Ps. 142 Josh. 14. 6-14 Matt. 12. 1-21 *or First EP of Luke* Ps. 33 Hos. 6. 1-3 2 Tim. 3. 10-end **R ct**	
	LUKE THE EVANGELIST			
R	Isa. 35. 3-6 Ps. 147. 1-6 2 Tim. 4. 5-15 Luke 10. 1-9 *or* Luke 7. 36-end	(Ps. 145; 146) Isa. ch. 55 Luke 1. 1-4	(Ps. 103) Ecclus. 38. 1-14 *or* Isa. 61. 1-6 Col. 4. 7-end	
G		2 Macc. 6. 12-end *or* 2 Chron. 34. 1-18 John 15. 12-17	2 Kings 22.1 - 23.3 1 Tim. 1.18 - 2.end	
G		2 Macc. 7. 1-19 *or* 2 Chron. 34. 19-end John 15. 18-end	2 Kings 23. 4-25 1 Tim. ch. 3	
G		2 Macc. 7. 20-41 *or* 2 Chron. 35. 1-19 John 16. 1-15	2 Kings. 23.36 - 24.17 1 Tim. ch. 4	
G		Tobit ch. 1 *or* 2 Chron. 35.20 - 36.10 John 16. 16-22	2 Kings 24.18 - 25.12 1 Tim. 5. 1-16	
G		Tobit ch. 2 *or* 2 Chron. 36. 11-end John 16. 23-end	2 Kings 25. 22-end 1 Tim. 5. 17-end **ct**	
	THE TWENTY-FIRST SUNDAY AFTER TRINITY			
G	Gen. 32. 24-29 Ps. 90. 1-12 Eph. 6. 10-20 John 4. 46b-end	Ps. 119. 89-104 Isa. 59. 9-20 Luke 14. 1-14	Ps. 119. 121-136 Eccles. chs 11 and 12 2 Tim. 2. 1-7	

		Sunday Principal Service Weekday Eucharist	Third Service Morning Prayer	Second Service Evening Prayer
24 Sunday	**THE LAST SUNDAY AFTER TRINITY** *(continued)*			
	or, if being observed as Bible Sunday:			
G		Isa. 55. 1–11 Ps. 19. 7–end 2 Tim. 3.14 - 4.5 John 5. 36b–end	Ps. 119. 89–104 Isa. 45. 22–end Matt. 24. 30–35 *or* Luke 14. 1–14	Ps. 119. 1–16 2 Kings ch. 22 Col. 3. 12–17 *Gospel*: Luke 4. 14–30
25 Monday	*Crispin and Crispinian, Martyrs at Rome, c. 287*			
G **DEL 30**		Rom. 8. 12–17 Ps. 68. 1–6, 19 Luke 13. 10–17	Ps. ***1***; 2; 3 Tobit ch. 3 *or* Mic. 1. 1–9 John 17. 1–5	Ps. ***4***; 7 Judith ch. 4 *or* Exod. 22. 21–27; 23. 1–17 1 Tim. 6. 1–10
26 Tuesday	**Alfred the Great, King of the West Saxons, Scholar, 899** *Cedd, Abbot of Lastingham, Bishop of the East Saxons, 664**			
Gw	Com. Saint *or* *also* 2 Sam. 23. 1–5 John 18. 33–37	Rom. 8. 18–25 Ps. 126 Luke 13. 18–21	Ps. ***5***; 6; (8) Tobit ch. 4 *or* Mic. ch. 2 John 17. 6–19	Ps. ***9***; 10† Judith 5.1 - 6.4 *or* Exod. 29.38 - 30.16 1 Tim. 6. 11–end
27 Wednesday				
G		Rom. 8. 26–30 Ps. 13 Luke 13. 22–30	Ps. 119. 1–32 Tobit 5. 1–6a *or* Mic. ch. 3 John 17. 20–end	Ps. ***11***; 12; 13 Judith 6.10 - 7.7 *or* Lev. ch. 8 2 Tim. 1. 1–14 *or First EP of Simon and Jude* Ps. 124; 125; 126 Deut. 32. 1–4 John 14. 15–26 **R ct**
28 Thursday	**SIMON AND JUDE, APOSTLES**			
R		Isa. 28. 14–16 Ps. 119. 89–96 Eph. 2. 19–end John 15. 17–end	*MP*: Ps. 116; 117 Wisd. 5. 1–16 *or* Isa. 45. 18–end Luke 6. 12–16	*EP*: Ps. 119. 1–16 1 Macc. 2. 42–66 *or* Jer. 3. 11–18 Jude 1–4, 17–end
29 Friday	**James Hannington, Bishop of Eastern Equatorial Africa, Martyr in Uganda, 1885**			
Gr	Com. Martyr *or* *esp.* Matt. 10. 28–39	Rom. 9. 1–5 Ps. 147. 13–end Luke 14. 1–6	Ps. 17; ***19*** Tobit ch. 7 *or* Mic. 5. 2–end John 18. 12–27	Ps. 22 Judith 8. 9–end *or* Lev. 16. 2–24 2 Tim. 2. 14–end
30 Saturday				
G		Rom. 11. 1–2, 11–12, 25–29 Ps. 94. 14–19 Luke 14. 1, 7–11	Ps. 20; 21; ***23*** Tobit ch. 8 *or* Mic. ch. 6 John 18. 28–end	Ps. ***24***; 25 Judith ch. 9 *or* Lev. ch. 17 2 Tim. ch. 3 **ct**

*Chad may be celebrated with Cedd on 26 October instead of 2 March.

	Calendar and Holy Communion	Morning Prayer	Evening Prayer	NOTES
	Crispin, Martyr at Rome, *c.* 287			
r	Com. Martyr	Tobit ch. 3 *or* Mic. 1. 1–9 John 17. 1–5	Judith ch. 4 *or* Exod. 22. 21–27; 23. 1–17 1 Tim. 6. 1–10	
G		Tobit ch. 4 *or* Mic. ch. 2 John 17. 6–19	Judith 5.1 – 6.4 *or* Exod. 29.38 – 30.16 1 Tim. 6. 11–end	
G		Tobit 5. 1–6a *or* Mic. ch. 3 John 17. 20–end	Judith 6.10 – 7.7 *or* Lev. ch. 8 2 Tim. 1. 1–14 *or First EP of Simon and Jude* (Ps. 124; 125; 126) Deut. 32. 1–4 John 14. 15–26 **R ct**	
	SIMON AND JUDE, APOSTLES			
R	Isa. 28. 9–16 Ps. 116. 11–end Jude 1–8 *or* Rev. 21. 9–14 John 15. 17–end	(Ps. 119. 89–96) Wisd. 5. 1–16 *or* Isa. 45. 18–end Luke 6. 12–16	(Ps. 119. 1–16) 1 Macc. 2. 42–66 *or* Jer. 3. 11–18 Eph. 2. 19–end	
G		Tobit ch. 7 *or* Mic. 5. 2–end John 18. 12–27	Judith 8. 9–end *or* Lev. 16. 2–24 2 Tim. 2. 14–end	
G		Tobit ch. 8 *or* Mic. ch. 6 John 18. 28–end	Judith ch. 9 *or* Lev. ch. 17 2 Tim. ch. 3 **ct**	

		Sunday Principal Service Weekday Eucharist	Third Service Morning Prayer	Second Service Evening Prayer
31 Sunday	**THE FOURTH SUNDAY BEFORE ADVENT**			
R *or* **G**		Deut. 6. 1–9 Ps. 119. 1–8 Heb. 9. 11–14 Mark 12. 28–34	Ps. 112; 149 Jer. 31. 31–34 1 John 3. 1–3	*First EP of All Saints* Ps. 1; 5 Ecclus. 44. 1–15 *or* Isa. 40. 27–end Rev. 19. 6–10 **𝔚 ct**
𝔚	*Or ALL SAINTS' SUNDAY (see readings for 1 November throughout the day)*			

November 2021

1 Monday	**ALL SAINTS' DAY**			
𝔚 **DEL 31**		Wisd. 3. 1–9 *or* Isa. 25. 6–9 Ps. 24. 1–6 Rev. 21. 1–6a John 11. 32–44	*MP*: Ps. 15; 84; 149 Isa. ch. 35 Luke 9. 18–27	*EP*: Ps. 148; 150 Isa. 65. 17–end Heb. 11.32 - 12.2
	or, if the readings above are used on Sunday 31 October:			
𝔚		Isa. 56. 3–8 *or* 2 Esdras 2. 42–end Ps. 33. 1–5 Heb. 12. 18–24 Matt. 5. 1–12	*MP*: Ps. 111; 112; 117 Wisd. 5. 1–16 *or* Jer. 31. 31–34 2 Cor. 4. 5–12	*EP*: Ps. 145 Isa. 66. 20–23 Col. 1. 9–14
	or, if kept as a feria:			
R *or* **G**		Rom. 11. 29–end Ps. 69. 31–37 Luke 14. 12–14	Ps. **2**; 146 *alt*. Ps. 27; ***30*** Isa. 1. 1–20 Matt. 1. 18–end	Ps. **92**; 96; 97 *alt*. Ps. 26; ***28***; 29 Dan. ch. 1 Rev. ch. 1
2 Tuesday	**Commemoration of the Faithful Departed (All Souls' Day)**			
Rp *or* **Gp**	Lam. 3. 17–26, 31–33 *or* *or* Wisd. 3. 1–9 Ps. 23 *or* Ps. 27. 1–6, 16–end Rom. 5. 5–11 *or* 1 Pet. 1. 3–9 John 5. 19–25 *or* John 6. 37–40	Rom. 12. 5–16 Ps. 131 Luke 14. 15–24	Ps. **5**; 147. 1–12 *alt*. Ps. 32; ***36*** Isa. 1. 21–end Matt. 2. 1–15	Ps. 98; 99; ***100*** *alt*. Ps. 33 Dan. 2. 1–24 Rev. 2. 1–11
3 Wednesday	**Richard Hooker, Priest, Anglican Apologist, Teacher, 1600** *Martin of Porres, Friar, 1639*			
Rw *or* **Gw**	Com. Teacher *or* *esp*. John 16. 12–15 *also* Ecclus. 44. 10–15	Rom. 13. 8–10 Ps. 112 Luke 14. 25–33	Ps. **9**; 147. 13–end *alt*. Ps. 34 Isa. 2. 1–11 Matt. 2. 16–end	Ps. 111; ***112***; 116 *alt*. Ps. 119. 33–56 Dan. 2. 25–end Rev. 2. 12–end
4 Thursday				
R *or* **G**		Rom. 14. 7–12 Ps. 27. 14–end Luke 15. 1–10	Ps. 11; ***15***; 148 *alt*. Ps. 37† Isa. 2. 12–end Matt. ch. 3	Ps. 118 *alt*. Ps. 39; ***40*** Dan. 3. 1–18 Rev. 3. 1–13
5 Friday				
R *or* **G**		Rom. 15. 14–21 Ps. 98 Luke 16. 1–8	Ps. ***16***; 149 *alt*. Ps. 31 Isa. 3. 1–15 Matt. 4. 1–11	Ps. 137; 138; ***143*** *alt*. Ps. 35 Dan. 3. 19–end Rev. 3. 14–end

	Calendar and Holy Communion	Morning Prayer	Evening Prayer	NOTES
	THE TWENTY-SECOND SUNDAY AFTER TRINITY			
G	Gen. 45. 1–7, 15 Ps. 133 Phil. 1. 3–11 Matt. 18. 21–end	Ps. 112; 149 Jer. 31. 31–34 1 John 3. 1–3	*First EP of All Saints* Ps. 1; 5 Ecclus. 44. 1–15 *or* Isa. 40. 27–end Rev. 19. 6–10 **W ct**	
	ALL SAINTS' DAY			
W	Isa. 66. 20–23 Ps. 33. 1–5 Rev. 7. 2–4 [5–8] 9–12 Matt. 5. 1–12	Ps. 15; 84; 149 Isa. ch. 35 Luke 9. 18–27	Ps. 148; 150 Isa. 65. 17–end Heb. 11.32 – 12.2	
	To celebrate All Souls' Day, see *Common Worship* provision.			
G		Isa. 1. 21–end Matt. 2. 1–15	Dan. 2. 1–24 Rev. 2. 1–11	
G		Isa. 2. 1–11 Matt. 2. 16–end	Dan. 2. 25–end Rev. 2. 12–end	
G		Isa. 2. 12–end Matt. ch. 3	Dan. 3. 1–18 Rev. 3. 1–13	
G		Isa. 3. 1–15 Matt. 4. 1–11	Dan. 3. 19–end Rev. 3. 14–end	

		Sunday Principal Service Weekday Eucharist	Third Service Morning Prayer	Second Service Evening Prayer
6 Saturday	*Leonard, Hermit, 6th century; William Temple, Archbishop of Canterbury, Teacher, 1944*			
R *or* **G**		Rom. 16. 3–9, 16, 22–end Ps. 145. 1–7 Luke 16. 9–15	Ps. ***18***. ***31–end***; 150 *alt.* Ps. 41; ***42***; 43 Isa. 4.2 – 5.7 Matt. 4. 12–22	Ps. 145 *alt.* Ps. 45; ***46*** Dan. 4. 1–18 Rev. ch. 4 **ct**
7 Sunday	**THE THIRD SUNDAY BEFORE ADVENT**			
R *or* **G**		Jonah 3. 1–5, 10 Ps. 62. 5–end Heb. 9. 24–end Mark 1. 14–20	Ps. 136 Mic. 4. 1–5 Phil. 4. 6–9	Ps. 46; [82] Isa. 10.33 – 11.9 John 14. 1–29 (*or* 23–29)
8 Monday	**The Saints and Martyrs of England**			
Rw *or* **Gw** **DEL 32**	Isa. 61. 4–9 *or* *or* Ecclus. 44. 1–15 Ps. 15 Rev. 19. 5–10 John 17. 18–23	Wisd. 1. 1–7 *or* Titus 1. 1–9 Ps. 139. 1–9 *or* Ps. 24. 1–6 Luke 17. 1–6	Ps. 19; ***20*** *alt.* Ps. 44 Isa. 5. 8–24 Matt. 4.23 – 5.12	Ps. 34 *alt.* Ps. ***47***; 49 Dan. 4. 19–end Rev. ch. 5
9 Tuesday	*Margery Kempe, Mystic,* c. *1440*			
R *or* **G**		Wisd. 2.23 – 3.9 *or* Titus 2. 1–8, 11–14 Ps. 34. 1–6 *or* Ps. 37. 3–5, 30–32 Luke 17. 7–10	Ps. ***21***; 24 *alt.* Ps. ***48***; 52 Isa. 5. 25–end Matt. 5. 13–20	Ps. 36; ***40*** *alt.* Ps. 50 Dan. 5. 1–12 Rev. ch. 6
10 Wednesday	**Leo the Great, Bishop of Rome, Teacher, 461**			
Rw *or* **Gw**	Com. Teacher *or* *also* 1 Pet. 5. 1–11	Wisd. 6. 1–11 *or* Titus 3. 1–7 Ps. 82 *or* Ps. 23 Luke 17. 11–19	Ps. ***23***; 25 *alt.* Ps. 119. 57–80 Isa. ch. 6 Matt. 5. 21–37	Ps. 37 *alt.* Ps. ***59***; 60; (67) Dan. 5. 13–end Rev. 7. 1–4, 9–end
11 Thursday	**Martin, Bishop of Tours, c. 397**			
Gw *or* **Rw**	Com. Bishop *or* *also* 1 Thess. 5. 1–11 Matt. 25. 34–40	Wisd. 7.22 – 8.1 *or* Philemon 7–20 Ps. 119. 89–96 *or* Ps. 146. 4–end Luke 17. 20–25	Ps. ***26***; 27 *alt.* Ps. 56; ***57***; (63†) Isa. 7. 1–17 Matt. 5. 38–end	Ps. 42; ***43*** *alt.* Ps. 61; ***62***; 64 Dan. ch. 6 Rev. ch. 8
12 Friday				
R *or* **G**		Wisd. 13. 1–9 *or* 2 John 4–9 Ps. 19. 1–4 *or* Ps. 119. 1–8 Luke 17. 26–end	Ps. 28; ***32*** *alt.* Ps. ***51***; 54 Isa. 8. 1–15 Matt. 6. 1–18	Ps. 31 *alt.* Ps. 38 Dan. 7. 1–14 Rev. 9. 1–12
13 Saturday	**Charles Simeon, Priest, Evangelical Divine, 1836**			
Rw *or* **Gw**	Com. Pastor *or* *esp.* Mal. 2. 5–7 *also* Col. 1. 3–8 Luke 8. 4–8	Wisd. 18. 14–16; 19. 6–9 *or* 3 John 5–8 Ps. 105. 1–5, 35–42 *or* Ps. 112 Luke 18. 1–8	Ps. 33 *alt.* Ps. 68 Isa. 8.16 – 9.7 Matt. 6. 19–end	Ps. 84; ***86*** *alt.* Ps. 65; ***66*** Dan. 7. 15–end Rev. 9. 13–end **ct**

	Calendar and Holy Communion	Morning Prayer	Evening Prayer	NOTES
	Leonard, Hermit, 6th century			
Gw	Com. Abbot	Isa. 4.2 – 5.7 Matt. 4. 12-22	Dan. 4. 1-18 Rev. ch. 4 **ct**	
	THE TWENTY-THIRD SUNDAY AFTER TRINITY			
G	Isa. 11. 1-10 Ps. 44. 1-9 Phil. 3. 17-end Matt. 22. 15-22	Ps. 136 Mic. 4. 1-5 Phil. 4. 6-9	Ps. 144 Isa. 10.33 – 11.9 John 14. 1-29 (*or* 23-29)	
G		Isa. 5. 8-24 Matt. 4.23 – 5.12	Dan. 4. 19-end Rev. ch. 5	
G		Isa. 5. 25-end Matt. 5. 13-20	Dan. 5. 1-12 Rev. ch. 6	
G		Isa. ch. 6 Matt. 5. 21-37	Dan. 5. 13-end Rev. 7. 1-4, 9-end	
	Martin, Bishop of Tours, *c.* 397			
Gw	Com. Bishop	Isa. 7. 1-17 Matt. 5. 38-end	Dan. ch. 6 Rev. ch. 8	
G		Isa. 8. 1-15 Matt. 6. 1-18	Dan. 7. 1-14 Rev. 9. 1-12	
	Britius, Bishop of Tours, 444			
Gw	Com. Bishop	Isa. 8.16 – 9.7 Matt. 6. 19-end	Dan. 7. 15-end Rev. 9. 13-end **ct**	

		Sunday Principal Service Weekday Eucharist	Third Service Morning Prayer	Second Service Evening Prayer
14 Sunday	**THE SECOND SUNDAY BEFORE ADVENT** (Remembrance Sunday)			
R *or* **G**		Dan. 12. 1-3 Ps. 16 Heb. 10. 11-14 [15-18] 19-25 Mark 13. 1-8	Ps. 96 1 Sam. 9.27 - 10.2a; 10. 17-26 Matt. 13. 31-35	Ps. 95 Dan. ch. 3 (*or* 3. 13-end) Matt. 13. 24-30, 36-43
15 Monday				
R *or* **G** **DEL 33**		1 Macc. 1. 10-15, 41-43, 54-57, 62-64 *or* Rev. 1. 1-4; 2. 1-5 Ps. 79. 1-5 *or* Ps. 1 Luke 18. 35-end	Ps. 46; ***47*** *alt*. Ps. 71 Isa. 9.8 - 10.4 Matt. 7. 1-12	Ps. 70; ***71*** *alt*. Ps. ***72***; 75 Dan. 8. 1-14 Rev. ch. 10
16 Tuesday	**Margaret, Queen of Scotland, Philanthropist, Reformer of the Church, 1093** *Edmund Rich of Abingdon, Archbishop of Canterbury, 1240*			
Rw *or* **Gw**	Com. Saint *or* *also* Prov. 31. 10-12, 20, 26-end 1 Cor. 12.13 - 13.3 Matt. 25. 34-end	2 Macc. 6. 18-end *or* Rev. 3. 1-6, 14-31 Ps. 11 *or* Ps. 15 Luke 19. 1-10	Ps. 48; ***52*** *alt*. Ps. 73 Isa. 10. 5-19 Matt. 7. 13-end	Ps. ***67***; 72 *alt*. Ps. 74 Dan. 8. 15-end Rev. 11. 1-14
17 Wednesday	**Hugh, Bishop of Lincoln, 1200**			
Rw *or* **Gw**	Com. Bishop *or* *also* 1 Tim. 6. 11-16	2 Macc. 7. 1, 20-31 *or* Rev. ch. 4 Ps. 116. 10-end *or* Ps. 150 Luke 19. 11-28	Ps. ***56***; 57 *alt*. Ps. 77 Isa. 10. 20-32 Matt. 8. 1-13	Ps. 73 *alt*. Ps. 119. 81-104 Dan. 9. 1-19 Rev. 11. 15-end
18 Thursday	**Elizabeth of Hungary, Princess of Thuringia, Philanthropist, 1231**			
Rw *or* **Gw**	Com. Saint *or* *esp*. Matt. 25. 31-end *also* Prov. 31. 10-end	1 Macc. 2. 15-29 *or* Rev. 5. 1-10 Ps. 129 *or* Ps. 149. 1-5 Luke 19. 41-44	Ps. 61; ***62*** *alt*. Ps. 78. 1-39† Isa. 10.33 - 11.9 Matt. 8. 14-22	Ps. 74; ***76*** *alt*. Ps. 78. 40-end† Dan. 9. 20-end Rev. ch. 12
19 Friday	**Hilda, Abbess of Whitby, 680** *Mechtild, Béguine of Magdeburg, Mystic, 1280*			
Rw *or* **Gw**	Com. Religious *or* *esp*. Isa. 61.10 - 62.5	1 Macc. 4. 36-37, 52-59 *or* Rev. 10. 8-11 Ps. 122 *or* Ps. 119. 65-72 Luke 19. 45-48	Ps. ***63***; 65 *alt*. Ps. 55 Isa. 11.10 - 12.end Matt. 8. 23-end	Ps. 77 *alt*. Ps. 69 Dan. 10.1 - 11.1 Rev. 13. 1-10
20 Saturday	**Edmund, King of the East Angles, Martyr, 870** *Priscilla Lydia Sellon, a Restorer of the Religious Life in the Church of England, 1876*			
R *or* **Gr**	Com. Martyr *or* *also* Prov. 20. 28; 21. 1-4, 7	1 Macc. 6. 1-13 *or* Rev. 11. 4-12 Ps. 124 *or* Ps. 144. 1-9 Luke 20. 27-40	Ps. 78. 1-39 *alt*. Ps. ***76***; 79 Isa. 13. 1-13 Matt. 9. 1-17	Ps. 78. 40-end *alt*. Ps. 81; ***84*** Dan. ch. 12 Rev. 13. 11-end **ct** *or First EP of Christ the King* Ps. 99; 100 Isa. 10.33 - 11.9 1 Tim. 6. 11-16 **R** *or* **W ct**

	Calendar and Holy Communion	Morning Prayer	Evening Prayer	NOTES
	THE TWENTY-FOURTH SUNDAY AFTER TRINITY			
G	Isa. 55. 6–11 Ps. 85. 1–7 Col. 1. 3–12 Matt. 9. 18–26	Ps. 96 1 Sam. 9.27 - 10.2a; 10. 17–26 Matt. 13. 31–35	Ps. 95 Dan. ch. 3 (*or* 3. 13–end) Matt. 13. 24–30, 36–43	
	Machutus, Bishop, Apostle of Brittany, *c.* 564			
Gw	Com. Bishop	Isa. 9.8 - 10.4 Matt. 7. 1–12	Dan. 8. 1–14 Rev. ch. 10	
G		Isa. 10. 5–19 Matt. 7. 13–end	Dan. 8. 15–end Rev. 11. 1–14	
	Hugh, Bishop of Lincoln, 1200			
Gw	Com. Bishop	Isa. 10. 20–32 Matt. 8. 1–13	Dan. 9. 1–19 Rev. 11. 15–end	
G		Isa. 10.33 - 11.9 Matt. 8. 14–22	Dan. 9. 20–end Rev. ch. 12	
G		Isa. 11.10 - 12.end Matt. 8. 23–end	Dan. 10.1 - 11.1 Rev. 13. 1–10	
	Edmund, King of the East Angles, Martyr, 870			
Gr	Com. Martyr	Isa. 13. 1–13 Matt. 9. 1–17	Dan. ch. 12 Rev. 13. 11–end	
			ct	

		Sunday Principal Service Weekday Eucharist	Third Service Morning Prayer	Second Service Evening Prayer
21 Sunday	**CHRIST THE KING** The Sunday Next Before Advent			
R *or* **W**		Dan. 7. 9–10, 13–14 Ps. 93 Rev. 1. 4b–8 John 18. 33–37	*MP*: Ps. 29; 110 Isa. 32. 1–8 Rev. 3. 7–end	*EP*: Ps. 72 (*or* 72. 1–7) Dan. ch. 5 John 6. 1–15
22 Monday	*Cecilia, Martyr at Rome, c. 230*			
R *or* **G** **DEL 34**		Dan. 1. 1–6, 8–20 *Canticle*: Bless the Lord Luke 21. 1–4	Ps. 92; ***96*** *alt.* Ps. ***80***; 82 Isa. 14. 3–20 Matt. 9. 18–34	Ps. ***80***; 81 *alt.* Ps. ***85***; 86 Isa. 40. 1–11 Rev. 14. 1–13
23 Tuesday	**Clement, Bishop of Rome, Martyr, c. 100**			
R *or* **Gr**	Com. Martyr *or* *also* Phil. 3.17 – 4.3 Matt. 16. 13–19	Dan. 2. 31–45 *Canticle*: Benedicite 1–3 Luke 21. 5–11	Ps. ***97***; 98; 100 *alt.* Ps. 87; ***89. 1–18*** Isa. ch. 17 Matt. 9.35 – 10.15	Ps. 99; ***101*** *alt.* Ps. 89. 19–end Isa. 40. 12–26 Rev. 14.14 – 15.end
24 Wednesday				
R *or* **G**		Dan. 5. 1–6, 13–14, 16–17, 23–28 *Canticle*: Benedicite 4–5 Luke 21. 12–19	Ps. 110; 111; ***112*** *alt.* Ps. 119. 105–128 Isa. ch. 19 Matt. 10. 16–33	Ps. 121; ***122***; 123; 124 *alt.* Ps. ***91***; 93 Isa. 40.27 – 41.7 Rev. 16. 1–11
25 Thursday	*Catherine of Alexandria, Martyr, 4th century; Isaac Watts, Hymn Writer, 1748*			
R *or* **G**		Dan. 6. 12–end *Canticle*: Benedicite 6–8a Luke 21. 20–28	Ps. ***125***; 126; 127; 128 *alt.* Ps. 90; ***92*** Isa. 21. 1–12 Matt. 10.34 – 11.1	Ps. 131; 132; ***133*** *alt.* Ps. 94 Isa. 41. 8–20 Rev. 16. 12–end
26 Friday				
R *or* **G**		Dan. 7. 2–14 *Canticle*: Benedicite 8b–10a Luke 21. 29–33	Ps. 139 *alt.* Ps. ***88***; (95) Isa. 22. 1–14 Matt. 11. 2–19	Ps. ***146***; 147 *alt.* Ps. 102 Isa. 41.21 – 42.9 Rev. ch. 17
27 Saturday				
R *or* **G**		Dan. 7. 15–27 *Canticle*: Benedicite 10b–end Luke 21. 34–36	Ps. 145 *alt.* Ps. 96; ***97***; 100 Isa. ch. 24 Matt. 11. 20–end	Ps. 148; 149; ***150*** *alt.* Ps. 104 Isa. 42. 10–17 Rev. ch. 18 **P ct**
28 Sunday	**THE FIRST SUNDAY OF ADVENT** *Common Worship* Year C begins			
P		Jer. 33. 14–16 Ps. 25. 1–9 1 Thess. 3. 9–end Luke 21. 25–36	Ps. 44 Isa. 51. 4–11 Rom. 13. 11–end	Ps. 9 (*or* 9. 1–8) Joel 3. 9–end Rev. 14.13 – 15.4 *Gospel*: John 3. 1–17

	Calendar and Holy Communion	Morning Prayer	Evening Prayer	NOTES
	THE SUNDAY NEXT BEFORE ADVENT To celebrate Christ the King, see *Common Worship* provision.			
G	Jer. 23. 5–8 Ps. 85. 8–end Col. 1. 13–20 John 6. 5–14	Ps. 29; 110 Isa. 32. 1–8 Rev. 3. 7–end	Ps. 72 (*or* 72. 1–7) Dan. ch. 5 Rev. 1. 4b–8	
	Cecilia, Martyr at Rome, c. 230			
Gr	Com. Virgin Martyr	Isa. 14. 3–20 Matt. 9. 18–34	Isa. 40. 1–11 Rev. 14. 1–13	
	Clement, Bishop of Rome, Martyr, c. 100			
Gr	Com. Martyr	Isa. ch. 17 Matt. 9.35 - 10.15	Isa. 40. 12–26 Rev. 14.14 - 15.end	
G		Isa. ch. 19 Matt. 10. 16–33	Isa. 40.27 - 41.7 Rev. 16. 1–11	
	Catherine of Alexandria, Martyr, 4th century			
Gr	Com. Virgin Martyr	Isa. 21. 1–12 Matt. 10.34 - 11.1	Isa. 41. 8–20 Rev. 16. 12–end	
G		Isa. 22. 1–14 Matt. 11. 2–19	Isa. 41.21 - 42.9 Rev. ch. 17	
G		Isa. ch. 24 Matt. 11. 20–end	Isa. 42. 10–17 Rev. ch. 18 **P ct**	
	THE FIRST SUNDAY IN ADVENT Advent 1 Collect until Christmas Eve			
P	Mic. 4. 1–4, 6–7 Ps. 25. 1–9 Rom. 13. 8–14 Matt. 21. 1–13	Ps. 44 Isa. 51. 4–11 Rom. 13. 11–end	Ps. 9 (*or* 9. 1–8) Joel 3. 9–end Rev. 14.13 - 15.4	

		Sunday Principal Service Weekday Eucharist	Third Service Morning Prayer	Second Service Evening Prayer
29 Monday	Daily Eucharistic Lectionary Year 2 begins			
P		Isa. 2. 1–5 Ps. 122 Matt. 8. 5–11	Ps. ***50***; 54 *alt.* Ps. ***1***; 2; 3 Isa. 25. 1–9 Matt. 12. 1–21	Ps. 70; ***71*** *alt.* Ps. ***4***; 7 Isa. 42. 18–end Rev. ch. 19 *or First EP of Andrew the Apostle* Ps. 48 Isa. 49. 1–9a 1 Cor. 4. 9–16 **R ct**
	Day of Intercession and Thanksgiving for the Missionary Work of the Church			
		Isa. 49. 1–6; Isa. 52. 7–10; Mic. 4. 1–5 Acts 17. 12–end; 2 Cor. 5.14 - 6.2; Eph. 2. 13–end Ps. 2; 46; 47 Matt. 5. 13–16; Matt. 28. 16–end; John 17. 20–end		
30 Tuesday	**ANDREW THE APOSTLE**			
R		Isa. 52. 7–10 Ps. 19. 1–6 Rom. 10. 12–18 Matt. 4. 18–22	*MP*: Ps. 47; 147. 1–12 Ezek. 47. 1–12 *or* Ecclus. 14. 20–end John 12. 20–32	*EP*: Ps. 87; 96 Zech. 8. 20–end John 1. 35–42

December 2021

1 Wednesday	*Charles de Foucauld, Hermit in the Sahara, 1916*			
P		Isa. 25. 6–10a Ps. 23 Matt. 15. 29–37	Ps. 5; ***7*** *alt.* Ps. 119. 1–32 Isa. 28. 1–13 Matt. 12. 38–end	Ps. 76; ***77*** *alt.* Ps. ***11***; 12; 13 Isa. 43. 14–end Rev. 21. 1–8
2 Thursday				
P		Isa. 26. 1–6 Ps. 118. 18–27a Matt. 7. 21, 24–27	Ps. ***42***; 43 *alt.* Ps. 14; ***15***; 16 Isa. 28. 14–end Matt. 13. 1–23	Ps. ***40***; 46 *alt.* Ps. 18† Isa. 44. 1–8 Rev. 21. 9–21
3 Friday	*Francis Xavier, Missionary, Apostle of the Indies, 1552*			
P		Isa. 29. 17–end Ps. 27. 1–4, 16–17 Matt. 9. 27–31	Ps. ***25***; 26 *alt.* Ps. 17; ***19*** Isa. 29. 1–14 Matt. 13. 24–43	Ps. 16; ***17*** *alt.* Ps. 22 Isa. 44. 9–23 Rev. 21.22 - 22.5
4 Saturday	*John of Damascus, Monk, Teacher, c. 749; Nicholas Ferrar, Deacon, Founder of the Little Gidding Community, 1637*			
P		Isa. 30. 19–21, 23–26 Ps. 146. 4–9 Matt. 9.35 - 10.1, 6–8	Ps. ***9***; (10) *alt.* Ps. 20; 21; ***23*** Isa. 29. 15–end Matt. 13. 44–end	Ps. ***27***; 28 *alt.* Ps. ***24***; 25 Isa. 44.24 - 45.13 Rev. 22. 6–end **ct**

	Calendar and Holy Communion	Morning Prayer	Evening Prayer	NOTES
P		Isa. 25. 1–9 Matt. 12. 1–21	Isa. 42. 18–end Rev. ch. 19 *or First EP of Andrew the Apostle* (Ps. 48) Isa. 49. 1–9a 1 Cor. 4. 9–16 **R ct**	
	To celebrate the Day of Intercession and Thanksgiving for the Missionary Work of the Church, see *Common Worship* provision.			
G				
	ANDREW THE APOSTLE			
R	Zech. 8. 20–end Ps. 92. 1–5 Rom. 10. 9–end Matt. 4. 18–22	(Ps. 47; 147. 1–12) Ezek. 47. 1–12 *or* Ecclus. 14. 20–end John 12. 20–32	(Ps. 87; 96) Isa. 52. 7–10 John 1. 35–42	
P		Isa. 28. 1–13 Matt. 12. 38–end	Isa. 43. 14–end Rev. 21. 1–8	
P		Isa. 28. 14–end Matt. 13. 1–23	Isa. 44. 1–8 Rev. 21. 9–21	
P		Isa. 29. 1–14 Matt. 13. 24–43	Isa. 44. 9–23 Rev. 21.22 – 22.5	
P		Isa. 29. 15–end Matt. 13. 44–end	Isa. 44.24 – 45.13 Rev. 22. 6–end **ct**	

			Sunday Principal Service Weekday Eucharist	Third Service Morning Prayer	Second Service Evening Prayer
5 Sunday	**THE SECOND SUNDAY OF ADVENT**				
P			Baruch ch. 5 *or* Mal. 3. 1–4 *Canticle*: Benedictus Phil. 1. 3–11 Luke 3. 1–6	Ps. 80 Isa. 64. 1–7 Matt. 11. 2–11	Ps. 75; [76] Isa. 40. 1–11 Luke 1. 1–25
6 Monday	**Nicholas, Bishop of Myra, *c.* 326**				
Pw	Com. Bishop *also* Isa. 61. 1–3 1 Tim. 6. 6–11 Mark 10. 13–16	*or*	Isa. ch. 35 Ps. 85. 7–end Luke 5. 17–26	Ps. 44 *alt.* Ps. 27; ***30*** Isa. 30. 1–18 Matt. 14. 1–12	Ps. ***144***; 146 *alt.* Ps. 26; ***28***; 29 Isa. 45. 14–end 1 Thess. ch. 1
7 Tuesday	**Ambrose, Bishop of Milan, Teacher, 397**				
Pw	Com. Teacher *also* Isa. 41. 9b–13 Luke 22. 24–30	*or*	Isa. 40. 1–11 Ps. 96. 1, 10–end Matt. 18. 12–14	Ps. ***56***; 57 *alt.* Ps. 32; ***36*** Isa. 30. 19–end Matt. 14. 13–end	Ps. ***11***; 12; 13 *alt.* Ps. 33 Isa. ch. 46 1 Thess. 2. 1–12
8 Wednesday	**The Conception of the Blessed Virgin Mary** Ember Day*				
Pw	Com. BVM	*or*	Isa. 40. 25–end Ps. 103. 8–13 Matt. 11. 28–end	Ps. ***62***; 63 *alt.* Ps. 34 Isa. ch. 31 Matt. 15. 1–20	Ps. ***10***; 14 *alt.* Ps. 119. 33–56 Isa. ch. 47 1 Thess. 2. 13–end
9 Thursday					
P			Isa. 41. 13–20 Ps. 145. 1, 8–13 Matt. 11. 11–15	Ps. 53; ***54***; 60 *alt.* Ps. 37† Isa. ch. 32 Matt. 15. 21–28	Ps. 73 *alt.* Ps. 39; ***40*** Isa. 48. 1–11 1 Thess. ch. 3
10 Friday	Ember Day*				
P			Isa. 48. 17–19 Ps. 1 Matt. 11. 16–19	Ps. 85; ***86*** *alt.* Ps. 31 Isa. 33. 1–22 Matt. 15. 29–end	Ps. 82; ***90*** *alt.* Ps. 35 Isa. 48. 12–end 1 Thess. 4. 1–12
11 Saturday	Ember Day*				
P			Ecclus. 48. 1–4, 9–11 *or* 2 Kings 2. 9–12 Ps. 80. 1–4, 18–19 Matt. 17. 10–13	Ps. 145 *alt.* Ps. 41; ***42***; 43 Isa. ch. 35 Matt. 16. 1–12	Ps. 93; ***94*** *alt.* Ps. 45; ***46*** Isa. 49. 1–13 1 Thess. 4. 13–end **ct**
12 Sunday	**THE THIRD SUNDAY OF ADVENT**				
P			Zeph. 3. 14–end *Canticle*: Isa. 12. 2–end *or* Ps. 146. 4–end Phil. 4. 4–7 Luke 3. 7–18	Ps. 12; 14 Isa. 25. 1–9 1 Cor. 4. 1–5	Ps. 50. 1–6; [62] Isa. ch. 35 Luke 1. 57–66 [67–end]
13 Monday	**Lucy, Martyr at Syracuse, 304** *Samuel Johnson, Moralist, 1784*				
Pr	Com. Martyr *also* Wisd. 3. 1–7 2 Cor. 4. 6–15	*or*	Num. 24. 2–7, 15–17 Ps. 25. 3–8 Matt. 21. 23–27	Ps. 40 *alt.* Ps. 44 Isa. 38. 1–8, 21–22 Matt. 16. 13–end	Ps. 25; ***26*** *alt.* Ps. ***47***; 49 Isa. 49. 14–25 1 Thess. 5. 1–11

* For Ember Day provision, see p. 11.

	Calendar and Holy Communion	Morning Prayer	Evening Prayer	NOTES
	THE SECOND SUNDAY IN ADVENT			
P	2 Kings 22. 8–10; 23. 1–3 Ps. 50. 1–6 Rom. 15. 4–13 Luke 21. 25–33	Ps. 40 Isa. 64. 1–7 Luke 3. 1–6	Ps. 75 [76] Mal. 3. 1–4 Luke 1. 1–25	
	Nicholas, Bishop of Myra, *c.* 326			
Pw	Com. Bishop	Isa. 30. 1–18 Matt. 14. 1–12	Isa. 45. 14–end 1 Thess. ch. 1	
P		Isa. 30. 19–end Matt. 14. 13–end	Isa. ch. 46 1 Thess. 2. 1–12	
	The Conception of the Blessed Virgin Mary			
Pw		Isa. ch. 31 Matt. 15. 1–20	Isa. ch. 47 1 Thess. 2. 13–end	
P		Isa. ch. 32 Matt. 15. 21–28	Isa. 48. 1–11 1 Thess. ch. 3	
P		Isa. 33. 1–22 Matt. 15. 29–end	Isa. 48. 12–end 1 Thess. 4. 1–12	
P		Isa. ch. 35 Matt. 16. 1–12	Isa. 49. 1–13 1 Thess. 4. 13–end **ct**	
	THE THIRD SUNDAY IN ADVENT			
P	Isa. ch. 35 Ps. 80. 1–7 1 Cor. 4. 1–5 Matt. 11. 2–10	Ps. 12; 14 Isa. 25. 1–9 Luke 3. 7–18	Ps. 62 Zeph. 3. 14–end Luke 1. 57–66 [67–end]	
	Lucy, Martyr at Syracuse, 304			
Pr	Com. Virgin Martyr	Isa. 38. 1–8, 21–22 Matt. 16. 13–end	Isa. 49. 14–25 1 Thess. 5. 1–11	

		Sunday Principal Service Weekday Eucharist	Third Service Morning Prayer	Second Service Evening Prayer
14 Tuesday	**John of the Cross, Poet, Teacher, 1591**			
Pw	Com. Teacher *or* *esp.* 1 Cor. 2. 1–10 *also* John 14. 18–23	Zeph. 3. 1–2, 9–13 Ps. 34. 1–6, 21–22 Matt. 21. 28–32	Ps. ***70***; 74 *alt.* Ps. ***48***; 52 Isa. 38. 9–20 Matt. 17. 1–13	Ps. ***50***; 54 *alt.* Ps. 50 Isa. ch. 50 1 Thess. 5. 12–end
15 Wednesday				
P		Isa. 45. 6b–8, 18, 21b–end Ps. 85. 7–end Luke 7. 18b–23	Ps. ***75***; 96 *alt.* Ps. 119. 57–80 Isa. ch. 39 Matt. 17. 14–21	Ps. 25; ***82*** *alt.* Ps. ***59***; 60; (67) Isa. 51. 1–8 2 Thess. ch. 1
16 Thursday				
P		Isa. 54. 1–10 Ps. 30. 1–5, 11–end Luke 7. 24–30	Ps. ***76***; 97 *alt.* Ps. 56; ***57***; (63†) Zeph. 1.1 – 2.3 Matt. 17. 22–end	Ps. 44 *alt.* Ps. 61; ***62***; 64 Isa. 51. 9–16 2 Thess. ch. 2
17 Friday	O Sapientia *Eglantyne Jebb, Social Reformer, Founder of 'Save the Children', 1928*			
P		Gen. 49. 2, 8–10 Ps. 72. 1–5, 18–19 Matt. 1. 1–17	Ps. 77; ***98*** *alt.* Ps. ***51***; 54 Zeph. 3. 1–13 Matt. 18. 1–20	Ps. 49 *alt.* Ps. 38 Isa. 51. 17–end 2 Thess. ch. 3
18 Saturday				
P		Jer. 23. 5–8 Ps. 72. 1–2, 12–13, 18–end Matt. 1. 18–24	Ps. 71 *alt.* Ps. 68 Zeph. 3. 14–end Matt. 18. 21–end	Ps. 42; ***43*** *alt.* Ps. 65; ***66*** Isa. 52. 1–12 Jude **ct**
19 Sunday	**THE FOURTH SUNDAY OF ADVENT**			
P		Mic. 5. 2–5a *Canticle*: Magnificat *or* Ps. 80. 1–8 Heb. 10. 5–10 Luke 1. 39–45 [46–55]	Ps. 144 Isa. 32. 1–8 Rev. 22. 6–end	Ps. 123; [131] Isa. 10.33 – 11.10 Matt. 1. 18–end
20 Monday				
P		Isa. 7. 10–14 Ps. 24. 1–6 Luke 1. 26–38	Ps. ***46***; 95 Mal. 1. 1, 6–end Matt. 19. 1–12	Ps. ***4***; 9 Isa. 52.13 – 53.end 1 Pet. 1. 1–15
21 Tuesday*				
P		Zeph. 3. 14–18 Ps. 33. 1–4, 11–12, 20–end Luke 1. 39–45	Ps. ***121***; 122; 123 Mal. 2. 1–16 Matt. 19. 13–15	Ps. 80; ***84*** Isa. ch. 54 2 Pet. 1.16 – 2.3
22 Wednesday				
P		1 Sam. 1. 24–end Ps. 113 Luke 1. 46–56	Ps. ***124***; 125; 126; 127 Mal. 2.17 – 3.12 Matt. 19. 16–end	Ps. 24; ***48*** Isa. ch. 55 2 Pet. 2. 4–end

*Thomas the Apostle may be celebrated on 21 December instead of 3 July.

	Calendar and Holy Communion	Morning Prayer	Evening Prayer	NOTES
P		Isa. 38. 9–20 Matt. 17. 1–13	Isa. ch. 50 1 Thess. 5. 12–end	
	Ember Day			
P	Ember CEG	Isa. ch. 39 Matt. 17. 14–21	Isa. 51. 1–8 2 Thess. ch. 1	
	O Sapientia			
P		Zeph. 1.1 – 2.3 Matt. 17. 22–end	Isa. 51. 9–16 2 Thess. ch. 2	
	Ember Day			
P	Ember CEG	Zeph. 3. 1–13 Matt. 18. 1–20	Isa. 51. 17–end 2 Thess. ch. 3	
	Ember Day			
P	Ember CEG	Zeph. 3. 14–end Matt. 18. 21–end	Isa. 52. 1–12 Jude **ct**	
	THE FOURTH SUNDAY IN ADVENT			
P	Isa. 40. 1–9 Ps. 145. 17–end Phil. 4. 4–7 John 1. 19–28	Ps. 144 Isa. 32. 1–8 Rev. 22. 6–end	Ps. 123; [131] Isa. 10.33 – 11.10 Matt. 1. 18–end	
P		Mal. 1. 1, 6–end Matt. 19. 1–12	Isa. 52.13 – 53.end 1 Pet. 1. 1–15 *or First EP of Thomas* (Ps. 27) Isa. ch. 35 Heb. 10.35 – 11.1 **R ct**	
	THOMAS THE APOSTLE			
R	Job 42. 1–6 Ps. 139. 1–11 Eph. 2. 19–end John 20. 24–end	(Ps. 92; 146) 2 Sam. 15. 17–21 *or* Ecclus. ch. 2 John 11. 1–16	(Ps. 139) Hab. 2. 1–4 1 Pet. 1. 3–12	
P		Mal. 2.17 – 3.12 Matt. 19. 16–end	Isa. ch. 55 2 Pet. 2. 4–end	

		Sunday Principal Service Weekday Eucharist	Third Service Morning Prayer	Second Service Evening Prayer
23 Thursday				
P		Mal. 3. 1–4; 4. 5–end Ps. 25. 3–9 Luke 1. 57–66	Ps. 128; 129; ***130***; 131 Mal. 3.13 - 4.end Matt. 23. 1–12	Ps. 89. 1–37 Isa. 56. 1–8 2 Pet. ch. 3
24 Friday	**CHRISTMAS EVE**			
P		*Morning Eucharist* 2 Sam. 7. 1–5, 8–11, 16 Ps. 89. 2, 19–27 Acts 13. 16–26 Luke 1. 67–79	Ps. 45; 113 Nahum ch. 1 Matt. 23. 13–28	Ps. 85 Zech. ch. 2 Rev. 1. 1–8
25 Saturday	**CHRISTMAS DAY**			
𝔚	*Any of the following sets of readings may be used on the evening of Christmas Eve and on Christmas Day. Set III should be used at some service during the celebration.*	*I* Isa. 9. 2–7 Ps. 96 Titus 2. 11–14 Luke 2. 1–14 [15–20] *II* Isa. 62. 6–end Ps. 97 Titus 3. 4–7 Luke 2. [1–7] 8–20 *III* Isa. 52. 7–10 Ps. 98 Heb. 1. 1–4 [5–12] John 1. 1–14	*MP*: Ps. ***110***; 117 Isa. 62. 1–5 Matt. 1. 18–end	*EP*: Ps. 8 Isa. 65. 17–25 Phil. 2. 5–11 *or* Luke 2. 1–20 *if it has not been used at the principal service of the day*
26 Sunday	**STEPHEN, DEACON, FIRST MARTYR** (or transferred to 29 December)			
R	*The reading from Acts must be used as either the first or second reading at the Eucharist.*	2 Chron. 24. 20–22 *or* Acts 7. 51–end Ps. 119. 161–168 Acts 7. 51–end *or* Gal. 2. 16b–20 Matt. 10. 17–22	*MP*: Ps. ***13***; 31. 1–8; 150 Jer. 26. 12–15 Acts ch. 6	*EP*: Ps. 57; ***86*** Gen. 4. 1–10 Matt. 23. 34–end
	or, for The First Sunday of Christmas			
W		1 Sam. 2. 18–20, 26 Ps. 148 (*or* 148. 1–6) Col. 3. 12–17 Luke 2. 41–end	Ps. 105. 1–11 Isa. 41.21 - 42.1 1 John 1. 1–7	Ps. 132 Isa. ch. 61 Gal. 3.27 - 4.7 *Gospel*: Luke 2. 15–21
27 Monday	**JOHN, APOSTLE AND EVANGELIST**			
W		Exod. 33. 7–11a Ps. 117 1 John ch. 1 John 21. 19b–end	*MP*: Ps. ***21***; 147. 13–end Exod. 33. 12–end 1 John 2. 1–11	*EP*: Ps. 97 Isa. 6. 1–8 1 John 5. 1–12

	Calendar and Holy Communion	Morning Prayer	Evening Prayer	NOTES
P		Mal. 3.13 - 4.end Matt. 23. 1–12	Isa. 56. 1–8 2 Pet. ch. 3	
	CHRISTMAS EVE			
P	Collect (1) Christmas Eve (2) Advent 1 Mic. 5. 2–5a Ps. 24 Titus 3. 3–7 Luke 2. 1–14	Nahum ch. 1 Matt. 23. 13–28	Zech. ch. 2 Rev. 1. 1–8	
	CHRISTMAS DAY			
𝔚	Isa. 9. 2–7 Ps. 98 Heb. 1. 1–12 John 1. 1–14	Ps. 110; 117 Isa. 62. 1–5 Matt. 1. 18–end	Ps. 8 Isa. 65. 17–25 Phil. 2. 5–11 *or* Luke 2. 1–20	
	STEPHEN, DEACON, FIRST MARTYR (or transferred to 29 December)			
R	Collect (1) Stephen (2) Christmas 2 Chron. 24. 20–22 Ps. 119. 161–168 Acts 7. 55–end Matt. 23. 34–end	Ps. ***13***; 31. 1–8; 150 Jer. 26. 12–15 Acts ch. 6	Ps. 57; ***86*** Gen. 4. 1–10 Matt. 10. 17–22	
	or, for The Sunday after Christmas Day			
W	Isa. 62. 10–12 Ps. 45. 1–7 Gal. 4. 1–7 Matt. 1. 18–end	Ps. 105. 1–11 Isa. 41.21 - 42.1 1 John 1. 1–7	Ps. 132 Isa. ch. 61 Luke 2. 15–21	
	JOHN, APOSTLE AND EVANGELIST			
W	Collect (1) John (2) Christmas Exod. 33. 18–end Ps. 92. 11–end 1 John ch. 1 John 21. 19b–end	(Ps. ***21***; 147. 13–end) Exod. 33. 7–11a 1 John 2. 1–11	(Ps. 97) Isa. 6. 1–8 1 John 5. 1–12	

		Sunday Principal Service Weekday Eucharist	Third Service Morning Prayer	Second Service Evening Prayer
28 Tuesday	**THE HOLY INNOCENTS**			
R		Jer. 31. 15–17 Ps. 124 1 Cor. 1. 26–29 Matt. 2. 13–18	*MP*: Ps. ***36***; 146 Baruch 4. 21–27 *or* Gen. 37. 13–20 Matt. 18. 1–10	*EP*: Ps. 123; ***128*** Isa. 49. 14–25 Mark 10. 13–16
29 Wednesday	**Thomas Becket, Archbishop of Canterbury, Martyr, 1170*** (For Stephen, Deacon, First Martyr, see provision on 26 December.)			
Wr	Com. Martyr *or* *esp*. Matt. 10. 28–33 *also* Ecclus. 51. 1–8	1 John 2. 3–11 Ps. 96. 1–4 Luke 2. 22–35	Ps. ***19***; 20 Jonah ch. 1 Col. 1. 1–14	Ps. 131; ***132*** Isa. 57. 15–end John 1. 1–18
30 Thursday				
W		1 John 2. 12–17 Ps. 96. 7–10 Luke 2. 36–40	Ps. 111; 112; ***113*** Jonah ch. 2 Col. 1. 15–23	Ps. ***65***; 84 Isa. 59. 1–15a John 1. 19–28
31 Friday	*John Wyclif, Reformer, 1384*			
W		1 John 2. 18–21 Ps. 96. 1, 11–end John 1. 1–18	Ps. 102 Jonah chs 3 & 4 Col. 1.24 - 2.7	Ps. ***90***; 148 Isa. 59. 15b–end John 1. 29–34 *or First EP of The Naming of Jesus* Ps. 148 Jer. 23. 1–6 Col. 2. 8–15 **ct**

*Thomas Becket may be celebrated on 7 July instead of 29 December.

	Calendar and Holy Communion	Morning Prayer	Evening Prayer	NOTES
	THE HOLY INNOCENTS			
R	Collect (1) Innocents (2) Christmas Jer. 31. 10–17 Ps. 123 Rev. 14. 1–5 Matt. 2. 13–18	(Ps. ***36***; 146) Baruch 4. 21–27 *or* Gen. 37. 13–20 Matt. 18. 1–10	(Ps. 124; ***128***) Isa. 49. 14–25 Mark 10. 13–16	
W		Jonah ch. 1 Col. 1. 1–14	Isa. 57. 15–end John 1. 1–18	
W		Jonah ch. 2 Col. 1. 15–23	Isa. 59. 1–15a John 1. 19–28	
	Silvester, Bishop of Rome, 335			
W	Com. Bishop	Jonah chs 3 & 4 Col. 1.24 – 2.7	Isa. 59. 15b–end John 1. 29–34 *or First EP of The Circumcision of Christ* (Ps. 148) Jer. 23. 1–6 Col. 2. 8–15 **ct**	

The *Common Worship* Additional Weekday Lectionary

The Additional Weekday Lectionary provides two readings on a one-year cycle for each day (except for Sundays, Principal Feasts and Holy Days, Festivals and Holy Week). They 'stand alone' and are intended particularly for use in those churches and cathedrals that attract occasional rather than regular congregations. The Additional Weekday Lectionary has been designed to complement rather than replace the existing Weekday Lectionary. Thus a church with a regular congregation in the morning and a congregation made up mainly of visitors in the evening would continue to use the Weekday Lectionary in the morning but might choose to use this Additional Weekday Lectionary for Evening Prayer.

Psalms are not provided, since the Weekday Lectionary already offers a variety of approaches with regard to psalmody. This Lectionary is not intended for use at the Eucharist; the Daily Eucharistic Lectionary is already authorized for that purpose.

On Sundays, Principal Feasts, other Principal Holy Days, Festivals, and in Holy Week, where no readings are provided in this table, the lectionary provision in the main part of this volume should be used.

Date		Old Testament	New Testament
November 2020			
29	S	THE FIRST SUNDAY OF ADVENT	
30	M	ANDREW	
December 2020			
1	Tu	Zeph. 3. 14–end	1 Thess. 4. 13–end
2	W	Isa. 65.17 – 66.2	Matt. 24. 1–14
3	Th	Mic. 5. 2–5a	John 3. 16–21
4	F	Isa. 66. 18–end	Luke 13. 22–30
5	Sa	Mic. 7. 8–15	Rom. 15.30 – 16.7, 25–end
6	S	THE SECOND SUNDAY OF ADVENT	
7	M	Jer. 7. 1–11	Phil. 4. 4–9
8	Tu	Dan. 7. 9–14	Matt. 24. 15–28
9	W	Amos 9. 11–end	Rom. 13. 8–end
10	Th	Jer. 23. 5–8	Mark 11. 1–11
11	F	Jer. 33. 14–22	Luke 21. 25–36
12	Sa	Zech. 14. 4–11	Rev. 22. 1–7
13	S	THE THIRD SUNDAY OF ADVENT	
14	M	Isa. 40. 1–11	Matt. 3. 1–12
15	Tu	Lam. 3. 22–33	1 Cor. 1. 1–9
16	W	Joel 3. 9–16	Matt. 24. 29–35
17	Th	Ecclus. 24. 1–9 *or* Prov. 8. 22–31	1 Cor. 2. 1–13
18	F	Exod. 3. 1–6	Acts 7. 20–36
19	Sa	Isa. 11. 1–9	Rom. 15. 7–13
20	S	THE FOURTH SUNDAY OF ADVENT	
21	M	Num. 24. 15b–19	Rev. 22. 10–21
22	Tu	Jer. 30. 7–11a	Acts 4. 1–12
23	W	Isa. 7. 10–15	Matt. 1. 18–23
24	Th	*At Evening Prayer the readings for Christmas Eve are used. At other services, the following readings are used:* Isa. 29. 13–18	1 John 4. 7–16
25	F	**CHRISTMAS DAY**	
26	Sa	STEPHEN	
27	S	JOHN THE EVANGELIST (THE FIRST SUNDAY OF CHRISTMAS)	
28	M	THE HOLY INNOCENTS	
29	Tu	Mic. 1. 1–4; 2. 12–13	Luke 2. 1–7
30	W	Isa. 9. 2–7	John 8. 12–20
31	Th	Eccles. 3. 1–13	Rev. 21. 1–8
January 2021			
1	F	**THE NAMING AND CIRCUMCISION OF JESUS**	
2	Sa	Isa. 66. 6–14 *Where, for pastoral reasons, The Epiphany is celebrated on Sunday 3 January, the readings for the Eve of Epiphany are used at Evening Prayer.*	Matt. 12. 46–50
3	S	THE SECOND SUNDAY OF CHRISTMAS (*or The Epiphany*)	
4	M	Isa. 63. 7–16 *Where, for pastoral reasons, The Epiphany is celebrated on Sunday 3 January, the following readings are used:* Deut. 6. 4–15	Gal. 3.23 – 4.7 / John 10. 31–end
5	Tu	*At Evening Prayer the readings for the Eve of the Epiphany are used. At other services, the following readings are used:* Isa. ch. 12 *Where, for pastoral reasons, The Epiphany is celebrated on Sunday 3 January, the following readings are used:* Isa. 63. 7–16	2 Cor. 2. 12–end / Gal. 3.23 – 4.7
6	W	**THE EPIPHANY** *Where, for pastoral reasons, The Epiphany is celebrated on Sunday 3 January, the following readings are used:* Isa. ch. 12	2 Cor. 2. 12–end
7	Th	Gen. 25. 19–end	Eph. 1. 1–6
8	F	Joel 2. 28–end	Eph. 1. 7–14
9	Sa	*At Evening Prayer the readings for the Eve of the Baptism of Christ are used. At other services, the following readings are used:* Prov. 8. 12–21	Eph. 1. 15–end
10	S	THE BAPTISM OF CHRIST (The First Sunday of Epiphany)	
11	M	Isa. 41. 14–20	John 1. 29–34
12	Tu	Exod. 17. 1–7	Acts 8. 26–end
13	W	Exod. 15. 1–19	Col. 2. 8–15
14	Th	Zech. 6. 9–15	1 Pet. 2. 4–10
15	F	Isa. 51. 7–16	Gal. 6. 14–18
16	Sa	Lev. 16. 11–22	Heb. 10. 19–25
17	S	THE SECOND SUNDAY OF EPIPHANY	
18	M	1 Kings. 17. 8–16	Mark 8. 1–10
19	Tu	1 Kings 19. 1–9a	Mark 1. 9–15
20	W	1 Kings 19. 9b–18	Mark 9. 2–13
21	Th	Lev. 11. 1–8, 13–19, 41–45	Acts 10. 9–16
22	F	Isa. 49. 8–13	Acts 10. 34–43
23	Sa	Gen. 35. 1–15	Acts 10. 44–end
24	S	THE THIRD SUNDAY OF EPIPHANY	
25	M	CONVERSION OF PAUL	
26	Tu	Ezek. 20. 39–44	John 17. 20–end
27	W	Neh. 2. 1–10	Rom. 12. 1–8
28	Th	Deut. 26. 16–end	Rom. 14. 1–9
29	F	Lev. 19. 9–28	Rom. 15. 1–7
30	Sa	Jer. 33. 1–11 *or, where The Presentation is celebrated on Sunday 31 January, First EP of Presentation of Christ*	1 Pet. 5. 5b–end
31	S	THE FOURTH SUNDAY OF EPIPHANY (*or The Presentation*)	
February			
1	M	Jonah ch. 3	2 Cor. 5. 11–21
2	Tu	**THE PRESENTATION** *or* Prov. 4. 10–end	Matt. 5. 13–20
3	W	Isa. 61. 1–9	Luke 7. 18–30
4	Th	Isa. 52. 1–12	Matt. 10. 1–15
5	F	Isa. 56. 1–8	Matt. 28. 16–end
6	Sa	Hab. 2. 1–4	Rev. 14. 1–7
7	S	THE SECOND SUNDAY BEFORE LENT	
8	M	Isa. 61. 1–9	Mark 6. 1–13
9	Tu	Isa. 52. 1–10	Rom. 10. 5–21

10	W	Isa. 52.13 – 53.6	Rom. 15. 14–21
11	Th	Isa. 53. 4–12	2 Cor. 4. 1–10
12	F	Zech. 8. 16–end	Matt. 10. 1–15
13	Sa	Jer. 1. 4–10	Matt. 10. 16–22
14	S	**THE SUNDAY NEXT BEFORE LENT**	
15	M	2 Kings 2. 13–22	3 John
16	Tu	Judges 14. 5–17	Rev. 10. 4–11
17	W	**ASH WEDNESDAY**	
18	Th	Gen. 2. 7–end	Heb. 2. 5–end
19	F	Gen. 4. 1–12	Heb. 4. 12–end
20	Sa	2 Kings 22. 11–end	Heb. 5. 1–10
21	S	**THE FIRST SUNDAY OF LENT**	
22	M	Gen. 6. 11–end; 7. 11–16	Luke 4. 14–21
23	Tu	Deut. 31. 7–13	1 John 3. 1–10
24	W	Gen. 11. 1–9	Matt. 24. 15–28
25	Th	Gen. 13. 1–13	1 Pet. 2. 13–end
26	F	Gen. 21. 1–8	Luke 9. 18–27
27	Sa	Gen. 32. 22–32	2 Pet. 1. 10–end
28	S	**THE SECOND SUNDAY OF LENT**	

March

1	M	1 Chron. 21. 1–17	1 John 2. 1–8
2	Tu	Zech. ch. 3	2 Pet. 2. 1–10a
3	W	Job 1. 1–22	Luke 21.34 – 22.6
4	Th	2 Chron. 29. 1–11	Mark 11. 15–19
5	F	Exod. 19. 1–9a	1 Pet. 1. 1–9
6	Sa	Exod. 19. 9b–19	Acts 7. 44–50
7	S	**THE THIRD SUNDAY OF LENT**	
8	M	Josh. 4. 1–13	Luke 9. 1–11
9	Tu	Exod. 15. 22–27	Heb. 10. 32–end
10	W	Gen. 9. 8–17	1 Pet. 3. 18–end
11	Th	Dan. 12. 5–end	Mark 13. 21–end
12	F	Num. 20. 1–13	1 Cor. 10. 23–end
13	Sa	Isa. 43. 14–end	Heb. 3. 1–15
14	S	**THE FOURTH SUNDAY OF LENT (Mothering Sunday)**	
15	M	2 Kings 24.18 – 25.7	1 Cor. 15. 20–34
16	Tu	Jer. 13. 12–19	Acts 13. 26–35
17	W	Jer. 13. 20–27	1 Pet. 1.17 – 2.3
18	Th	Jer. 22. 11–19	Luke 11. 37–52
19	F	**JOSEPH OF NAZARETH**	
20	Sa	Ezra ch. 1	2 Cor. 1. 12–19
21	S	**THE FIFTH SUNDAY OF LENT (Passiontide begins)**	
22	M	Joel 2. 12–17	2 John
23	Tu	Isa. 58. 1–14	Mark 10. 32–45
24	W	Job 36. 1–12	John 14. 1–14
25	Th	**THE ANNUNCIATION**	
26	F	Lam. 5. 1–3, 19–22	John 12. 20–26
27	Sa	Job 17. 6–end	John 12. 27–36
28	S	**PALM SUNDAY** HOLY WEEK	

April

4	S	**EASTER DAY**	
5	M	Isa. 54. 1–14	Rom. 1. 1–7
6	Tu	Isa. 51. 1–11	John 5. 19–29
7	W	Isa. 26. 1–19	John 20. 1–10
8	Th	Isa. 43. 14–21	Rev. 1. 4–end
9	F	Isa. 42. 10–17	1 Thess. 5. 1–11
10	Sa	Job 14. 1–14	John 21. 1–14
11	S	**THE SECOND SUNDAY OF EASTER**	
12	M	Ezek. 1. 22–end	Rev. ch. 4
13	Tu	Prov. 8. 1–11	Acts 16. 6–15
14	W	Hos. 5.15 – 6.6	1 Cor. 15. 1–11
15	Th	Jonah ch. 2	Mark 4. 35–end
16	F	Gen. 6. 9–end	1 Pet. 3. 8–end
17	Sa	1 Sam. 2. 1–8	Matt. 28. 8–15
18	S	**THE THIRD SUNDAY OF EASTER**	
19	M	Exod. 24. 1–11	Rev. ch. 5
20	Tu	Lev. 19. 9–18, 32–end	Matt. 5. 38–end
21	W	Gen. 3. 8–21	1 Cor. 15. 12–28
22	Th	Isa. 33. 13–22	Mark 6. 47–end
23	F	**GEORGE**	
24	Sa	Isa. 61.10 – 62.5	Luke 24. 1–12
25	S	**THE FOURTH SUNDAY OF EASTER**	
26	M	**MARK** (transferred)	
27	Tu	Job 31. 13–23	Matt. 7. 1–12
28	W	Gen. 2. 4b–9	1 Cor. 15. 35–49
29	Th	Prov. 28. 3–end	Mark 10. 17–31
30	F	Eccles. 12. 1–8	Rom. 6. 1–11

May

1	Sa	**PHILIP AND JAMES**	
2	S	**THE FIFTH SUNDAY OF EASTER**	
3	M	Gen. 15. 1–18	Rom. 4. 13–end
4	Tu	Deut. 8. 1–10	Matt. 6. 19–end
5	W	Hos. 13. 4–14	1 Cor. 15. 50–end
6	Th	Exod. 3. 1–15	Mark 12. 18–27
7	F	Ezek. 36. 33–end	Rom. 8. 1–11
8	Sa	Isa. 38. 9–20	Luke 24. 33–end
9	S	**THE SIXTH SUNDAY OF EASTER**	
10	M	Prov. 4. 1–13	Phil. 2. 1–11
11	Tu	Isa. 32. 12–end	Rom. 5. 1–11
12	W	*At Evening Prayer the readings for the Eve of Ascension Day are used. At other services, the following readings are used*: Isa. 43. 1–13	Titus 2.11 – 3.8
13	Th	**ASCENSION DAY**	
14	F	**MATTHIAS** *The following readings are used where Matthias is celebrated on Wednesday 24 February*: Exod. 35.30 – 36.1	Gal. 5. 13–end
15	Sa	Num. 11. 16–17, 24–29	1 Cor. ch. 2
16	S	**THE SEVENTH SUNDAY OF EASTER** (Sunday after Ascension Day)	
17	M	Num. 27. 15–end	1 Cor. ch. 3
18	Tu	1 Sam. 10. 1–10	1 Cor. 12. 1–13
19	W	1 Kings 19. 1–18	Matt. 3. 13–end
20	Th	Ezek. 11. 14–20	Matt. 9.35 – 10.20
21	F	Ezek. 36. 22–28	Matt. 12. 22–32
22	Sa	*At Evening Prayer the readings for the Eve of Pentecost are used. At other services, the following readings are used*: Mic. 3. 1–8	Eph. 6. 10–20
23	S	**PENTECOST** (Whit Sunday)	
24	M	Gen. 12. 1–9	Rom. 4. 13–end
25	Tu	Gen. 13. 1–12	Rom. 12. 9–end
26	W	Gen. ch. 15	Rom. 4. 1–8
27	Th	Gen. 22. 1–18	Heb. 11. 8–19
28	F	Isa. 51. 1–8	John 8. 48–end
29	Sa	*At Evening Prayer the readings for the Eve of Trinity Sunday are used. At other services, the following readings are used*: Ecclus. 44. 19–23 *or* Josh. 2. 1–15	James 2. 14–26
30	S	**TRINITY SUNDAY**	
31	M	**THE VISITATION** *Where The Visitation is celebrated on 2 July*: Exod. 2. 1–10	Heb. 11. 23–31

June

1	Tu	Exod. 2. 11–end	Acts 7. 17–29
2	W	Exod. 3. 1–12	Acts 7. 30–38
3	Th	*Day of Thanksgiving for the Institution of the Holy Communion (Corpus Christi), or, where Corpus Christi is celebrated as a Lesser Festival*: Exod. 6. 1–13	John 9. 24–38
4	F	Exod. 34. 1–10	Mark 7. 1–13
5	Sa	Exod. 34. 27–end	2 Cor. 3. 7–end
6	S	**THE FIRST SUNDAY AFTER TRINITY**	
7	M	Gen. 37. 1–11	Rom. 12. 9–21
8	Tu	Gen. 41. 15–40	Mark 13. 1–13
9	W	Gen. 42. 17–end	Matt. 18. 1–14
10	Th	Gen. 45. 1–15	Acts 7. 9–16
11	F	**BARNABAS**	
12	Sa	Gen. 50. 4–21	Luke 15. 11–end

13	S	**THE SECOND SUNDAY AFTER TRINITY**	
14	M	Isa. ch. 32	James 3. 13–end
15	Tu	Prov. 3. 1–18	Matt. 5. 1–12
16	W	Judg. 6. 1–16	Matt. 5. 13–24
17	Th	Jer. 6. 9–15	1 Tim. 2. 1–6
18	F	1 Sam. 16. 14–end	John 14. 15–end
19	Sa	Isa. 6. 1–9	Rev. 19. 9–end
20	S	**THE THIRD SUNDAY AFTER TRINITY**	
21	M	Exod. 13. 13b–end	Luke 15. 1–10
22	Tu	Prov. 1. 20–end	James 5. 13–end
23	W	Isa. 5. 8–24	James 1. 17–25
24	Th	**THE BIRTH OF JOHN THE BAPTIST**	
25	F	Jer. 15. 15–end	Luke 16. 19–31
26	Sa	Isa. 25. 1–9	Acts 2. 22–33
27	S	**THE FOURTH SUNDAY AFTER TRINITY**	
28	M	Exod. 20. 1–17	Matt. 6. 1–15
29	Tu	**PETER AND PAUL**	
30	W	Isa. 24. 1–15	1 Cor. 6. 1–11

July

1	Th	Job ch. 7	Matt. 7. 21–29
2	F	Jer. 20. 7–end	Matt. 27. 27–44
3	Sa	**THOMAS**	
		Where Thomas is celebrated on 21 December:	
		Job ch. 28	Heb. 11.32 – 12.2
4	S	**THE FIFTH SUNDAY AFTER TRINITY**	
5	M	Exod. 32. 1–14	Col. 3. 1–11
6	Tu	Prov. 9. 1–12	2 Thess. 2.13 – 3.5
7	W	Isa. 26. 1–9	Rom. 8. 12–27
8	Th	Jer. 8.18 – 9.6	John 13. 21–35
9	F	2 Sam. 5. 1–12	Matt. 27. 45–56
10	Sa	Hos. 11. 1–11	Matt. 28. 1–7
11	S	**THE SIXTH SUNDAY AFTER TRINITY**	
12	M	Exod. 40. 1–16	Luke 14. 15–24
13	Tu	Prov. 11. 1–12	Mark 12. 38–44
14	W	Isa. 33. 2–10	Phil. 1. 1–11
15	Th	Job ch. 38	Luke 18. 1–14
16	F	Job 42. 1–6	John 3. 1–15
17	Sa	Eccles. 9. 1–11	Heb. 1. 1–9
18	S	**THE SEVENTH SUNDAY AFTER TRINITY**	
19	M	Num. 23. 1–12	1 Cor. 1. 10–17
20	Tu	Prov. 12. 1–12	Gal. 3. 1–14
21	W	Isa. 49. 8–13	2 Cor. 8. 1–11
22	Th	**MARY MAGDALENE**	
23	F	2 Sam. 18. 18–end	Matt. 27. 57–66
24	Sa	Isa. 55. 1–7	Mark 16. 1–8
25	S	**JAMES** *or* **THE EIGHTH SUNDAY AFTER TRINITY**	
26	M	Joel 3. 16–21	Mark 4. 21–34
27	Tu	Prov. 12. 13–end	John 1. 43–51
28	W	Isa. 55. 8–end	2 Tim. 2. 8–19
29	Th	Isa. 38. 1–8	Mark 5. 21–43
30	F	Jer. 14. 1–9	Luke 8. 4–15
31	Sa	Eccles. 5. 10–19	1 Tim. 6. 6–16

August

1	S	**THE NINTH SUNDAY AFTER TRINITY**	
2	M	Josh. 1. 1–9	1 Cor. 9. 19–end
3	Tu	Prov. 15. 1–11	Gal. 2. 15–end
4	W	Isa. 49. 1–7	1 John 1
5	Th	Prov. 27. 1–12	John 15. 12–27
6	F	**THE TRANSFIGURATION**	
7	Sa	Zech. 7.8 – 8.8	Luke 20. 27–40
8	S	**THE TENTH SUNDAY AFTER TRINITY**	
9	M	Judg. 13. 1–23	Luke 10. 38–42
10	Tu	Prov. 15. 15–end	Matt. 15. 21–28
11	W	Isa. 45. 1–7	Eph. 4. 1–16
12	Th	Jer. 16. 1–5	Luke 12. 35–48
13	F	Jer. 18. 1–11	Heb. 1. 1–9
14	Sa	Jer. 26. 1–19	Eph. 3. 1–13
15	S	**THE BLESSED VIRGIN MARY** *or* **THE ELEVENTH SUNDAY AFTER TRINITY**	
16	M	Ruth 2. 1–13	Luke 10. 25–37
17	Tu	Prov. 16. 1–11	Phil. 3. 4b–end
18	W	Deut. 11. 1–21	2 Cor. 9. 6–end
19	Th	Ecclus. ch. 2	John 16. 1–15
		or Eccles. 2. 12–25	
20	F	Obad. 1–10	John 19. 1–16
21	Sa	2 Kings 2. 11–14	Luke 24. 36–end
22	S	**THE TWELFTH SUNDAY AFTER TRINITY**	
23	M	1 Sam. 17. 32–50	Matt. 8. 14–22
24	Tu	**BARTHOLOMEW**	
25	W	Jer. 5. 20–end	2 Pet. 3. 8–end
26	Th	Dan. 2. 1–23	Luke 10. 1–20
27	F	Dan. 3. 1–28	Rev. ch. 15
28	Sa	Dan. ch. 6	Phil. 2. 14–24
29	S	**THE THIRTEENTH SUNDAY AFTER TRINITY**	
30	M	2 Sam. 7. 4–17	2 Cor. 5. 1–10
31	Tu	Prov. 18. 10–21	Rom. 14. 10–end

September

1	W	Judg. 4. 1–10	Rom. 1. 8–17
2	Th	Isa. 49. 14–end	John 16. 16–24
3	F	Job 9. 1–24	Mark 15. 21–32
4	Sa	Exod. 19. 1–9	John 20. 11–18
5	S	**THE FOURTEENTH SUNDAY AFTER TRINITY**	
6	M	Hag. ch. 1	Mark 7. 9–23
7	Tu	Prov. 21. 1–18	Mark 6. 30–44
8	W	Hos. 11. 1–11	1 John 4. 9–end
9	Th	Lam. 3. 34–48	Rom. 7. 14–end
10	F	2 Kings 19. 4–18	1 Thess. ch. 3
11	Sa	Ecclus. 4. 1–28	2 Tim. 3. 10–end
		or Deut. 29. 2–15	
12	S	**THE FIFTEENTH SUNDAY AFTER TRINITY**	
13	M	Wisd. 6. 12–21	Matt. 15. 1–9
		or Job 12. 1–16	
14	Tu	**HOLY CROSS DAY**	
15	W	Prov. 2. 1–15	Col. 1. 9–20
16	Th	Baruch 3. 14–end	John 1. 1–18
		or Gen. 1. 1–13	
17	F	Ecclus. 1. 1–20	1 Cor. 1. 18–end
		or Deut. 7. 7–16	
18	Sa	Wisd. 9. 1–12	Luke 2. 41–end
		or Jer. 1. 4–10	
19	S	**THE SIXTEENTH SUNDAY AFTER TRINITY**	
20	M	Gen. 21. 1–13	Luke 1. 26–38
21	Tu	**MATTHEW**	
22	W	2 Kings 4. 1–7	John 2. 1–11
23	Th	2 Kings 4. 25b–37	Mark 3. 19b–35
24	F	Judith 8. 9–17, 28–36	John 19. 25b–30
		or Ruth 1. 1–18	
25	Sa	Exod. 15. 19–27	Acts 1. 6–14
26	S	**THE SEVENTEENTH SUNDAY AFTER TRINITY**	
27	M	Exod. 19. 16–end	Heb. 12. 18–end
28	Tu	1 Chron. 16. 1–13	Rev. 11. 15–end
29	W	**MICHAEL AND ALL ANGELS**	
30	Th	Neh. 8. 1–12	1 Cor. 14. 1–12

October

1	F	Isa. 1. 10–17	Mark 12. 28–34
2	Sa	Dan. 6. 6–23	Rev. 12. 7–12
3	S	**THE EIGHTEENTH SUNDAY AFTER TRINITY**	
4	M	2 Sam. 22. 4–7, 17–20	Heb. 7.26 – 8.6
5	Tu	Prov. 22. 17–end	2 Cor. 12. 1–10
6	W	Hos. ch. 14	James 2. 14–26
7	Th	Isa. 24. 1–15	John 16. 25–33
8	F	Jer. 14. 1–9	Luke 23. 44–56
9	Sa	Zech. 8. 14–end	John 20. 19–end
10	S	**THE NINETEENTH SUNDAY AFTER TRINITY**	
11	M	1 Kings 3. 3–14	1 Tim. 3.14 – 4.8
12	Tu	Prov. 27. 11–end	Gal. 6. 1–10
13	W	Isa. 51. 1–6	2 Cor. 1. 1–11
14	Th	Ecclus. 18. 1–14	1 Cor. 11. 17–end
		or Job ch. 26	
15	F	Ecclus. 28. 2–12	Mark 15. 33–47
		or Job 19. 21–end	
16	Sa	Isa. 44. 21–end	John 21. 15–end

17	S	**THE TWENTIETH SUNDAY AFTER TRINITY**	
18	M	**LUKE**	
19	Tu	Prov. 31. 10–end	Luke 10. 38–42
20	W	Jonah ch. 1	Luke 5. 1–11
21	Th	Exod. 12. 1–20	1 Thess. 4. 1–12
22	F	Isa. ch. 64	Matt. 27. 45–56
23	Sa	2 Sam. 7. 18–end	Acts 2. 22–33
24	S	**THE LAST SUNDAY AFTER TRINITY**	
25	M	Isa. 42. 14–21	Luke 1. 5–25
26	Tu	1 Sam. 4. 12–end	Luke 1. 57–end
27	W	Baruch 5 *or* Hag. 1. 1–11	Mark 1. 1–11
28	Th	**SIMON AND JUDE**	
29	F	2 Sam. 11. 1–15	Matt. 14. 1–12
30	Sa	Isa. 43. 15–21	Acts 19. 1–10
31	S	**THE FOURTH SUNDAY BEFORE ADVENT**	

November

1	M	**ALL SAINTS' DAY**	
		or, where All Saints' Day is celebrated on Sunday 31 October only:	
		Esther 3. 1–11; 4. 7–17	Matt. 18. 1–10
2	Tu	Ezek. 18. 21–end	Matt. 18. 12–20
3	W	Prov. 3. 27–end	Matt. 18. 21–end
4	Th	Exod. 23. 1–9	Matt. 19. 1–15
5	F	Prov. 3. 13–18	Matt. 19. 16–end
6	Sa	Deut. 28. 1–6	Matt. 20. 1–16
7	S	**THE THIRD SUNDAY BEFORE ADVENT**	
8	M	Isa. 40. 21–end	Rom. 11. 25–end
9	Tu	Ezek. 34. 20–end	John 10. 1–18
10	W	Lev. 26. 3–13	Titus 2. 1–10
11	Th	Hos. 6. 1–6	Matt. 9. 9–13
12	F	Mal. ch. 4	John 4. 5–26
13	Sa	Mic. 6. 6–8	Col. 3. 12–17
14	S	**THE SECOND SUNDAY BEFORE ADVENT**	
15	M	Mic. 7. 1–7	Matt. 10. 24–39
16	Tu	Hab. 3. 1–19a	1 Cor. 4. 9–16
17	W	Zech. 8. 1–13	Mark 13. 3–8
18	Th	Zech. 10. 6–end	1 Pet. 5. 1–11
19	F	Mic. 4. 1–5	Luke 9. 28–36
20	Sa	*At Evening Prayer the readings for the Eve of Christ the King are used. At other services, the following readings are used:*	
		Exod. 16. 1–21	John 6. 3–15
21	S	**CHRIST THE KING** (The Sunday next before Advent)	
22	M	Jer. 30. 1–3, 10–17	Rom. 12. 9–21
23	Tu	Jer. 30. 18–24	John 10. 22–30
24	W	Jer. 31. 1–9	Matt. 15. 21–31
25	Th	Jer. 31. 10–17	Matt. 16. 13–end
26	F	Jer. 31. 31–37	Heb. 10. 11–18
27	Sa	Isa. 51.17 – 52.2	Eph. 5. 1–20
28	S	**THE FIRST SUNDAY OF ADVENT**	
29	M	Mal. 3. 1–6	Matt. 3. 1–6
30	Tu	**ANDREW**	

December

1	W	Isa. 65.17 – 66.2	Matt. 24. 1–14
2	Th	Mic. 5. 2–5a	John 3. 16–21
3	F	Isa. 66. 18–end	Luke 13. 22–30
4	Sa	Mic. 7. 8–15	Rom. 15.30 – 16.7, 25–end
5	S	**THE SECOND SUNDAY OF ADVENT**	
6	M	Jer. 7. 1–11	Phil. 4. 4–9
7	Tu	Dan. 7. 9–14	Matt. 24. 15–28
8	W	Amos 9. 11–end	Rom. 13. 8–14
9	Th	Jer. 23. 5–8	Mark 11. 1–11
10	F	Jer. 33. 14–22	Luke 21. 25–36
11	Sa	Zech. 14. 4–11	Rev. 22. 1–7
12	S	**THE THIRD SUNDAY OF ADVENT**	
13	M	Isa. 40. 1–11	Matt. 3. 1–12
14	Tu	Lam. 3. 22–33	1 Cor. 1. 1–9
15	W	Joel 3. 9–16	Matt. 24. 29–35
16	Th	Isa. ch. 62	1 Thess. 3. 6–13
17	F	Ecclus. 24. 1–9 *or* Prov. 6. 22–31	1 Cor. 2. 1–13
18	Sa	Exod. 3. 1–6	Acts 7. 20–36
19	S	**THE FOURTH SUNDAY OF ADVENT**	
20	M	Isa. 22. 21–23	Rev. 3. 7–13
21	Tu	Num. 24. 15b–19	Rev. 22. 10–21
22	W	Jer. 30. 7–11a	Acts 4. 1–12
23	Th	Isa. 7. 10–15	Matt. 1. 18–23
24	F	*At Evening Prayer the readings for Christmas Eve are used. At other services, the following readings are used:*	
		Isa. 29. 13–18	1 John 4. 7–16
25	Sa	**CHRISTMAS DAY**	
26	S	**STEPHEN** (or transferred to 29th) *or* **THE FIRST SUNDAY OF CHRISTMAS**	
27	M	**JOHN THE EVANGELIST**	
28	Tu	**THE HOLY INNOCENTS**	
29	W	Mic. 1. 1–4; 2. 12–13	Luke 2. 1–7
30	Th	Isa. 9. 2–7	John 8. 12–20
31	F	Eccles. 3. 1–13	Rev. 21. 1–8

CALENDAR 2021

JANUARY

Su	..	X^2	B	E^2	E^3	E^4
M	..	4	11	18	25	..
Tu	..	5	12	19	26	..
W	..	E	13	20	27	..
Th	..	7	14	21	28	..
F	1	8	15	22	29	..
Sa	2	9	16	23	30	..

FEBRUARY

Su	..	L^{-2}	L^{-1}	L^1	L^2	..
M	1	8	15	22	..	..
Tu	Pr	9	16	23	..	..
W	3	10	A	24	..	..
Th	4	11	18	25	..	..
F	5	12	19	26	..	..
Sa	6	13	20	27	..	..

MARCH

Su	..	L^3	L^4	L^5	P	..
M	1	8	15	22	29	..
Tu	2	9	16	23	30	..
W	3	10	17	24	31	..
Th	4	11	18	An	..	..
F	5	12	19	26	..	..
Sa	6	13	20	27	..	..

APRIL

Su	..	E	E^2	E^3	E^4	..
M	..	5	12	19	26	..
Tu	..	6	13	20	27	..
W	..	7	14	21	28	..
Th	M	8	15	22	29	..
F	G	9	16	23	30	..
Sa	3	10	17	24	..	..

MAY

Su	..	E^5	E^6	E^7	W	T
M	..	3	10	17	24	31
Tu	..	4	11	18	25	..
W	..	5	12	19	26	..
Th	..	6	A	20	27	..
F	..	7	14	21	28	..
Sa	1	8	15	22	29	..

JUNE

Su	..	T^1	T^2	T^3	T^4	..
M	..	7	14	21	28	..
Tu	1	8	15	22	29	..
W	2	9	16	23	30	..
Th	3	10	17	24	..	..
F	4	11	18	25	..	..
Sa	5	12	19	26	..	..

JULY

Su	..	T^5	T^6	T^7	T^8	..
M	..	5	12	19	26	..
Tu	..	6	13	20	27	..
W	..	7	14	21	28	..
Th	1	8	15	22	29	..
F	2	9	16	23	30	..
Sa	3	10	17	24	31	..

AUGUST

Su	T^9	T^{10}	T^{11}	T^{12}	T^{13}	..
M	2	9	16	23	30	..
Tu	3	10	17	24	31	..
W	4	11	18	25	..	..
Th	5	12	19	26	..	..
F	6	13	20	27	..	..
Sa	7	14	21	28	..	..

SEPTEMBER

Su	..	T^{14}	T^{15}	T^{16}	T^{17}	..
M	..	6	13	20	27	..
Tu	..	7	14	21	28	..
W	1	8	15	22	29	..
Th	2	9	16	23	30	..
F	3	10	17	24	..	..
Sa	4	11	18	25	..	..

OCTOBER

Su	..	T^{18}	T^{19}	T^{20}	T^L	A^{-4}
M	..	4	11	18	25	..
Tu	..	5	12	19	26	..
W	..	6	13	20	27	..
Th	..	7	14	21	28	..
F	1	8	15	22	29	..
Sa	2	9	16	23	30	..

NOVEMBER

Su	..	A^{-3}	A^{-2}	A^{-1}	A	..
M	AS	8	15	22	29	..
Tu	2	9	16	23	30	..
W	3	10	17	24	..	..
Th	4	11	18	25	..	..
F	5	12	19	26	..	..
Sa	6	13	20	27	..	..

DECEMBER

Su	..	A^2	A^3	A^4	X^1	..
M	..	6	13	20	27	..
Tu	..	7	14	21	28	..
W	1	8	15	22	29	..
Th	2	9	16	23	30	..
F	3	10	17	24	31	..
Sa	4	11	18	X	..	..

A = Ash Wednesday, Ascension, Advent
A^- = Before Advent
A^{-4} = also All Saints, 2021, and 2022 (if trans.)
A^{-1} = Christ the King
An = Annunciation
AS = All Saints
B = Baptism
E = Epiphany, Easter
E^4 = also Presentation, 2021 and 2022 (if trans.)
G = Good Friday
L = Lent
L^- = Before Lent

CALENDAR 2022

JANUARY

Su	..	X^2	B	E^2	E^3	E^4
M	..	3	10	17	24	31
Tu	..	4	11	18	25	..
W	..	5	12	19	26	..
Th	..	E	13	20	27	..
F	..	7	14	21	28	..
Sa	1	8	15	22	29	..

FEBRUARY

Su	..	L^{-4}	L^{-3}	L^{-2}	L^{-1}	..
M	..	7	14	21	28	..
Tu	1	8	15	22	..	..
W	Pr	9	16	23	..	..
Th	3	10	17	24	..	..
F	4	11	18	25	..	..
Sa	5	12	19	26	..	..

MARCH

Su	..	L^1	L^2	L^3	L^4	..
M	..	7	14	21	28	..
Tu	1	8	15	22	29	..
W	A	9	16	23	30	..
Th	3	10	17	24	31	..
F	4	11	18	An	..	..
Sa	5	12	19	26	..	..

APRIL

Su	..	L^5	P	E	E^2	..
M	..	4	11	18	25	..
Tu	..	5	12	19	26	..
W	..	6	13	20	27	..
Th	..	7	M	21	28	..
F	1	8	G	22	29	..
Sa	2	9	16	23	30	..

MAY

Su	E^3	E^4	E^5	E^6	E^7	..
M	2	9	16	23	30	..
Tu	3	10	17	24	31	..
W	4	11	18	25	..	..
Th	5	12	19	A	..	..
F	6	13	20	27	..	..
Sa	7	14	21	28	..	..

JUNE

Su	..	W	T	T^1	T^2	..
M	..	6	13	20	27	..
Tu	..	7	14	21	28	..
W	1	8	15	22	29	..
Th	2	9	16	23	30	..
F	3	10	17	24	..	..
Sa	4	11	18	25	..	..

JULY

Su	..	T^3	T^4	T^5	T^6	T^7
M	..	4	11	18	25	..
Tu	..	5	12	19	26	..
W	..	6	13	20	27	..
Th	..	7	14	21	28	..
F	1	8	15	22	29	..
Sa	2	9	16	23	30	..

AUGUST

Su	..	T^8	T^9	T^{10}	T^{11}	..
M	1	8	15	22	29	..
Tu	2	9	16	23	30	..
W	3	10	17	24	31	..
Th	4	11	18	25	..	..
F	5	12	19	26	..	..
Sa	6	13	20	27	..	..

SEPTEMBER

Su	..	T^{12}	T^{13}	T^{14}	T^{15}	..
M	..	5	12	19	26	..
Tu	..	6	13	20	27	..
W	..	7	14	21	28	..
Th	1	8	15	22	29	..
F	2	9	16	23	30	..
Sa	3	10	17	24	..	..

OCTOBER

Su	..	T^{16}	T^{17}	T^{18}	T^L	A^{-4}
M	..	3	10	17	24	31
Tu	..	4	11	18	25	..
W	..	5	12	19	26	..
Th	..	6	13	20	27	..
F	..	7	14	21	28	..
Sa	1	8	15	22	29	..

NOVEMBER

Su	..	A^{-3}	A^{-2}	A^{-1}	A^1	..
M	..	7	14	21	28	..
Tu	AS	8	15	22	29	..
W	2	9	16	23	30	..
Th	3	10	17	24	..	..
F	4	11	18	25	..	..
Sa	5	12	19	26	..	..

DECEMBER

Su	..	A^2	A^3	A^4	X	..
M	..	5	12	19	26	..
Tu	..	6	13	20	27	..
W	..	7	14	21	28	..
Th	1	8	15	22	29	..
F	2	9	16	23	30	..
Sa	3	10	17	24	31	..

M = Maundy Thursday
P = Palm Sunday
Pr = Presentation
T = Trinity
(T^3 = also Thomas)
(T^8 = also James, 2021)
(T^{11} = also Blessed Virgin Mary, 2021)
T^L = Last Sunday after Trinity
W = Pentecost (Whit Sunday)
X = Christmas
X^2 = also Epiphany, 2021 and 2022 (if trans.)